Competing for Knowledge

Knowledge is the primary means of wealth creation for a rapidly growing number of individuals, firms, and economies. This book focuses on the dynamics of the knowledge economy, providing an overview of the knowledge creation capabilities of economies. It examines the growth performance of leading knowledge economies, and presents a detailed analysis of how the creation and connection of knowledge is becoming the key means of growing productivity.

Huggins and Izushi introduce the concepts of network capital and knowledge communities to explain and understand how knowledge is connected and transferred across firms, organizations, and economies, whilst taking issue with the accepted concepts of business clusters, social capital, and endogenous growth theory. This book demonstrates how the knowledge economy has fundamentally shifted the way in which the value of both firms and economies are measured, and points to the way in which the knowledge race has become global due to increasing parts of the developing world being integrated with the advanced world through international trade and investment.

This book will be of interest to students and researchers engaged with the knowledge economy, management, and economic geography, as well as managers and public policy makers interested in competitiveness and economic development.

Robert Huggins is a Director of the Enterprise and Regional Development Unit and Senior Lecturer in Enterprise and Regional Development at the University of Sheffield's Management School, UK. **Hiro Izushi** is Senior Lecturer in Innovation for the Economics and Strategy Group at Aston Business School in Birmingham, UK. They are also the Co-Directors of the Centre for International Competitiveness, which they founded in 2007.

Routledge studies in global competition

Edited by John Cantwell

University of Reading, UK

and

David Mowery

University of California, Berkeley, USA

1 **Japanese Firms in Europe**
Edited by Frédérique Sachwald

2 **Technological Innovation, Multinational Corporations and New International Competitiveness**
The case of intermediate countries
Edited by José Molero

3 **Global Competition and the Labour Market**
Nigel Driffield

4 **The Source of Capital Goods Innovation**
The role of user firms in Japan and Korea
Kong-Rae Lee

5 **Climates of Global Competition**
Maria Bengtsson

6 **Multinational Enterprises and Technological Spillovers**
Tommaso Perez

7 **Governance of International Strategic Alliances**
Technology and transaction costs
Joanne E. Oxley

8 **Strategy in Emerging Markets**
Telecommunications establishments in Europe
Anders Pehrsson

9 **Going Multinational**
The Korean experience of direct investment
Edited by Frédérique Sachwald

10 **Multinational Firms and Impacts on Employment, Trade and Technology**
New perspectives for a new century
Edited by Robert E. Lipsey and Jean-Louis Mucchielli

11 **Multinational Firms**
The global–local dilemma
Edited by John H. Dunning and Jean-Louis Mucchielli

12 **MIT and the Rise of Entrepreneurial Science**
Henry Etzkowitz

13 **Technological Resources and the Logic of Corporate Diversification**
Brian Silverman

14 **The Economics of Innovation, New Technologies and Structural Change**
Cristiano Antonelli

15 **European Union Direct Investment in China**
Characteristics, challenges and perspectives
Daniel Van Den Bulcke, Haiyan Zhang and Maria do Céu Esteves

16 **Biotechnology in Comparative Perspective**
Edited by Gerhard Fuchs

17 **Technological Change and Economic Performance**
Albert L. Link and Donald S. Siegel

18 **Multinational Corporations and European Regional Systems of Innovation**
John Cantwell and Simona Iammarino

19 **Knowledge and Innovation in Regional Industry**
An entrepreneurial coalition
Roel Rutten

20 **Local Industrial Clusters**
Existence, emergence and evolution
Thomas Brenner

21 **The Emerging Industrial Structure of the Wider Europe**
Edited by Francis McGowen, Slavo Radosevic and Nick Von Tunzelmann

22 **Entrepreneurship**
A new perspective
Thomas Grebel

23 **Evaluating Public Research Institutions**
The US advanced technology program's intramural research initiative
Albert N. Link and John T. Scott

24 **Location and Competition**
Edited by Steven Brakman and Harry Garretsen

25 **Entrepreneurship and Dynamics in the Knowledge Economy**
Edited by Charlie Karlsson, Börje Johansson and Roger R. Stough

26 **Evolution and Design of Institutions**
Edited by Christian Schubert and Georg von Wangenheim

27 **The Changing Economic Geography of Globalization**
Reinventing space
Edited by Giovanna Vertova

28 **Economics of the Firm**
Analysis, evolution and history
Edited by Michael Dietrich

29 **Innovation, Technology and Hypercompetition**
Hans Gottinger

30 **Mergers and Acquisitions in Asia**
A global perspective
Roger Y. W. Tang and Ali M. Metwalli

31 Competitiveness of New Industries
Institutional framework and learning in information technology in Japan, the US and Germany
Edited Cornelia Storz and Andreas Moerke

32 Entry and Post-Entry Performance of Newborn Firms
Marco Vivarelli

33 Changes in Regional Firm Founding Activities
A theoretical explanation and empirical evidence
Dirk Fornahl

34 Risk Appraisal and Venture Capital in High Technology New Ventures
Gavin C. Reid and Julia A. Smith

35 Competing for Knowledge
Creating, connecting, and growing
Robert Huggins and Hiro Izushi

Competing for Knowledge

Creating, connecting, and growing

Robert Huggins and Hiro Izushi

Routledge
Taylor & Francis Group
LONDON AND NEW YORK

First published 2007
by Routledge
2 Park Square, Milton Park, Abingdon, Oxon OX14 4RN

Simultaneously published in the USA and Canada
by Routledge
270 Madison Ave, New York, NY 10016

Routledge is an imprint of the Taylor & Francis Group, an informa business

Typeset in Times by Wearset Ltd, Boldon, Tyne and Wear
Printed and bound in Great Britain by TJI Digital, Padstow, Cornwall

British Library Cataloguing in Publication Data
A catalogue record for this book is available from the British Library

Library of Congress Cataloging in Publication Data
A catalog record for this book has been requested

ISBN10: 0-415-37512-6 (hbk)
ISBN10: 0-203-94059-8 (ebk)

ISBN13: 978-0-415-37512-2 (hbk)
ISBN13: 978-0-203-94059-8 (ebk)

Contents

Illustrations

Figures

Tables

Preface

We first discussed the idea for this book at a conference in Trento (Italy) in October 2000. At that time, notions of the *new economy* were still very hot, with the full implications of the dot.com crash and the bursting of the so-called economic bubble yet to be fully realized. The period within which this book was subsequently researched and written was remarkable, as the fad of the new economy shifted to a more considered and balanced outlook of the changes occurring in economies across the globe. In this book we have attempted to take an overarching view of what we term the *knowledge economy* and its composition, seeking to explore its long-term development as well as its more recent evolution. The format and style of the book is such that it can be easily digested by informed readers, while those with a special interest in certain areas are able to gain further insight from the detailed notes and references we provide. The theoretical scope of the book principally draws on concepts from economics, strategic management, innovation studies, sociology, as well as economic and human geography. These theories are utilized to provide the backdrop for understanding the link between knowledge and competitiveness, and how firms and economies can enhance both.

The writing of this book developed from our work in launching the *World Knowledge Competitiveness Index (WKCI)*, which was published for the first time in 2002. The *WKCI* was aimed at filling a particular research gap – the lack of intelligence on the composition and performance of the knowledge economy at the sub-national and regional level. Since 2002, the *WKCI* has established itself as an important indicator of the *knowledge competitiveness* of high-performing regions across the globe. The publication of the *WKCI* has its root in a study commissioned by South East England Development Agency (SEEDA) in the UK. We are grateful to Paul Lovejoy and Rashid Bashir, our clients at SEEDA, who allowed us the scope to develop some initial frameworks adopted in this book. The *WKCI* also gave us a platform to carry out further research on the knowledge economy for a range of organizations including the European Commission, the Organisation for Economic Co-operation and Development (OECD), the European Centre for the Development of Vocational Training, the Government of Alberta, London Development Agency, Scottish Enterprise, and the Welsh Development Agency. In particular, we would like to thank Mikel

Landabaso, Jonathan Potter, Manfred Tessaring, Patrick McVeigh, Madeline Smith, and Mark Barry, who commissioned us to undertake a number of related studies, the fruits of which helped shape much of the thinking and analysis in this book. Also, we wish to give special thanks to all those who worked with us on these studies, in particular Nia Emlyn-Jones, Jonathan Day, and Will Davies, who proved to be researchers of remarkable quality given their tender years – we were very lucky indeed to have their assistance as we pursued our knowledge economy project. Special mention is also due to Stuart Harries, Jean Gordon, and Martin Jones.

Finally, our biggest thanks go to our respective families. Robert would like to thank Alison, Richard, Eleanor, and James for their continuing love and tolerance, and Lindy and Alan for all their support and efforts over the years. Hiro offers special thanks to Keiko, Keiichi, Usa, Neko, and Usaaka for their love and unfailing support; Lala for his keen intellectual interest and critique; Toyohiko for showing the importance of daily practice; and Inuaka and Ki for their cheering over the years.

Robert Huggins
Hiro Izushi

1 Introduction

Knowledge is the primary means of wealth creation for a rapidly growing number of individuals, firms, and economies. Key industries in advanced economies in the late twentieth century – microelectronics, telecommunications, and computer software – as well as the twenty-first century's high hopes – such as biotechnology and nanotechnology – are intensive users of brainpower.[1] A significant proportion of workers in these industries are devoted to the creation and use of state-of-the-art knowledge, earning higher wages than their counterparts in less skill-demanding occupations. An ability to understand, process, and generate advanced knowledge is crucial to the success of these workers. Similarly, firms in high-technology industries rely heavily on the production and use of advanced knowledge as a key source of their value-added.[2] Endowments of natural resources such as minerals, coal, and oil no longer determine the fortunes of economies. Today, knowledge is the key source of competitive advantage.

Knowledge-based competition is akin to a marathon race – fought over the long-run, but with the possibility of disruptions that radically change the rules of the race. Even in markets where steep learning curves and scale economies help incumbents to fend off competition, new entrants with novel products often dethrone them as market leaders.[3] A key to successfully competing in this long yet unpredictable race is through the careful and long-term management of core capabilities and expertise by investing in a range of knowledge-based resources, such as research and development (R&D), education and training, collaborative relationships with other businesses, and information and communication technology infrastructure. To compete in a knowledge-based environment, workers need to continually improve their skills, while firms need to continually upgrade their knowledge base and develop new products and processes. At a macro level, regions and nations compete with one another by raising the standards of their infrastructure in the hope of attracting and retaining skilled workers and blue-chip firms.

As knowledge-based competition becomes evermore global, many firms may find it tempting to try and settle into a market for low quality products, taking advantage of short-run opportunities to satisfy demand. However, in the long-run this will cost them their prosperity, as they fail to adapt to the emergence of new knowledge and innovations. Once a firm is excluded from the knowledge race, it will sooner or later witness a decline in performance and profits, resulting in lower wages and loss of jobs. For those regions and nations accommodating such firms, the inability to compete in the knowledge race creates the probability of increases in social disorder and a growing burden upon fiscal balance. Therefore, however tough it is, stakeholders – individual workers, businesses, and governments – must remain in the race if they are to raise or even keep their current standards of living.[4]

The race has become global due to increasing parts of the developing world becoming integrated with the developed world through international trade and investment. Advances in telecommunications and logistics have made possible the global sourcing of skills, goods, and services. Automotive factory workers in Germany, France, and the United Kingdom now compete with their counterparts in Eastern Europe, based on a combination of available skills and wages. French and Italian workers in apparel and leather workshops are faced with competition from workers in China who are able to do their jobs for significantly lower wages. Call centers in India, which are now drifting to Philippines, deal with customers in the United Kingdom and the United States, replacing local operators in those countries where the customers are located. This cross-border competition is increasingly spreading toward high-technology jobs. Due to the growing cross-national outsourcing of software programming, programmers in North America now have to share the global pool of jobs with programmers in India. Although there are different capitalist models at work across the globe, varying in social responsibility and income distribution across their societies, the basic principle of demand and supply is universal. If a worker can offer the same skills at a lower price, the worker wins the competition against others with the same skill levels. Given this, the choice available for workers in today's advanced economies is to either upgrade their skill levels or lose out to similarly skilled workers in lower-wage economies.

Global competition is witnessing a power shift in the map of knowledge creation capacity across nations. By 2001, Taiwan and South Korea, two of Asia's Tiger economies, had already caught up with or almost surpassed the UK in the number of new patents granted by US Patent and Trademark Office (USPTO). These two Tiger economies also recorded a faster growth rate in new patents than the United States.[5] A growing proportion of USPTO patents are granted to overseas inventors, indicating a growth in innovation capabilities outside the traditionally strong United States. In 1963, foreign inventors outside the United States accounted for only 18.6 percent of the total patents granted by USPTO. This percentage steadily grew from that time and broke the mark of 40 percent in 1981. In 2001, 47.1 percent of the new patents were awarded to overseas inventors.[6] This mirrors the fading dominance of the United States in human capital development. From 1993 to 1999, the number of researchers in other member countries of the Organisation for Economic Co-operation and Development (OECD) increased from approximately 1.50 million to 2.04 million, an average annual growth rate of 5.3 percent.[7] During the same period, the United States failed to match this pace, with the number of researchers growing from approximately 965,000 to 1.26 million at an average annual growth rate of 4.6 percent, 0.7 percent lower than the other OECD countries.[8] The number of researchers in the US labor force might appear large enough to ensure that it keeps its lead in the global race. However, when combined, the total number of workers with university degrees or equivalents in the three largest non-OECD countries – China, India, and Russia – now equals that of the United States.[9] Coupled with the rise of China and India in high-technology sectors, the failure to keep up with the human capital development taking place outside of its borders creates great concern among US business managers. For instance, Microsoft CEO Steven Ballmer states: 'The US is No. 3 in the world and falling behind quickly No. 1 [India] and No. 2 [China] in terms of computer-science graduates.'[10]

Growing

The focus of this book is the dynamics of what is called the knowledge-based economy. As in the past, economic growth remains a crucial goal in the knowledge-based economy. While the finite amount of natural resources and environmental problems have emerged as global concerns, economic growth, and more precisely productivity growth, continues to be the motor that maintains the fabric of society. As Benjamin Friedman, a Harvard economist, writes, economic growth is essential for greater opportunity, tolerance of diversity, social mobility, commitment to fairness, and dedication to democracy.[11] During times of expansion, nations tend to liberalize – increasing rights, reducing restrictions, and expanding benefits for the needy. During times of stagnation, they change direction toward authoritarianism. Not only does economic growth raise living standards and make liberal social policies possible, it also causes people to be optimistic about the future.[12] What has changed from the old, traditional economy is that productivity growth, driven by technological and organizational innovations, has become the key source of economic growth. In many advanced economies, population growth has slowed down significantly or even turned negative. Economic growth propelled by population growth has long faded from the picture in advanced economies. With environmental concerns, we are increasingly aware of the constraints upon the use of natural resources in our economic activities. It is imperative to create a greater amount of economic value under the constraints of these limited natural resources coupled with stagnating population growth. The source that allows us to achieve this is knowledge, and it is the creation and connection of knowledge that underpins the development of new commercial products and services.

Creating

The capacity for knowledge creation and commercialization is being developed at a different rate today than in the past. One example is the growth of investment in individual skills and organizational competencies related to handling and generating knowledge. A growing number of the young in advanced economies now receive higher education or equivalent levels of vocational education, increasing the proportion of the labor force equipped with skills in handling knowledge-intensive tasks. In 1950, only 6.2 percent of those aged 25 years and over in the United States had a bachelor's or higher degree. By 2005, the proportion had shot up to 27.6 percent.[13] With the average educational qualification of individual workers becoming higher than ever, firms now assign a growing proportion of their employees to knowledge-creating tasks. For instance, while only 25 out of 10,000 workers in the United States were engaged in R&D in 1950, there were 91 R&D scientists and engineers for every 10,000 workers in 1999.[14] Management has shifted its competitive focus from the control of markets, through entry barriers under relatively stable conditions, to the creation of internal competencies aimed at coping with fast-changing market conditions.[15] In particular, not only is the effective management of the existing knowledge base important, but equally crucial are the organizational capabilities for creating new knowledge in a sustainable manner.[16]

In a similar vein, we are witnessing growing efforts to cultivate those knowledge sources that are yet to be fully commercially exploited. An example of this is the growth in industrial research at universities, which is often mediated and facilitated by government. While universities have long supplied industry with the outputs of basic research as a public source of knowledge, industrial links were seen primarily as an essential part of the teaching process, assisting staff in understanding the industry requirements for graduate skills.[17] However, there has been a renewed emphasis by universities upon industrial research and collaboration with industry in advanced economies, particularly since the 1980s in the United States.[18] In the United States, the drive toward commercial and industrial research at higher-education institutions was cemented by the enactment of the Bayh-Dole Act in 1980.[19] The act allowed nonprofit research groups to patent and commercialize technologies developed with federal funds. This has given rise to 'academic entrepreneurs' who use their research outputs for commercial products to set up their own businesses.[20] Furthermore, many universities have assumed a more proactive role in commercializing their research outputs through licensing and collaborative research agreements with industry. This change in the role of universities is partly the result of government policy that aims to fully integrate a previously unexploited knowledge source into the knowledge-based economy, raising international competitiveness.

Connecting

Most importantly, in this book we explore the growing efforts to connect knowledge within and across organizational units and sectors, aimed at maximizing the sharing and further creation of knowledge. Knowledge is often 'sticky' and difficult to transfer, which arises in part from a significant proportion of it being *stuck* in the heads of individuals. Such difficult-to-transfer knowledge is referred to as tacit and is embodied in individuals as skills they possess. Jeff Hawkins describes three epochs of intelligence, each of which was marked by the use of a new medium for memory. The first epoch is traced back to the use of DNA as a medium. Primitive species passed on their DNA-based memory of the world to their offspring through their genes, but individuals could not yet learn and adapt within their lifetime. The second epoch began when nature invented modifiable nervous systems that could quickly form memories. This allows, for example, an animal – such as a dog – to learn about the structure of its world and adapt its behavior accordingly within its lifetime. The third and final epoch is unique to humans. This began with the invention of language and the expansion of the large neocortex area of our brain. This allows us to learn the structure of the world within our lifetime and effectively communicate this to other humans via language.[21] However, this unparalleled ability to use languages masks the fact that a significant proportion of our knowledge is still embedded in our brains in a form that is not reliant on language.

As the scientist and philosopher Michael Polanyi stated, 'we can know more than we can tell'.[22] A familiar example to illustrate this fact is our almost infallible ability to recognize a human face.[23] When we see a friend's face, we automatically recognize the person in less than a second. It does not matter if the friend is close or far away, facing us, turned a little to the side, or in profile. The friend's visage can appear in countless positions and variations, yet in every case we know instantly that we are looking at the particular friend. We find it hard to describe in words or any other forms of coding what that recognition entails. Also, robots and computer programs, which are products of our codified knowledge (i.e. knowledge which is relatively easily transferable), are usually poor in handling the variation in visual inputs and recognizing a person's face.[24] As this case illustrates, a significant proportion of knowledge remains tacit and can be gained only through experience. To become an expert wine taster, or to acquire knowledge of innumerable blends of tea, we must go through a long course of experience building, often under the guidance of an expert.[25] We also acquire a lot of knowledge with the aid of texts, such as this book, but later forget them. However, even if we forget those texts that conveyed the original knowledge, the knowledge is often retained in a tacit form. Polanyi, a native of Hungary, wrote that although he had forgotten most of the medical terms he learned in that country when training in radiology, and acquired no others in place of them when he subsequently left Hungary, he could still make sense of and comprehend an X-ray if asked to do so.[26] In other words, we know a lot in a form that has yet to be articulated for transfer to others.

Ikujiro Nonaka and Hirotaka Takeuchi's *knowledge spiral* model, one of the most influential works in the field of knowledge management, is a reflection of the 'sticky' nature of knowledge.[27] Nonaka and Takeuchi adopt the distinction between tacit and explicit knowledge (i.e. knowledge expressed in languages and codes), further recognizing the following four modes of knowledge conversion:

1. from tacit to tacit
2. from tacit to explicit
3. from explicit to explicit
4. from explicit to tacit.

While most previous knowledge management models focused upon explicit knowledge, Nonaka and Takeuchi stress that the organization has to mobilize tacit knowledge created and accumulated at the individual level and amplify knowledge 'organizationally' through the four modes of knowledge conversion. Processes of extracting, combining, and creating tacit knowledge often require particularly intensive interactions among an organization's members. For instance, sharing experience and learning-by-observing requires opportunities for interaction, such as in the form of apprenticeships and brainstorming sessions. Transferring and combining knowledge, particularly tacit knowledge, within an organization is not a costless and spontaneous process. Therefore, organizations need to devise and manage the process of knowledge transfer and combination effectively if they are to make the best use of their knowledge.

Network capital

Beyond organizational units where every member knows each other, individuals mobilize what we call *network capital* to share and connect different sources and forms of knowledge. Our contention is that before connection of knowledge happens, individuals and firms have to know the source of the knowledge they require. Knowing the source of knowledge is a resource-consuming activity. When seeking knowledge, individuals and firms may start by scanning their environment and identifying 'who knows what'. While publications such as *Who's Who* and the *Yellow Pages* and, increasingly, Internet search engines such as *Google* serve as scanning tools, such information is not always readily available. Sources of useful information, such as industry insiders, do not always publicize themselves to everyone. Instead, they sometimes attempt to increase their value by staying hidden from the public scene and, therefore, hard for outsiders to find. Knowing the source of knowledge does not end here. After identifying the source, knowledge seekers have to establish relationships with it. The creation of such relationships can be instant if the source sells its knowledge as a commercial service. However, this is not always the case, since knowledge seekers often have to prove to the source that they are a 'worthy' recipient of the source's knowledge. Such worthiness may be achieved through, for example, the high likelihood of reciprocity, that is, the seeker providing the source with knowledge in due course. Once relationships are established, sought-after knowledge starts to flow from the source.

Although this ability to know and access the source of knowledge is intangible, it is nevertheless a very valuable asset. It is the foundation upon which knowledge is obtained and connected across individuals and organizations as well as decisions relating to the mobilization of other types of resource. That is why we call it network capital; it is a type of capital equivalent to physical capital or human capital. The rise of electronics-based communication tools such as the Internet does not reduce the value of this capital. Instead, given the flood of information circulated through such electronic tools, as well as the growth of individuals involved in knowledge creation, the significance of network capital is increasing since it is often becoming more difficult to establish relationships with the right knowledge sources that are able to spark innovation.

A point we would like to stress is that the accumulation of network capital is based on the initiative of individuals and firms, being strategically motivated by their economic concerns. A similar but distinct concept that has gained currency in the last two decades is social capital. According to this concept, communities, which are often spatially-defined (such as cities or regions), possess social norms and customs that lubricate the transfer and connection of knowledge. These social norms and customs – such as obligations and expectations relating to networking and collaboration – are embedded in the social environment. The trustworthiness of any environment is often tacit and specific to each community. The more trustworthy a community is, the likelier it may be to facilitate the transfer and connection of knowledge, in turn reinforcing the cycle of knowledge creation. While we do not deny the existence of social capital, we recognize a key difference between network capital and social capital. Social capital is a place-based external force influencing connection of knowledge across organizations through the generation of localized trust. By contrast, network capital is what firms invest in to establish the networks and relationships required to meet their economic expectations, thus creating significant differences between firms in their innovation performance. While firms can strategically influence their network capital resources, they are less able to influence their social capital.

Knowledge community

The other concept we propose is what we call *knowledge community*. In our analysis of efforts aimed at transferring and connecting knowledge, we focus upon the diversity in skills and expertise among individuals and firms involved in these processes. Hawkins suggests that in terms of the workings of our brains, 'creativity is mixing and matching patterns of everything you've ever experienced or come to know in your lifetime'.[28] We store sequences of patterns in our memories in a form (which Hawkins calls the 'invariant' form) such that the knowledge of past events can be applied to new situations. Applying our memories, we predict and understand new situations, or in other words, 'we predict the future by analogy to the past'.[29] Novel ideas are born out of this act of making predictions by analogy, yet they break some expected patterns while simultaneously teaching us new ones. Frans Johansson argues that novel, breakthrough ideas most often occur when we bring concepts from one field into new, unfamiliar territories.[30] Studies support the view that communication between individuals (or groups of individuals) who are mutually distant in their skills, backgrounds, and status are more likely to produce fresh and novel ideas and approaches to problem solving.[31] Outsiders provide a more critical perspective, in part because they are less subject to convergence pressures within a group of individuals. A recent study suggests that the use of cross-functional teams increases innovation success by as much as 30 percent.[32]

Yet, such diversity is often lost in the developmental path of firms and industries. Repeated interactions and exchanges of information between individuals within a group lead to a convergence of their norms, values, and behaviors through the creation of local languages. The evolution of local languages through iterative communication within an organizational unit further lubricates the exchange of information among its members and improves efficiency in communication. This gives rise to a cumulative cycle of growing homogeneity and increased efficiency. At an industry or sector level, the loss of diversity often takes place through the evolution of an industry. At an early stage, an industry enjoys varieties in products, firms, and organizations, which is followed by their replication and selection in the market place.[33] Toward the end of its life cycle, many firms in the industry come to share the same ideas about who their customers are and what products and services they want. Clayton Christensen suggests that the more they share this conventional wisdom about how they compete, the more they fight for incremental improvements in cost reductions and quality and the more they avoid discontinuous disruptive new products.[34]

We consider that those who are engaged in innovation activity are divided into a large number of specialist groups working on their own areas of knowledge, and it is these groups we call knowledge communities. Although geniuses like Leonardo Da Vinci and Albert Einstein broke the barrier and produced outstanding achievements in multiple disciplines, more average individuals specialize and create new knowledge in a small area due to the limited amount of resources available to them and the increasing amount of knowledge they need to master.[35] Individuals engaged in innovation often gain inspiration from outside of their specialized area, yet develop and polish these inspirations to the point of finalized product forms using the skills and expertise they have acquired through long periods of education and training. These latter processes force them to use shared codes of practice that reinforce their specialized discipline. A key issue here is how to strike a balance between communication within their own discipline and connection with knowledge in other disciplines.

In general, managers and policy makers need to maintain diversity in skills and competencies when they endeavor to connect knowledge within and across organizational units. This idea has come to find some acceptance within managerial circles, as evidenced by the use of cross-functional teams and concurrent engineering within a growing number of firms. However, it is harder to put the idea into practice when connecting knowledge across firms, as the herd mentality comes into effect at the industry and sector level. In fact, policy programs aimed at stimulating innovation often produce opposite effects. A broad range of policy programs now exist across the world that try to help facilitate the transfer and connection of knowledge across organizations.[36] One of the prominent programs in recent years has concerned attempts to develop 'clusters', or spatial agglomerations of firms operating in related sectors, with Harvard Business School's Michael Porter being the key architect.[37] However, in regions whose key industries have entered a mature phase, blind faith in cluster development may be counter-productive. As Christensen argues, mature industries need to break away from existing patterns of connecting knowledge and seek new knowledge outside clusters of similar businesses.

Structure of the book

In this book, we strive to provide a bird's eye view of the knowledge-based economy with several detailed analyses of the above three processes: *creating* and *connecting* knowledge for *growing* productivity. A good few books are already published that look into one or two of these processes. While we appreciate these works for their depth of analysis and the sophistication of analytical tools employed, they do not always give a 'feel' of the magnitude with which these three processes permeate today's economy. There are also publications such as the OECD's *Science, Technology and Industry Scoreboard*, which provides an overview of the knowledge-based economy by presenting a wide range of statistical indicators.[38] Again, while we find these publications useful, they are thin in their coverage of those aspects that do not lend themselves to quantitative descriptions. Our goal is to bridge these two approaches.

The structure of the book is as follows. In Chapter 2, we provide an overview of growth in the knowledge creation capabilities of advanced economies before examining their growth performance. In spite of the greater number of individuals being devoted to the creation of new ideas in recent decades, rates of productivity growth in advanced economies, such as the US, Japan, France, and Germany, have remained more or less the same. We introduce the idea of knowledge community to understand this contradiction. The picture emerging from this analysis is a hyper-competitive economy where the gap between 'haves' and 'have-nots' of knowledge and skills is growing.

Silicon Valley, 'the Hollywood of high tech', is the focus of Chapter 3. We compare over 100 best-performing regional economies across the globe in terms of the knowledge-based capacity of firms and explore why Silicon Valley leads the rest. The capacity of firms to use knowledge can be measured by the amount of value they produce through a combined unit of their physical capital (i.e. equipment, machinery, buildings) and labor. Our analysis reveals that Silicon Valley is the best all-round player in the world. It excels in information technology–related knowledge creation and scores high in all the other aspects associated with measures of the knowledge-based capacity of businesses. Although there are some regions that excel in one knowledge-based aspect, none show the all-roundness of Silicon Valley. This implies that a competence in one particular area alone is not enough to lift the innovation performance of an economy.

In Chapter 4, we discuss in greater depth the concept of network capital. Our discussion of network capital centers on clusters of knowledge-based businesses as the arena where both network capital and social capital are most likely generated and, in turn, underpin a cluster's operation. The focus upon knowledge-based clusters continues in Chapter 5, in which we examine important examples of knowledge-based business clusters around the globe, including Silicon Valley, San Francisco, Tokyo, Ottawa, Cambridge, and Helsinki, as well as newly emerging clusters in China and India. While our analysis of best-performing regions in Chapter 3 is a snapshot at the turn of the twenty-first century, the case studies presented in Chapter 5 are concerned with their genesis and evolution over time. The case studies demonstrate that the formation of relationships and the exchange and interaction between groups of like-minded businesses are the foundation upon which the development and evolution of knowledge clusters is based. Moreover, we argue it is the generation of these communication networks that policies aimed at developing knowledge clusters give insufficient attention to creating and facilitating.

If network capital is the force that sustains knowledge-based clusters, skills and talent are their basic unit. The emergence of the knowledge economy has placed education and training in a position of paramount importance throughout the world. The importance of developing and maintaining a skilled workforce has become heightened by the increasing mobility of capital resulting in the allocation of corporate resources at a global level. In Chapter 6, we argue that individuals seeking education and training, and policy makers assisting them, require the foresight to identify those skills that should be demanded, rather than merely those that are demanded by firms. We also trace a shift in Foreign Direct Investment (FDI) attraction policy from its previous emphasis upon job creation to focus upon creating opportunities to connect the advanced knowledge of inward investors to local indigenous firms.

In Chapter 7, we return to the subject of network capital. The focus of this chapter is the management of external knowledge sourcing. We examine two key forces shaping the knowledge sourcing behaviors of firms – clusters and industry life cycles – as well as the influence of management style. We argue that knowledge sourcing is an evolutionary process dependent upon the nature of the relationships built with the knowledge source. These relationships are a productive asset, or what is termed network capital. However, we contend that these relationships can sometimes constrain firms in their innovation activity and make them vulnerable to disruptive changes.

A key element in the success of knowledge commercialization is the availability of suitable finance. There is increasing evidence that academic and research institutions, corporations, and individuals alike are facing significant problems in accessing finance to fund knowledge-based venturing. In Chapter 8, we examine the development of seed and early stage funds as a means of bridging the equity gap. While there is clear evidence of market failure in the provision of seed finance to knowledge-intensive business ventures, government intervention also suffers from a number of shortcomings. In particular, it should be recognized that seed finance alone is not sufficient to stimulate successful knowledge-based entrepreneurship, as evidenced by our analysis of Silicon Valley as the world's leading knowledge-based region.

Finally, we conclude our analysis of the knowledge-based economy in Chapter 9 by discussing key future management and policy implications. In particular, we focus upon the implications of changes in the global distribution of knowledge and the new flows and connections emerging between the traditionally knowledge-intensive regions of North America and Europe and their rapidly emerging counterparts in Asia, especially in China and India.

2 The origin and reality of the knowledge-based economy

> The modern world is swept by change. New technologies emerge constantly, new markets are opening up. There are new competitors but also great new opportunity … Our success depends on how well we exploit our most valuable assets: our knowledge, skills, and creativity. These are the key to designing high-value goods and services and advanced business practices. They are at the heart of a modern, knowledge driven economy.
>
> (Tony Blair, foreword for *Our Competitive Future: Building the Knowledge Driven Economy*)[1]

The term *knowledge-based economy*, or its equivalents the *knowledge economy* and *knowledge-driven economy*, frequently shows up in government reports and policy speeches these days. It has become a cliché in policy circles, which always points to a bright side of the modern economy or a model of the future economy. While the positive image has some truth, the knowledge-based economy is not necessarily what the image conveys. This chapter reviews how the knowledge-based economy has come to the fore in the current discussion of economic development. It shows how the knowledge-based economy is distinct from the old, traditional economy. It also explores the recent trend of knowledge-based economic growth, referring to the performance of advanced economies, particularly in the US and the UK. In spite of its image of hyper performance, the knowledge-based economy grows only at a moderate pace. Another clear and disturbing feature of the knowledge-based economy is the polarization in the wealth distribution between the 'haves' and the 'have-nots' with a capacity to utilize knowledge.

Origin of the knowledge-based economy

It has been a long time since economists first recognized contributions of knowledge to the growth of productivity through technical change and the associated increase of per capita income. In the production of goods and services, individuals or organizations combine knowledge of a range of technologies relevant to their production circumstances with knowledge about the markets they operate in, such as demand characteristics and competing firms. Back in the late eighteenth century, Adam Smith already recognized the economic contribution of knowledge through the division of labor. He saw increases in labor productivity (i.e. output per worker) as arising from divisions of labor in the following three ways: (1) the increased dexterity of each worker (2) the saving of time lost in a shift from one task to another, and (3) the invention of higher-productivity machines and equipment.[2] Of the three sources, the first refers to the formation of skills embodied in each worker. The third points to technical progress embodied in machinery and equipment as a result of advances in engineering at that time. In addition, the division of labor itself (and particularly the saving of time in the changeover between different production tasks) represents a new way of organizing the work process. This foresaw a source of productivity increases as accruing from the present-day just-in-time system. All these arose from the knowledge bases of those individuals and organizations that introduced and implemented the idea. Following Smith's observation of the variety of sources contributing to productivity growth, a number of economists – such as Karl Marx, Walt Rostow, and Simon Kuznets, to name a few – argued that structural changes driven by technological and organizational innovations are a source of economic growth.[3] The most well-known architect of such a vision is Joseph Schumpeter who coined the evolution of a capitalist economy as 'creative destruction'. Schumpeter says:

> Capitalism ... is by nature a form or method of economic change and not only never is but never can be stationary.... The fundamental impulse that sets and keeps the capitalist engine in motion comes from the new consumers' goods, the new methods of production or transportation, the new markets, the new forms of industrial organization that capitalist enterprise creates.[4]

However, innovation was relegated to the background of mainstream economics in a greater part of the twentieth century. The efforts of neoclassical economists were primarily aimed at accounting for how scarce resources are allocated among their alternative uses. This focus excluded from their analytical framework the question of how firms choose and develop technologies, processes, and products.[5] Factors causing a change in technology were considered external to their framework (i.e. 'exogenous'), while a change in labor and capital was seen as internal ('endogenous') and was to be accounted for. For instance, Robert Solow found that over 80 percent of labor productivity growth in the US in the first half of the twentieth century was due to something other than investment in plants and equipment. He called this the 'residual' and suggested that it included the effects of technical change. However, he did not account for how the technical change occurred, seeing it as residing outside his analytical framework.[6] Growth accounting with this neoclassical view ensued, including the studies of Edward Denison in the 1960s and John Kendrick in the 1970s.[7] Like their predecessor, however, they did not come to terms with the question of how firms make investment decisions to create technological knowledge through research and development (R&D).[8] It was not until the mid 1980s that this changed with the appearance of *new growth theory*. New growth theory attempted to 'endogenize' technical progress in a neoclassical framework. Given the dominance of the neoclassical paradigm in Anglo-Saxon countries (particularly the US), the birth of new growth theory, led by the Stanford economist Paul Romer, caused a sensation in academic circles and beyond. It is new growth theory that sheds new light upon knowledge-based economic growth.

The concept of the knowledge-based economy originally emerged out of the depths of the early 1980s recession in the US.[9] By the end of the 1970s, the US economy had experienced a considerable slowdown in productivity growth. Whereas the labor productivity of US private business sector grew at an average annual rate of 3.5 percent between 1948 and 1965, its growth declined to 2.8 percent in the period between 1965 and 1972. After the first oil price shock, US labor productivity further fell to an annual rate of less than one percent and came to a virtual halt at the end of the 1970s.[10] The productivity slowdown in the US was accompanied by deindustrialization with widespread and systematic disinvestment in the country's basic productive capacity. Capital was diverted from productive investment in basic industries toward speculation, mergers and acquisitions, and foreign investment. This resulted in ageing capital stock (such as equipment, machinery, and buildings) at home and a growth in the resources made available to US corporate subsidiaries operating abroad. As a consequence, plants were closed in basic industries such as steel and automotive, leaving workers displaced and communities abandoned.[11]

The combination of the slowdown in productivity and deindustrialization created doubts about service-led growth in the postindustrial era in the United States. Earlier than this, some economists had already foreseen the potential for productivity slowdown, pointing out gaps in productivity growth between two groups of activities within the economy. One is technologically progressive activities in which innovations, capital accumulation, and scale economies result in a cumulative rise in productivity. The other group includes activities which by their very nature permit only sporadic increases in productivity. While the first group includes manufacturing and some other services, the second non-progressive group encompasses a wide range of labor-intensive services, such as municipal government, education, performing arts, restaurants, and leisure-time activity.[12] This gave rise to the popular idea that productivity growth and standards of living were doomed to slow in the service-led economy. Several studies estimated how much the shift of labor force from manufacturing to services accounted for the slowing down of productivity in the US economy. According to these estimates, the manufacturing-to-services shift in employment accounted for anywhere between 10 and 40 percent of the slowing down in productivity.[13] Although this was less than might have been anticipated, the pessimists in the US were fixated with the country's deindustrialization and what appeared to be the irrevocable decline of the US economic system.[14] Some saw a weakness in the country's mass production system and advocated a shift towards an economy consisting of flexibly specialized small- and medium-sized firms.[15] Others focused upon a lack of integration of R&D into production and criticized the 'get-rich-quick' mentality embedded in the US system of venture capitalists and high-tech entrepreneurs.[16] Government policy did not escape from criticism either. Through comparison with 'developmental states' in Asia, some held the US government responsible for the lack of a concerted effort to proactively engage with industry in the area of industrial and trade policy.[17]

However, the psyche in the US started to change in the late 1980s. A number of observers took note of the rapid application of the silicon chip and digital technology in a wide range of areas.[18] With such icons in the computer industry as Bill Gates of Microsoft and Steven Jobs of Apple, the rise of entrepreneurship and small start-ups was hailed as a new source of economic vitality.[19] The combination of high technology and entrepreneurship gave rise to new, bright visions of the postindustrial era. The knowledge-based economy is one such vision. In the simplest terms, the knowledge-based economy centers its vitality on the capacity to create new ideas, innovate processes and products, and translate these into economic value and wealth.

'Weightless economy' and 'information economy'

The vision of the knowledge-based economy has a number of variants. Two popular ones are the *weightless economy* and the *information economy*.[20] In the weightless economy, a process of progressive dematerialization is under way. Its proponents argue that as developed economies continue to grow, a greater fraction of their gross domestic product (GDP) resides in economic commodities that have little or no physical manifestation. Such weightless products range from low technology activities such as haircuts and gardening through to financial services and high technology activities such as software development and telecommunications. Most importantly, the dematerialization process is positively associated with growth in the market for information and communication technologies (that is, ICT spending).[21]

In a similar vein, the information economy emphasizes the emergence of new information and communication technologies (ICTs) and the revolutionary role they have come to play in the modern economy. The concept generally focuses upon service sectors and occupations that make intensive use of information and ICTs. By distinguishing information-intensive services from the rest, it addresses the weakness of the post-industrial thesis that treats services as effectively homogeneous.[22] A number of studies have attempted to measure the share of the economic wealth originating from information-intensive activities.[23] A study of the information sector in the US suggests that it represented over 30 percent of GDP in 1997, up from 12 percent in 1950.[24] Another measure of the information economy is ICT-income share: the ratio of the value-added attributable to ICT equipment to the total value-added. In the US, the income share of ICT was 5.50 percent in 2000, up from 4.29 percent in 1990. The share in the UK increased more dramatically by almost 50 percent, rising from 4.30 percent in 1990 to 6.26 percent in 2000.[25]

Although the concept of the knowledge-based economy embraces the weightless economy and the information economy, it is distinguished from them on a number of accounts. Most importantly, the knowledge-based economy focuses upon the role of knowledge in innovation and economic growth, and pays attention to both technologically progressive manufacturing sectors and information-intensive service sectors as a major source of innovations. In spite of the growing presence of some innovative service sectors, innovations in the service sector as a whole often capitalizes on technical progress made by the manufacturing sector. A majority of innovation efforts in the form of formal R&D still takes place in manufacturing industries. However, R&D performances in services has made steady growth due to high levels of technological intensity in services related to ICTs.[26] In 1988, the number of qualified scientists and engineers employed in US private-sector service-producing industries, many of whom were software specialists in finance and retailing, amounted to 359,000 and 446,000 respectively, compared with 225,000 and 830,000 in private-sector goods-producing industries.[27] By 2001, the combined total of scientists and engineers employed in service-producing industries had overtaken their counterparts in goods-producing industries – 1,533,100 scientists and 511,500 engineers were employed in service-producing industries, while their counterparts in goods-producing industries numbered 326,500 and 593,800 respectively.[28] However, in terms of formal R&D expenditures, the service sector is still a smaller spender than the manufacturing sector. The share of R&D expenditures made by the service industry stood at 38.3 percent in the US in 2001, up from 24.3 percent in 1991. For the UK, the share of R&D expenditures made by service industry was 18.7 percent in 2001, up from 15.1 percent in 1991.[29]

In general, the innovation activity of service firms relies less on formal R&D than manufacturing firms. Instead, service firms are much more likely to claim an orientation towards organizational innovation.[30] A greater proportion of their innovation investment takes the form of the acquisition of machinery and equipment, software and technology, and expenditure on training, design, and marketing. Service firms in the UK spend on average 4.0 percent of their turnover on such acquisitions and R&D, while manufacturing firms spend 3.2 percent.[31] The purchase of productivity-enhancing machinery and equipment by services industries also shows a route through which manufacturing contributes to productivity growth.

Increased investment in innovation efforts by services industries, and particularly by the information sector, in turn gives rise to growth in the sales of manufactured goods to service industries. In the US, the share of manufacturing output sold to the information sector recorded an almost three-fold increase from 1972 to 1996.[32] In contrast, output from the information sector as a percentage of GDP grew by no more than 70 percent during the period.[33] This trend continued in the more recent period of 1998–2005.[34] The significantly faster growth of manufacturing sales to the information sector indicates the growing importance of manufactured goods (and particularly ICT equipment) to innovation efforts and productivity growth in service industries.[35] Complementarities exist between services and manufacturing in their growth process.[36]

Given its focus on the role of knowledge for innovation and productivity growth, the idea of the knowledge-based economy is distinct from the weightless economy and the information economy. The idea covers not only 'weightless' products but also technology-intensive heavy products. For instance, aircraft and spacecraft produced by the aerospace industry are the culmination of complex systems and sophisticated technologies in the modern era. However, they are neither dematerialized nor weightless, which excludes them from the weightless economy thesis.[37] The information economy emphasizes the low reproduction costs of information and its near instantaneous transmission by ICTs.[38] This often leads to a conjecture that the exchange and transfer of knowledge is almost effortless and unrestricted, which, as we demonstrate in the following chapters, is untrue. In a similar vein, the focus of the information economy upon ICTs neglects the significance of knowledge carried through means other than ICTs.[39] An illustrative example showing the significance of non-ICT communication is the idea of 'clusters'. The geographical clustering of firms in related sectors facilitates the exchange of information through face-to-face communication, as well as savings in transportation costs, due to proximity. This leads to the development of a common knowledge base which businesses in a cluster share, providing them with a significant competitive advantage in the global economy.[40] Furthermore, firms cannot benefit from ICT equipment and devices to their fullest extent simply by setting them up in their workplace. They need to reorganize production and create *intangible capital* in the form of organizational knowledge. The availability of cheap ICT equipment and devices is likely to effect major changes only if firms can deploy other inputs in radically different ways.[41] Creation of such productivity-enhancing organizational knowledge takes place outside the production of ICT hardware and software. While the weightless economy and the information economy have their own merits in terms of their focus, they exclude from consideration some of the important aspects knowledge plays in the growth processes of the modern economy.

The unique nature of knowledge

Two unique characteristics of knowledge, – *non-rivalry* and *non-excludability* – come into play in the dynamics of economic growth in a more intricate way than is often presumed. Rivalry refers to whether consumption of a good by one person precludes its consumption by another or not: if it does, the good is 'rival' and if not, the good is 'non-rival'. When a person eats an apple, the particular apple is in the person's stomach and not available for consumption by another person. Normal goods, such as energy and raw materials, are rival. On the other hand, knowledge, such as a recipe for a fruitcake, can be used infinite times. Even if someone makes a fruitcake by using a recipe for it, the recipe still exists for another to use. The consumption of knowledge by one person does not preclude its consumption by another; knowledge is non-rival.

The second characteristic, 'excludability', refers to whether an owner of a good can prevent others from using it: if an owner can, the good is 'excludable', and if not, the good is 'non-excludable'. When a person purchases a car, the person can protect its use by another person by keeping the car key at hand or even parking the car in a locked garage. A car, like other normal goods, is excludable. On the other hand, air in the open space is normally non-excludable, because one cannot prevent others from breathing it. Furthermore, there is a type of economic good called a 'public good', which consists of items such as public roads, bridges, and parks. Public goods are by definition non-excludable, as any member of the public cannot keep other members from using them. As for knowledge, it is non-excludable once its creator discloses it to others. When someone creates a recipe for a new type of fruitcake, the creator can protect it by not telling anyone else. However, if a new recipe's creator discloses it (e.g. telling the recipe to friends), then the creator cannot prevent others from using it any more. Knowledge becomes subject to non-excludability when its creator makes the knowledge known to others or sells a product embodying the knowledge that will allow others to do 'reverse engineering'.[42] One way of preventing this non-excludability from coming into effect is patenting. In those countries where intellectual property rights (IPR) laws are in place, an inventor of a new product (e.g. a chemical formula, a mechanical device, a computer program) can apply for a patent so that the invention is protected from others copying it for free, and receives financial rewards in the shape of payments from licensees who have to make payments to use the knowledge created by the inventor. However, every person is free to study the patent and learn the knowledge that makes the product possible. Such individuals, or firms and organizations, can further develop the knowledge and create a new product. In this sense, knowledge is non-excludable, although regulatory systems such as patenting protect and reward the creators of knowledge.

New growth theory (or modern endogenous growth theory) takes into account these two characteristics of knowledge when explaining economic growth. Unlike natural resources that can be depleted through consumption, knowledge can accumulate without bounds. Those workers who are engaged in innovative activity create new knowledge, which adds to a common knowledge base within an economy. New knowledge added to the base then increases the productivity of those workers engaged in innovation activity and stimulates further innovation. In this way, the two characteristics of knowledge are presumed to give rise to a virtuous cycle of innovation and knowledge accumulation. Proponents of new growth theory assume that the process is a key driver of long-run economic growth.[43]

While new growth theory came into the spotlight in the early 1990s, contributions of knowledge to economic growth were not new. As noted earlier, in the 1950s Robert Solow produced some indicative evidence that technical progress accounted for a significant proportion of economic growth in the US in the first half of the twentieth century. What distinguishes the present era from the previous ones is the primary position of the capacity to create and utilize knowledge as a determinant of wealth. Looking back at economic history of the last two centuries, Lester Thurow writes that knowledge and human capital have replaced natural resources as the primary resources for wealth creation in advanced economies.[44] In the nineteenth and early twentieth century, wealthy countries were endowed with natural resources or had preferential, and often exclusive, access to natural resources in other places through colonial systems. These wealthy countries often maintained their positions through large savings from natural resource–based industries and their investment into plant and equipment, which led to productivity growth. In contrast, key industries in advanced economies in the late twentieth century – microelectronics, biotechnology, telecommunications, new materials, aerospace, robots, and computer hardware and software – are all what Thurow calls 'man-made brainpower industries'. In the equation of determining the competitiveness of economies, natural resource endowments have lost much of their previous significance. Modern products often require fewer amounts of natural resources. Natural resources can be also sourced in a global market and moved cheaply at increasingly lower transportation costs. Capital availability has also fallen out of the competitive equation to a large extent, as anyone can borrow through the world's capital markets. Thurow says, 'today knowledge and skills stand alone as the source of comparative advantage' and 'become the key ingredient in the late twentieth century's location of economic activity'.[45]

The début of new growth theory in the US in the early 1990s could not have been timelier. After the US economy experienced negative growth in real GDP terms in 1980 and 1982, it staged a recovery and showed a steady growth until 2000, with the exception of a short slump in 1991. In the period from 1985 to 2000, the economy grew by 60 percent in real GDP terms with an average annual growth rate of 3.1 percent.[46] The recovery and growth of the US economy was paralleled by a rise in productivity. After labor productivity came to a virtual halt at the end of the 1970s, it resumed growth in the 1980s at an average annual rate of 1.3 percent and then made a further recovery to 2.1 percent in the 1990s.[47] The recovery and rapid growth renewed enthusiasm in the US economic system that tends to reward risk-taking and entrepreneurship. With the 'technology boom' in the US stock market in the 1990s, new growth theory came to the fore in academic and policy circles in the US and elsewhere as a key foundation to explain technology-based growth.[48] What if new growth theory had originated in Japan whose economy suffered a recession for most of the 1990s?

Why the knowledge-based economy has not grown more rapidly?

The popularity of new growth theory as a theoretical foundation of knowledge-based economic growth has brought its assumptions under scrutiny. This derives from one of the realities of the knowledge-based economy: a relatively modest growth rate. There is little doubt that the US is one of the leading knowledge-based economies, if not the most advanced of them all. In 2000, the US invested 6.8 percent of GDP in knowledge creation and utilization, measured by the sum of R&D expenditures, software purchases, and public and private spending on higher education. This was the second highest among OECD economies, following only Sweden which spent 7.2 percent of its GDP on these activities.[49] Also, the US boasts the most highly educated labor force of all OECD economies. Twenty-seven percent of the US population aged 25 to 64 had a bachelor's or higher degree in 1999. This was by far the highest percentage of all OECD economies.[50] Furthermore, 90 out of every 10,000 persons in the labor force worked as researchers in the US in 1999, surpassed only by three countries – Finland, Sweden, and Japan.[51]

The US economy has also become more knowledge-based in all the above aspects. The investment in knowledge creation and utilization (i.e. sum of R&D expenditures, software purchases, and public and private spending on higher education) as a percentage of GDP grew from 5.8 percent in 1991 to 6.8 percent in 2000.[52] Those with a bachelor's or higher degree as a percentage of the population aged 25 and over grew from 4.6 percent in 1940 to 24.4 percent by 2000.[53] The number of R&D scientists and engineers per 10,000 persons in the labor force hit an all-time high of 90 persons in 1999, up from 25 in 1950 and 75 in 1987.[54] With the US possessing such a large knowledge base by the 1990s, accompanied by the technology boom and the state of economic euphoria surrounding it, this might lead one to expect that the US grew at an unprecedented pace during this period. However, productivity growth in the US in the 1990s was modest when compared with the golden age of the 1950s and 1960s. The labor productivity of the US private business sector grew at an annual average rate of 3.5 percent between 1948 and 1965 and 2.8 percent between 1965 and 1972. By contrast, the average growth rate from 1990 to 2000 stood at only 2.1 percent.[55] The trend is the same with total factor productivity, which measures the ratio of the output of goods and services to a combination of inputs including labor and capital. In the period from 1990 to 2000, total factor productivity of US private businesses grew at an average annual rate of 1 percent. This growth rate is significantly lower than 2.4 percent in the period 1948–65 and 1.6 percent in the period 1965–72.[56] If knowledge is cumulative, and the number of people in the US receiving higher education or engaged in knowledge-based occupations is at its highest, why did productivity not grow at a record-breaking rate?

Increased difficulty in creating innovations

One of the factors that explain this slower than expected growth is the possibility of increased difficulty in creating innovations.[57] In the past, economists of the so-called 'acceleration school' thought that the generation of a new piece of knowledge would increase the probability of creating new products, processes, and ideas from novel and unanticipated combinations. In other words, the more knowledge is invented, the easier it becomes to invent still more. By contrast, the 'retardation school' of economics predicts the opposite: the more knowledge is invented, the less easy it becomes to invent still more.[58] If R&D activities are considered to be a main source of new knowledge useful to the production of goods and services, increased difficulties in creating new knowledge and innovations may be manifested by a decline of productivity in R&D, that is, the ratio of R&D output (i.e. new knowledge) to R&D input (e.g. professional labor) becomes smaller than before. For measuring R&D output, the number of patents is often used as a proxy.[59]

There are a number of pitfalls associated with equating the number of patents with the level of R&D output.[60] To start with, recent changes in the coverage of patent registrations makes historical analysis difficult.[61] In particular, a shift in the regime for the protection of intellectual property in computer software has led to an explosive growth of software patents since the early 1990s.[62] Because of this, any historical analysis of changes in patent counts needs care when identifying a trend of growth or decline.

Second, not all inventions are patented, as industries vary in their propensity to seek patents. Firms protect inventions with a range of mechanisms, including secrecy, lead-time advantages, and the use of complementary marketing and manufacturing capabilities. Patent protection is really important only in a few industries, most notably pharmaceuticals.[63] Large R&D industries with significant governmental research support, such as automotive and aircraft, tend to patent very much less than their R&D inputs would predict. Furthermore, some low technology sectors, such as the manufacturers of screws, nuts, and bolts, take out occasional patents in spite of their almost non-existent R&D activities.[64] Patented inventions also vary greatly in the magnitude of their technical and economic significance. Granting patents to inventions means that these inventions qualify for the standard set by the patent office in terms of novelty and potential usefulness. While some patents prove extremely valuable, a large majority reflect minor improvements of little economic value.[65] Though patents statistics are widely used as the best R&D-output proxy in terms of their quantity and accessibility, we need to take into account all the difficulties relating to their use and interpretation.

If we take patenting as a proxy for outputs of inventive activity, long-run trends show a decline in the ratio of R&D outputs to inputs until recently. As far back as the 1930s, economists have noticed the slackening in the growth rate of technical progress relative to R&D inputs in the US.[66] They found that the number of patents scarcely kept pace with the growth of population or the growth in the numbers of researchers since the late nineteenth century. In the 1960s, Fritz Machlup compiled evidence on the number of patents per worker engaged in R&D in the US for the period 1870–1960. If 1900 is taken as a base year, the number of scientists and engineers in 1954 was 16 times larger. In contrast, the number of patents granted in 1954 was only 37 percent higher than in 1900.[67] These declining trends continued through the 1970s. While the number of researchers in the US has grown by nearly 5 percent every year since the early 1950s, the number of patents granted to US residents was roughly constant for four decades with some fluctuations.[68] The decline in patents per researcher is also observed globally. A study by Robert Evenson reveals that, from 1964 to 1979–80, the ratio of patents granted per scientist/engineer engaged in R&D fell in almost all of the 50 countries covered by his study.[69]

The number of utility patents (i.e. patents for inventions) granted by the US Patent and Trademark Office (USPTO) to patentees of US origin peaked at 55,976 in 1971 and then gradually declined to a low of 30,078 in 1979. It has picked up pace since then and broke the previous record in 1996 with 61,104 patents registered. The number continued to climb and reached a high of 87,607 in 2001.[70] However, when measured in terms of per dollar spent on R&D, the level of patenting activity has not improved.[71] In a similar vein, the number of USPTO patent grants per 1,000 R&D scientists and engineers remained around 50 during most of the 1990s, which is similar to levels in the early 1980s.[72] A recent study of national innovative capacity of 17 OECD countries also suggests that average global R&D productivity declined during the period 1973–95.[73]

The long-run decline in the ratio of patents to workers engaged in R&D suggests a possibility of increased difficulty in producing innovations. Faced with puzzling statistics on these long-run trends, economists have offered a number of potential explanations. One is a decline in the propensity of firms to patent their inventions due to the increasing cost of obtaining and enforcing patents. However, this does not account for the universal observation of the drop in patent numbers relative to R&D workers, since many countries have not experienced rises in patent enforcement costs.[74] Another possibility is that the composition of industrial sectors has moved toward an increase in the activities of those sectors that are less likely to patent inventions. However, against this hypothesis, patenting relative to real R&D expenditures has fallen in all manufacturing sectors.[75] A further possible explanation is the rise in the average quality of patents, which would require more R&D inputs per patent.[76] Again, however, there is little evidence of universal changes in patent systems that would support this 'shrinking yardstick' explanation.

This leaves the possibility that technological breakthroughs have become increasingly hard to find as knowledge frontiers continue to advance. In any narrowly defined field or product area, the pool of inventive possibilities is likely to become depleted over time, until the field or product area is redefined anew by other major breakthroughs.[77] This is consistent with case studies of a number of industries that experienced technological booms and then entered a period of maturity.[78] Inventive effort moves from one 'fishing' ground to another and opens up new fishing grounds for inventions. However, the discovery of new fishing grounds may not keep pace with the depletion of old grounds. Declining patenting relative to R&D inputs indicates a sign of increased difficulty in creating innovations.

Knowledge spills over, but how far?

A further area of enquiry concerning moderate knowledge productivity growth is concerned with the extent to which workers engaged in R&D share a piece of knowledge. One of the key tenets of new growth theory is the assumption that a piece of knowledge *spills over* from its creator to others, with few associated costs. As already noted, knowledge has non-rival and non-excludable characteristics. Once an invention is disclosed, any person can study and gain from it. Although patenting prohibits the commercial use of an invention, the knowledge contained in the invention can be further utilized to create new products and processes.[79] If a greater number of R&D workers share the knowledge, then there will be a greater chance of successfully developing new products and processes based on the initial knowledge. In theory, the greater the number of workers engaged in R&D in a particular economy, the greater should be the number of product and process innovations and the faster the pace of knowledge-based productivity growth.

The *spillover* effects of knowledge can take place through time and across space. First, we can examine how spillovers take place through time. A study of 100 American firms by Edwin Mansfield revealed that information about decisions to develop a new product or process is, on average, in the hands of rivals within about 12 to 18 months. Also, information about the detailed nature and operation of a new product or process generally leaked within about a year after the completion of its development.[80] There are many channels through which information spreads. They include the movement of personnel from one firm to another, informal communication networks among engineers and scientists working at various firms, as well as professional meetings at which those workers gather and exchange information. In some industries, suppliers and customers pass on a great deal of information about one firm to its rivals. In other industries, patent applications are scrutinized very carefully, and reverse engineering is carried out. Although the basic information concerning the nature and operation of an innovation is not sufficient in many cases to permit the immediate introduction of an imitative product or process, it is a valuable source of ideas for the innovator's rivals.[81] Another study by Mansfield and his colleagues found that about 60 percent of patented successful innovations were imitated within four years of their introduction.[82] In one way or another, the creators of ideas today 'stand on the shoulders of the giants' that preceded them.[83]

Another dimension of spillovers is geographic distance. The general argument is that knowledge spills over more easily locally than at a distance. A study by Adam Jaffe and his colleagues discovered that citations to domestic patents were more likely to be domestic and more likely to come from the same region and locality as the cited patents. They also found that the localization of patent citations was significant even when the existing concentration of related research activity was taken into account.[84] This suggests that local firms are often embedded in knowledge-sharing networks.[85] Proximity to critical sources of knowledge reduces the costs of coordinating different sources and overcoming information gaps between knowledge-seekers and knowledge-providers. This takes place both horizontally between different firms operating at a particular stage in the production chain and vertically between firms operating at different stages in the production chain.[86] Also, ready access to local public or private research institutes and universities is another route through which knowledge flows. Such knowledge spillovers are especially important in highly R&D-intensive industries that deal with knowledge at the frontier of research. A study conducted by David Audretsch and Maryann Feldman shows that innovative activity tends to geographically cluster more in R&D-intensive industries where knowledge spillovers play a decisive role. Although such industries tend to exhibit a geographic concentration of production activity, clustering of their innovation activities tends to be even greater.[87]

Knowledge spillovers also take place internationally, but usually through more selective routes. Leading-edge technology constantly changes, resulting in new, better products and processes. Unless local networks keep abreast of different technological options emerging outside, they run the risk of becoming rigid and outdated.[88] In particular, the success of entrepreneurial endeavors – those taking the risk of starting up new ventures and tapping into new areas outside established technologies and markets – will depend on the firm's ability to access major markets from other localities and regions outside the cluster.[89] While firms benefit from local knowledge spillovers as an undirected, spontaneous 'buzz' in their cluster, they also need to consciously build non-local 'pipelines' to tap into knowledge from outside.[90] A study of innovative firms in the South East region of England, in fact, indicates that such firms seek knowledge from their overseas contacts, such as clients and distributors.[91] However, effects of international knowledge spillovers are smaller in scale than spillovers at the local level. According to a study of European regions, spillovers of knowledge from R&D and their effects in the form of patent generation are quite localized, usually within a distance of 300 kilometers.[92] Similarly, another study examining how R&D undertaken by G-5 countries influences the productivity of other OECD countries suggests that the productivity effect of spillovers is halved at a distance of 1,200 kilometers from the source of the R&D.[93]

There is little doubt that a virtuous cycle of knowledge spillovers tends to 'lift all boats'.[94] However, a question remains as to the role of such spillovers in the rise of the knowledge-based economy: Have the effects of knowledge spillovers become greater than before? One way of approaching this question is to examine changes in the balance between codified knowledge and tacit knowledge. Codified knowledge refers to information that can be easily communicated among individuals. Conversion of knowledge into information is a necessary condition for easy transmission, replication, and storage. By contrast, tacit knowledge – such as skills, competence, and talents – cannot be directly communicated to someone else in a verbal or other symbolic form. Science and technology draws crucially upon sets of human skills and techniques that are acquired experientially and transferred through demonstration, personal instruction, and movement of technical personnel.[95] The type of information contained in patents, blueprints, and other codified forms of knowledge is often, by itself, insufficient to successfully implement the technological innovations it aims to describe. There are tacit elements in technical knowledge, and the more tacit the knowledge is, the more it behaves like an ordinary private good that is rival and excludable.[96]

Some writers argue that economic incentives and available technologies largely determine whether knowledge is codified. In their view, more knowledge is becoming codified due to technological change and economic growth.[97] In particular, advances in ICTs have made it far easier to convert knowledge into readily-transmissible information and disseminate it on a greater scale than before. The increased availability of codified knowledge can bring the science base (i.e. universities and research institutes) into tighter and quicker interaction with the technological development of firms. It also increases the pace of product and process innovation by allowing testing and evaluation to be conducted through simulations, such as the use of computer simulation in the process of designing and evaluating a product's prototypes, rather than through practice.[98] A greater amount of codified knowledge implies an accelerated scale of knowledge spillovers and a faster pace of productivity growth.

However, a different picture emerges from a study of the knowledge sourcing behavior of firms. According to a study conducted by Stefano Brusoni and his colleagues at Sussex University, sources of codified knowledge are seen by firms to be relatively unimportant as sources of innovation. There are significant differences among industries of the extent to which firms rely on codified sources of information (such as patent disclosures and computer-based information networks). The use of sources of codified knowledge is closely associated with the use of other sources of knowledge involving more tacit elements, with firms that rely on sources of codified knowledge also investing heavily in R&D. This results from the fact that codified knowledge can be expensive to access and use.[99]

The results of the study highlight the importance of 'absorptive capacity' to identifying, assimilating, and exploiting knowledge from the environment. Individuals and organizations can have a particular kind of system to draw meaning and structure from (or 'understand') information consisting of explicit symbols. They have to acquire such systems over time through a process of 'apprenticeship' and trial-and-error learning. For example, even if Chinese characters can be beautifully written with pen and ink as symbols, the system necessary to read these characters and understand their meaning will have taken many years of skills training to be built.[100] The need for absorptive capacity is particularly strong at the frontier of new technologies. Lynne Zucker and her collaborators at the University of California in Los Angeles demonstrate that during the first ten to 15 years the US biotechnology industry was concentrated into a small initial group of discoverers and their coworkers. These discoverers possessed the genius and vision to continuously innovate and define the research frontier and apply the techniques of recombinant DNA in the most promising areas. Knowledge of the recombinant DNA techniques produced extraordinary returns only when used by those *star scientists* possessing an appropriate set of *intellectual human capital*.[101] A greater amount of codified *information* in modern society does not necessarily mean that we are able to observe an equally greater amount of codified *knowledge* than previous generations.[102] It is the absorptive capacity of individuals and organizations that determines the amount of knowledge they are able to understand and use.

Knowledge community

This calls into question the relevance of the stock of public knowledge which new growth theory assumes as one of its theoretical building blocks. The use of knowledge by R&D workers is not simply an outcome of the access to existing knowledge stocks, but their ability to learn and understand how to effectively apply knowledge to create commercial value. Such learning and understanding is a costly process, which results in the tendency of R&D worker to specialize in a particular area of knowledge. The process requires skills that R&D workers form through long periods of often costly education and training.[103] Given the limited amount of resources (including money and time) that can be invested in education and training, each R&D worker obviously has a limited capacity to understand and use differing forms of knowledge at any particular point in time.[104]

Indeed, the costly investment in skills formation means that R&D workers can benefit most by specializing in particular areas of knowledge. If an R&D worker participates in a number of projects that require different areas of knowledge, switching from one project to another is likely to incur costs. When an R&D worker does not work on a particular project, the worker may forget the best way of doing it, and it takes a while to relearn this knowledge. Such *switching costs* may be sufficiently high that R&D workers who are assigned many projects have little time to improve their performance and create new knowledge in any one of them.[105] The preferable knowledge set possessed by R&D workers becomes T-shaped as it is both deep at the frontier of a particular area of knowledge (the stem of the *T*) and, yet broad enough in related areas (the cross of the *T*). This skill structure enables R&D workers to explore the interface between a worker's own specialized knowledge area and various applications of this knowledge in particular products.[106] The skills structure is evident in the organization of work, whereby knowledge-based workers gain a competitive edge over others by pursuing an area of specialty.[107]

It is among workers specialized in the same area of knowledge that the sharing of knowledge contributes to creating new, state-of-the-art knowledge. This means that although knowledge resides within individuals, it is also embedded in *knowledge communities*.[108] New knowledge develops as individuals actively participate in the practices of a community of professionals who have received common training, share a language, and have a similar base of knowledge.[109] Iterations of interaction and exchange of information within a community leads to a convergence of the norms, values, and behaviors of its members through the further creation of local languages and coding schemes.[110] For example, mathematics is underpinned by its own language, using special characters. The evolution of local languages and coding schemes further lubricates the exchange of information among community members, allowing speedier and more accurate exchange of information. Members of these communities sooner or later learn from the accomplishments and failures of their predecessors. While accomplishments can be ascribed to particular individuals, new knowledge will often be shared as a common property by the communities within which these individuals are members.[111] The sharing of knowledge can also take place across knowledge communities, as well as within them. However, such cross-community knowledge sharing takes place mostly at a relatively elementary or intermediate level of knowledge. Given the need for individuals to devote their limited resources to efforts to stay at the respective knowledge frontier, most R&D workers understand state-of-the-art knowledge and contribute to its advancement only within their own community.

Variations in the number of knowledge communities within an industry are primarily influenced by two forces. One is the level of technical progress in each knowledge community. As technology advances in its sophistication and complexity, a greater amount of knowledge will accumulate along with the demand for individuals to learn more, resulting in more communities. For instance, examining data on Nobel Prize winners and great inventors, Benjamin Jones finds that the great minds at the start of the twentieth century began innovating, on average, at age 23, while the average for great minds at the end of the century rose to 31 years of age. Jones suggests that successive generations of researchers face an increasing educational burden and focus upon narrower expertise.[112] Such a force subsequently leads knowledge communities to focus on the increasingly narrower and more specialized areas of knowledge.

Another force is the widening technological base of an industry. Innovation rarely involves a single technology, but rather a bundle of knowledge brought together into a configuration.[113] Technological opportunities are generated through the combination and recombination of various technologies, new and old. Although not all combinations are technically and/or economically feasible, technological opportunities grow progressively due to the exponential growth of the number of possible technological combinations.[114] This gives rise to multi-technology products and processes involving larger numbers of technologies at the industry level, as well as increasing technology diversification and multidisciplinary R&D at the firm level. Many consumer and business products now contain a larger number of technologies than previously. The automotive industry's technology base has expanded from mechanical engineering to electro-mechanical systems, now stretching to include fuel cell technology.[115] Another example is more recent models of mobile phones, which now include digital cameras, music, and game players, representing a fusion of previously separate technologies.

These two forces – specialization of R&D workers and the widening technological base of industries – shape the number of knowledge communities operating in an industry, as well as the average number of R&D workers belonging to a community. Given the two forces, the growth of the R&D workforce does not necessarily lead to a higher rate of productivity growth. As technologies advance, knowledge communities focus on even narrower areas. This, combined with the widening technological base of an industry, increases the number of knowledge communities within an industry, spreading the industry's R&D workforce more thinly. Because of this, the average number of R&D workers within a knowledge community does not grow as fast as the industry's R&D workforce, since the number of knowledge communities is likely to proliferate. Our study of productivity growth in European regions shows that this model fits well with their recent performance.[116]

In general, the issues we have considered above point to a possible slowing down of productivity growth in the future. In advanced economies, productivity growth will arise from the growth of highly educated workers who are engaged in innovation activities. However, there is obviously a limit to the growth of this type of human capital. Not all employees of firms can be technologists and engineers. Workers cannot spend all of their time acquiring and developing skills through education and training either. At some point in time, the proportion of workers engaged in innovation activities within advanced economies will hit a ceiling. Then the growth in the number of R&D workers will be dependent solely on population growth. Although this scenario will not arise soon, we may see productivity grow more slowly in the future.[117]

A major route left for economies to stay innovative is better coordination among knowledge communities aimed at sparking synergy creation. As knowledge communities grow in number, it becomes more important to integrate diverse streams of the state-of-the-art knowledge residing within them. For individual firms, this means management's ability to combine knowledge of individual technologies and consolidate corporate-wide technologies and skills within their organizations.[118] Such coordination is also extended to their external environment. Given the growing technological complexity of products and processes, firms – small businesses and even large corporations – cannot source all necessary technologies in-house, and working with other players providing complementary technologies is an issue we discuss in subsequent chapters.

The bipolarization of 'haves' and 'have-nots' of knowledge and skills

The grim prospects for growth in the supercompetitive, knowledge-based race may discourage stakeholders from making long-term, and uncertain, investments in the future through R&D, training, and education. However, they would make a grave mistake by shunning these investments. We are already witnessing a growing polarization in wages between the 'haves' and 'have-nots' of knowledge and skills, and a lack of knowledge-based investment will only serve to accentuate this gap.

For a couple of decades after World War II, inequality, measured by wages or income, either remained stable or diminished in the US and Europe. For instance, in the US the wages of the top 10 percent earners and bottom 10 percent earners grew in tandem during the period, keeping the relative gap between the two groups stable.[119] Most European countries also witnessed a reduction of income inequality during the period.[120] This pattern was first broken in the US where overall wage inequality rose sharply in the early 1970s. In 1971, the top 10 percent of earners earned 266 percent more than the bottom 10 percent. By 1995, this gap had risen to 366 percent.[121] Furthermore, median wages stagnated from 1975 onwards, while the wages of the bottom 10 percent earners fell in real terms to levels below those in 1963.[122] Europe soon followed the trend set by the US, and by the second half of the 1980s most European countries saw increasing income inequality. In particular, a sharp rise in inequality has been most evident in the UK and Sweden, where inequality rose at a more rapid pace than in the US.[123] In the UK, the wages received by male manual workers reached a historical low, compared with the national average for all occupations, in 1990.[124]

This reflects the fast pace of wage growth among 'skilled' workers relative to 'less-skilled' workers, where the skills of workers is measured by years of schooling and labor market experience. In the US, for example, average weekly wages for the most-skilled workers rose by about 40 percent between 1963 and 1989. In contrast, the least skilled workers saw their wages decline by about five percent during the period.[125] More recently, the *college premium* – the wages of college graduates relative to the wages of high school graduates – increased by over 25 percent between 1979 and 1995.[126] Likewise, returns to education showed a clear increase in the UK during the 1980s. The increase in returns was largest particularly for high- and mid-level qualifications, such as university degrees and vocational qualifications from colleges.[127] The fast growth of skilled worker wages relative to less-skilled worker wages also occurred in other OECD countries. According to a study of manufacturing industries in ten developed countries, skilled, non-production workers saw their wages increase faster than less-skilled, production workers. The ratio of non-production wages to production wages rose at an average of 4 percent in these countries during the 1980s. Of the seven European countries analyzed, the rise of the differential in wages was the fastest in the UK, followed by Luxembourg, Denmark, and Austria, all of which marked a faster rise than the 4 percent average.[128]

Along with the faster rise of skilled worker wages, advanced economies also witnessed large reductions in the employment of less-skilled workers, which caused an increase in the share of skilled workers in industries producing exportable goods. For instance, since the 1970s, manufacturing industries in the US and the UK have shed a large number of less-skilled workers who worked on shop floors undertaking tasks such as fabricating, processing, assembling, and inspecting. This pushes up the proportion of skilled workers who are engaged in management, administration, and product development, as well as marketing, servicing, sales, and delivery.[129] Information technology equipment, electrical machinery, and printing and publishing are cases of industries undertaking skills upgrading most intensively.[130] Furthermore, skills upgrading has taken place outside of manufacturing as well.[131]

A market rule of thumb tells that a rise in the supply of a good pushes down its price. In light of this, it is puzzling to observe the long-run rise in wages for skilled workers relative to less-skilled workers when the supply of skilled worker is growing. In the US, for example, the wage premium of college graduates over high school graduates has grown substantially since 1950, even though there has been more than threefold increase in the employment share of college graduates.[132] If the wages of skilled workers kept rising relative to less-skilled workers, employers might be expected to reduce demand for skilled workers by replacing them with less-skilled workers. However, the double rise of both wages and demand for skilled workers can occur if the productivity of skilled workers grows at a faster pace than the productivity of less-skilled workers. If technical progress does not favor any particular group of workers, this would not happen. In reality, the faster productivity growth of skilled workers has occurred because technological progress has been more complementary to skilled than less-skilled workers. This is what economists call 'skill-biased technical progress'. The recent consensus is that technical change favors skilled workers, with the effect of boosting their productivity at a faster pace than the productivity of less-skilled workers, and replacing tasks previously performed by the latter.[133] The behavior of wages and returns to education indicates that technical change has been skill-biased during the past 60 years and probably for most of the twentieth century.[134]

There is much evidence to suggest that the relative growth in the share of skilled workers has a positive association with capital intensity (i.e. the amount of physical capital, such as computers and other ICT devices, per worker) and the implementation of new technologies across both industries and companies.[135] In particular, the rate of skills upgrading has been greater in those manufacturing and service sectors that use computers more intensively. Personal computers, computer-assisted production techniques, and robotics complement skilled workers by replacing many labor-intensive, low-skill tasks. Indicators of employee computer usage, computer investment per worker, and the proportion of computer investment to total investment are higher in industries with rapid rates of skills upgrading.[136] Changes in production processes through the use of ICTs are evident both in manufacturing and service sector activity. For example, in printing and publishing, the use of computers shifts almost all composition and keyboarding to professional and clerical employees, bypassing typesetting employees.[137] ICTs have also dramatically changed accounting and secretarial work in services such as the retail and financial sectors.[138] Furthermore, there is evidence at an individual level indicating a link between computer usage and higher wages. A study of employees in the US estimates that direct users of a computer at work earn 10 to 15 percent more than non-users.[139] As skilled workers are more likely to use computers than less-skilled workers, it is difficult to deny that technical progress in ICTs is more favorable to growth of both the productivity and wages of skilled workers.[140] Although skill-biased technical progress is not limited to the ICT revolution alone, ICTs have been at the centre of the phenomenon in recent decades.

Skills formation and skill-biased technical progress reinforce each other in the knowledge-based economy. However, technical progress has not always been favorable to skilled workers. In the nineteenth century, workshops run by skilled artisans were replaced first by factories and then by assembly lines and interchangeable parts. Many previously complex tasks were simplified, and workers with relatively few skills came to produce products previously manufactured by skilled artisans, reducing the demand for skilled workers.[141] Why did technical change shift away from being biased against to being biased in favor of skilled workers in the twentieth century – a feature which accelerated in the second half of the century? Daron Acemoglu argues that the rapid increase in the supply of skilled workers has induced the development of skill-complementary technologies.[142] Also, it is well documented that large-scale market demand has been crucial to the development of many technologies.[143] In early nineteenth century Britain, technical progress was characterized by skills replacement due to the migration of labor from agrarian villages to towns, which created a large inflow of unskilled workers and made profitable the introduction of technologies that assisted unskilled workers rather than skilled workers (e.g. skilled artisans at workshops were replaced by unskilled workers at new factories). By contrast, advanced economies in the second half of the twentieth century produced a large supply of well-educated workers through the mass higher-education system, creating a market for technologies complementary to them. This gave rise to a self-perpetuating process in which new skill-complementary technologies improve the productivity of skilled workers and raise their wages, making schooling and training more rewarding.

Skill-biased technical progress also increases wage inequality through changes in the way firms are organized: growth in the number of small firms employing skilled workers alone. There are three forces at play in this process. First, in large corporations where skilled workers often collaborate with less-skilled workers, there are situations that create downward pressures upon the productivity of skilled workers. For instance, new production processes designed by skilled workers may not achieve their potential when implemented by less-skilled workers, due to a lack of absorptive capacity on the part of the latter group. Second, labor unions at large corporations, representing the interests of less-skilled workers, apply upward pressures on their wages. With skill-biased technical change progressing further, it becomes more costly to adjust their wages upwardly in line with the wages of skilled workers. Third, skill-biased technical progress often enables skilled workers to automate tasks previously undertaken by less-skilled workers. These three forces make it more profitable for skilled workers to leave large corporations and set up their own businesses without their less-skilled counterparts.[144] This results in a reduction in the level of productivity at the large corporations from which skilled workers exit, pushing down the wages of remaining less-skilled workers. As a result, wage inequality is more accentuated in Anglo-Saxon countries that promote entrepreneurship through tax breaks and other support mechanisms, and deregulate labor markets than in, for example, continental Europe.[145]

In the US, men and women with four years of college experience earn, on average, nearly 45 percent more than those with only a high school diploma. This gap is as high as it has ever been, but it has been stuck in the range since the late 1990s, indicating a leveling off.[146] What may underlie such a leveling off is the interplay between advances in technology implementation and changes in organizations and their skill demands. The successful implementation of a technology requires skilled labor, the demand for which may gradually decrease and be followed by their replacement with less-skilled labor or even lower-wage workers abroad through offshoring. For instance, the introduction of a point-of-sale (POS) system in retailing initially requires the writing of a program to meet a retailer's specific needs, the program's test run and debugging, as well as the planning of overall implementation and employee training. Once the system is up and running, the initial demand for skilled labor gradually diminishes, leaving less skill-demanding tasks such as the use of the system at a check-out counter by a cashier. When the burst of technological changes and investment in ICTs subsides, demand for skilled labor may well decrease.[147] However, implementation of a new technology also brings about organizational changes and new skill demands which do not necessarily save on skill requirements. David Autor and his colleagues argue that organizational changes caused by ICT implementation create two types of skill demands. At a lower end of the skill spectrum, ICT investment reduces the labor input of routine manual and cognitive tasks that can be accomplished by following explicit rules and can be offshored to lower-wage countries. At a higher end, ICTs complement workers in performing non-routine problem solving and complex communications tasks, thus keeping, if not increasing, skilled jobs.[148]

Recent evidence suggests that in spite of the growth of outsourcing and offshoring of production tasks, the demand for skilled workers remains strong in the US labor market, supporting the two processes described above. A study by Robert Feenstra and Gordon Hanson suggests that foreign outsourcing of intermediate inputs, particularly production tasks performed by less-skilled workers, reduces demand for less-skilled workers in the US.[149] This makes the labor market structure more skill-intensive and raises the productivity level in the US with ripple effects through the supply chain. If a firm moves production tasks abroad either through outsourcing or foreign direct investment, it is also likely to source other inputs from there. This not only leads to an initial reduction in employment but also, in the long-run, stimulates productivity growth in upstream activity in the home country, as it forces upstream firms in the home country to compete with lower-cost competitors abroad.[150] The net effects are job growth, coupled with the reallocation of resources toward more technologically intensive sectors. A study by Global Insight finds that while global software and information technology (IT) service outsourcing has displaced some IT workers in the US, total employment has actually increased as the benefits ripple through the economy. The incremental economic activity that follows offshore outsourcing in the US is expected to create over 337,000 net new jobs by 2010.[151] However, to remain a highly productive economy, access to high level skills continues to be of paramount importance.

Conclusions

The picture of the knowledge economy we have drawn in this chapter is one in which a greater amount of resources are invested in knowledge creation and utilization than ever before, but which is operating under significant constraints, in particular increased difficulties in creating innovations, and limitations to knowledge sharing due to increased specialization. While the first constraint suggests the need to further invest in knowledge creation capacities, the second calls for strategies aimed at creating more mechanisms to facilitate the flow and sharing of knowledge both within a specialized area of expertise and across such specialized areas. Furthermore, technical progress in recent decades has favored knowledge workers, enhancing their productivity at a faster pace than the productivity of their less-skilled counterparts. Given the projected increase in the world supply of well-educated workers, skill-biased technical change is likely to continue. Therefore, although competition in the knowledge economy is a grueling affair, it is far better to stay in the race than quit.

3 Knowledge-based capacity of best-performing regions

> In 1940, Santa Clara County was a peaceful agricultural valley. By 1960, the electronics industry had taken root and it had become one of the fastest growing urban areas in the country. By 1970, it had gained its reputation as Silicon Valley, the world capital of the semiconductor industry.[1]

When AnnaLee Saxenian, an expert on the Silicon Valley economy at Berkeley, wrote this in 1981, she drew attention to the urban problems that plagued the region at the time, such as skyrocketing housing costs, traffic congestion, and high levels of air and water pollution. Today, these problems still persist in the region.[2] The region has also experienced a number of setbacks, most recently the biggest job losses in its history, with the collapse of the Internet boom in 2001.[3] Nonetheless, Silicon Valley has repeatedly shown resilience and is still best known as the world center of innovation or the 'Hollywood of high tech'.[4] For business managers, it leads the world in being able to combine scientific invention with a robust business plan, and for policy makers it represents a model of the innovative high-tech economy to imitate.[5]

This chapter compares Silicon Valley with over 100 other leading regional economies across the globe and analyzes its strengths in terms of the capacity of its businesses to use knowledge in production, to create and translate new ideas into economic value, and to sustain knowledge-based wealth creation. As the basis of competition shifts away from natural resources to brainpower, these abilities are key to the success of individual workers, firms, and national and regional economies. In this chapter, we ask: What is the position of Silicon Valley in today's knowledge-based economy? How does Silicon Valley really fare when compared with a range of other leading regional economies in terms of its knowledge-based capacity? The usefulness, accuracy, and practicality of such a comparison depends upon how we make the concept of the knowledge-based capacity operational and express it in quantitative terms, for which either statistics are available or robust estimates are obtained. Without a solid framework underlying the concept, a comparison would be prone to biases and errors. We start this chapter by reviewing issues regarding the establishment of such a framework in relation to the wider concept of *competitiveness*, which has gained increasing importance in understanding firm, industry, national or regional economic performance.

The competitiveness debate

Difficulties in designing a reliable indicator based on a new concept are found in the debates relating to competitiveness. A standard definition of competitiveness at the firm level is 'the capacity of a firm to compete, grow, and be profitable in the market place'.[6] A quantitative expression of this capability could be sought in either the price/performance attributes of current products or traditional accounting indicators such as profitability ratios. However, such an expression does not cover all the three aspects of the capability – 'to compete', 'to grow', and 'to be profitable'. For instance, a profitable firm does not necessarily grow; it may stay in a niche market without growth. A firm competes, grows, and is profitable at the same time only in certain conditions. This leads one to ask what enables a firm to achieve such conditions.

In his 1979 *Harvard Business Review* article, Michael Porter explored the sources of competitiveness at the firm level with his 'competitiveness forces' framework.[7] In this framework, the performance of a firm is determined by the structure of the industry within which it operates. The industry structure determining a firm's competitiveness consists of five 'forces' – entry barriers, substitutes, buyers' and suppliers' bargaining power, and intra-industry rivalry. By making use of scale economies and steep learning curves, a firm creates entry barriers. The creation of entry barriers is influenced by conditions such as the availability of substitutes, a firm's bargaining power relative to buyers and suppliers, and rivalry in the industry within which it operates. With entry barriers, a firm fends off competition from other firms and gains extra profits known as monopoly rents. If a firm establishes such a position at an early stage of the product/industry life cycle, it also enjoys good growth prospects, thus meeting all three aspects of competitiveness.

In *The Competitive Advantage of Nations* published in 1990, Porter extended the framework of firm competitiveness to the national economy.[8] A consensus definition of a nation's competitiveness would be its capacity to secure a high standard of living for its residents relative to the residents of other nations. At the same time, it is usually assumed that the concept is related to international trade.[9] Applying the competitiveness forces framework, which focuses on a firm's position within an industry, Porter sets a nation within the arena of international trade. Support for linking national competitiveness to international trade can be found in the idea of multiplier effects of income from exports and policy based on export-led growth. External income from exports produces additional demands for domestic activities through its spending, which is likely to create jobs and improve standards of living. This emphasis upon international trade performance, however, runs the risk of neglecting industries which do not generally compete in international markets. For instance, a great majority of services are traded locally and their producers do not compete in international markets. Yet, most of our employment and production are now in services, and lagging productivity in services is seen as the single most important factor in the stagnation of living standards in advanced economies.[10]

It is noteworthy that the definition of competitiveness at either the firm or the national level is not fully captured by a single quantitative indicator. A firm is regarded as competitive if it successfully fends off competition through entry barriers and enjoys benefits of imperfect competition. A firm's market share for a product may describe this, but a high level of market share does not necessarily mean growth in the case of a mature industry. Similarly, a high market share of international trade for a certain industry does not in general guarantee a high standard of living, since the indicator does not reflect those industries that do not compete in international markets. Clearly, the inability to express a concept in quantitative terms does not render it useless. However, concepts that do not lend themselves to quantitative expression leave room for ambiguities, contradictions, and misinterpretations.

One attempt to measure national competitiveness is World Economic Forum's (WEF) *Global Competitiveness Report*. Published since 1979, the report measures the comparative strengths and weaknesses of economies across the world. Michael Porter is codirector of the report and without doubt exerts a great influence on the design of its indices. In the report, WEF uses per capita gross domestic product (GDP) at purchasing power parity values as a variable with which a nation's competitive performance is measured. Sanjaya Lall, the late economics professor at Oxford, throws doubt upon the use of GDP per capita, as it loses a focus upon direct market competition between nations and simply measures a nation's income and growth.[11] This arises from a contradiction inherent in the consensus definition of a nation's competitiveness. The definition includes two distinct elements – competition in international trade and standards of living – which cannot be tied into one.

Knowledge-based capacity

As already highlighted, in many industries and countries the basis of competition has shifted from natural resources to brainpower. We showed in Chapter 2, at the level of individual workers, those who have received a high level of education and training earn significantly higher wages than those who have not, with the gap between them widening during the last three decades. There is little doubt that the capacity to understand and use knowledge and technology is a key to success for individuals in today's business environment. At the corporate level, a firm's competitive advantage arises not only from the sum of the capacities of its workers but also from management's ability to coordinate the diverse skills of workers and integrate multiple streams of technology.[12] Furthermore, a firm cannot afford to remain stationary with an existing range of products. It has to source knowledge, create new ideas, and translate them into commercial products. Since successful innovation quickly attracts imitation, a firm needs to sustain its innovative capacity over time.[13] The capacity to use knowledge in production, to create and translate new ideas into economic value, and to sustain knowledge-based wealth creation is a key to success for individual workers and firms, as well as the national and regional economies within which they operate.

Our focus upon knowledge-based capacity departs from Michael Porter's competitiveness forces framework in its approach. In the competitiveness forces framework, the primary determinants of success are external to the firm, resting on the characteristics of industry structure. By contrast, we assume that a firm is best viewed as a collection of sticky, difficult-to-imitate resources and capabilities.[14] In our view, those capabilities internal to a firm are crucial to its long-run success. We describe today's competition by an analogy of the differences between marathon running and boxing. In boxing, the principal aim of a player is to beat and drive the opponent out of the ring. It is characterized by direct conflict. Victory is expressed as standing alone in the ring with the opponent unable to fight any more. In a marathon, the primary goal is to stay ahead of your opponents. It is also a long-term race, whereas a boxing match may finish at any moment when the opponent is knocked out. We see today's competition among firms as a marathon race based on knowledge capacity. Firms harness their capacities over time and aim to stay ahead of others by producing better goods in terms of cost and/or qualities, and functions. Lagging behind competitors in a particular product market does not preclude a firm from catching up with the leader through creating and selling a new product. While ownership of a limited natural resource often gave a long-lasting advantage in the past, continuous innovation is required to win today's knowledge-based economic race. With fast changing technologies, a firm's dominant position can be easily lost if it fails to innovate continuously.[15]

We define the capacity to use knowledge in production in quantitative terms by the value of output per combined input of both labor and physical capital. This definition is distinct from labor productivity, which is a more widely used type of productivity measuring how much output each worker produces. The measurement of labor productivity requires two sets of data: the amount of output measured by value-added and amount of labor usually measured by counts of workers or total hours of work. Given a relative ease in collecting the statistics, labor productivity is widely used as an indicator of firm or economic performance.[16] However, labor productivity is not an accurate indicator of the brainpower used in production. For instance, semi-skilled production workers at a manufacturing factory may produce a large amount of output per hour using machinery and equipment. In contrast, highly skilled consultants at financial institutions or scientists at R&D laboratories may produce the same amount of value per hour relying upon their knowledge and skills. When measured by labor productivity, their performances are the same. However, there are different economic implications for the two groups of workers, particularly in terms of the wages they receive. It is most likely that highly skilled financial consultants and R&D workers earn higher wages than semi-skilled production workers. Similarly, labor productivity does not accurately capture progress in technology and management over time. We have witnessed rapid progress in a wide range of technologies, which translate into falling prices for the same production capacity (e.g. lower-cost silicon chips with the same memory size). Labor productivity measures do not tell us how much changes in production capacity derive either from technical progress or from the use of a greater amount of physical capital. The inability of labor productivity to identify sources of economic gain is crucial when examining contributions of knowledge to corporate and economic growth. By taking output per combined input of labor and physical capital, we can resolve this problem.

How we measure it? – total factor productivity

The objective of productivity measurement is to identify output differences that cannot be explained by input differences.[17] A firm or nation is more productive than another if it is able to produce the same output with less inputs, or if it produces more output using the same inputs. Similarly, a firm experiences productivity growth if its output increases at a greater rate than a fixed bundle of inputs. The comparison is more difficult when two firms use different bundles of inputs (e.g. one firm uses more labor while the other relies more on machinery and equipment) but produce the same amount of output.[18] To compare the two firms, there has to be a common yardstick with which a firm's ratio of output to its bundle of inputs is compared. This yardstick, called the production function, should define for all combinations of inputs (e.g. ratios of labor to physical capital) the standard amount of output they produce. If a firm produces a greater (or smaller) amount of output than this yardstick defines for the firm's combination of inputs, then something else must account for the difference between them. This 'something else' is the firm's productivity and derives from a number of sources, such as the technology underpinning the product's qualities and functions, the organization of workers adopted at the office/factory to produce the product, and market intelligence used to identify consumer demands.

Methods of measuring productivity are broadly divided into three groups – stochastic frontier production function models, data envelopment analysis, and total factor productivity.[19] The three groups vary in their ways of specifying a production function, although they generate surprisingly similar results in practice.[20] Of them, the third approach, total factor productivity (TFP), is most often employed in national and regional economic analysis, as it is simple to use and easy to interpret.[21] The concept of TFP was first introduced in the economics literature by Jan Tinbergen in 1942.[22] However, it is Robert Solow who provided the basics of growth accounting using TFP.[23] In his constructs of TFP, the growth rate of output per bundle of inputs (i.e. the growth rate of TFP) is simply obtained by subtracting the sum of the growth rates of inputs (i.e. labor and physical capital) from the growth rate of output. The formula developed by Solow became the growth accounting standard, spawning a large number of studies in the field.[24]

As with the two other approaches, TFP has some limitations. For one thing,

TFP itself does not explain how changes in inputs and improvements in TFP relate to elements such as economic incentives and government policies.[25] A growth rate of TFP, which is obtained by subtracting the growth rates of inputs from the growth rate of output, is called the 'Solow residual'. Solow thought that this arises mainly from technical progress, but his model does not account for what gives rise to it (i.e. 'manna from heaven' view of technology). In operational terms, although it is simpler to use than the other two approaches, TFP is more demanding in its data requirements than labor productivity measures. TFP requires data on physical capital in its calculations. An ideal measure of physical capital is the flow of 'services' provided by physical capital, such as the amount of machine hours used in the production process during a specific period. Since the available data do not usually permit this measurement, the typical procedure calculates the quantity of physical capital and assumes that the flow of 'services' is proportional to the stock of physical capital. A method of measuring physical capital stock, called the perpetual inventory method, estimates an initial figure of stock at a point in the past and then adds up figures on gross physical investment in the subsequent years with the estimated depreciation of existing stocks.[26] In practice, estimates of initial stock are harder to come by from official sources at the regional level than at the national level. This poses a problem especially when we compare regional economies from a wide range of countries across the globe.

However, the use of TFP as a measure of knowledge-based capacity has its own advantages, being the standard in the literature on productivity. Although it does not offer a theory of productivity growth by itself, it has developed a body of literature that looks into relationships between productivity and its sources, particularly human capital and technology. By examining those sources underlying TFP and its growth and sustainability, we would be able to analyze and gain insights into the relative strengths and weaknesses of regional economies across the globe.

Sources of total factor productivity

In his classic 1957 article, Solow estimated that growth of TFP accounted for nearly 87 percent of the labor productivity growth recorded in the US from 1910 to 1949.[27] More recently, the US Bureau of Labor Statistics made an estimate that from 1948 to 2002 labor productivity of the US non-farm private sector grew at an average annual compound rate of 2.29 percent. During the period, physical capital grew at a rate of 0.85 percent, accounting for 37 percent of the labor productivity growth. The US Bureau of Labor Statistics further broke down the remaining labor productivity growth. The Bureau estimated that the composition of labor improved at a rate of 0.24 percent annually, accounting for another 10 percent of the labor productivity growth. Accordingly, the rest of the labor productivity growth (53 percent), at an annual growth rate of 1.20 percent, comes from other sources, which are considered as technological change and other factors.[28]

As these examples show, TFP consists of two source groups: the quality of labor, commonly referred to as human capital, and the rest.[29] Human capital theory views education and training as investments in skills and competencies.[30] Skills and competencies gained from education and training are distinguished from 'labor', which provides the hand-eye coordination required for simple tasks. Based on rational expectations of returns from investment, individuals make decisions on their education and training as a way of augmenting their productivity.

By contrast, there is some disagreement as to technology's primary role in accounting for the rest of TFP. Some take the position that technology spreads quickly across the globe. According to this view, what accounts for cross-national variations in productivity levels and growth rates is not technology but other factors. For example, Gregory Mankiw argues that cross-country variations in growth rates can be accounted for by the rate of capital accumulation, even assuming that all countries share identical technologies independently of their individual R&D efforts.[31] For others, the 'Solow residual' is a measure of our ignorance, and TFP is 'anything or everything in a list that includes income inequality, political stability, democracy, property rights regimes, climate, geography, openness of the economy, financial depth, ethno-linguistic fractionalization, and many others'.[32] Arguing against this position, Danny Quah writes that while some of the work that looks into non-technology factors can be informative, a considerable fraction falls into 'what some have called "a blaze of mediocre sociology" '.[33]

Cross-national and regional variations in R&D efforts, such as the number of R&D workers, are highly correlated with cross-national/regional variations in TFP level. A study of European regions also shows that R&D efforts alone account for nearly half of the cross-regional variations in TFP growth rates.[34] The capacity of scientists and engineers to understand existing knowledge and create new knowledge develops as a result of their cumulative R&D efforts.[35] Instead of existing in a vacuum, technological knowledge only becomes useful when it is understood by those individuals with such a capacity. Because of this, knowledge accompanies skilled individuals, who are much less mobile than electronic signals. A growing number of studies have demonstrated that technological knowledge is 'sticky', traveling through selected routes and often to locations in proximity.[36] When these facts are combined, they suggest that the stock of knowledge resides in a way conducive to utilization within high-productivity locations where R&D efforts have been made over time. This provides a link between technology and TFP. There is little doubt that technology is a primary factor of TFP, although some factors other than R&D efforts also shape the process of generation and diffusion of technological knowledge.

Coming back to human capital, it is important to note that it has two faces in its contribution to TFP. It is used for producing goods and services, as well as for improving technology. Both aspects of human capital matter and each separately can influence TFP in a distinct way.[37] In the production of goods and services, the skills and competencies possessed by individuals account for part of productivity. As a result, the growth of human capital gives rise to the growth of productivity, and differences in the rates at which countries accumulate human capital over time create differences in productivity growth rates.[38] This view, inspired by Gary Becker and revisited by Robert Lucas Jr., underpins the US Bureau of Labor Statistics estimates of human capital contributions to productivity growth mentioned above.[39]

Human capital also facilitates the adoption of new technology. In their seminal 1966 article, Richard Nelson and Edmund Phelps argued that a more educated or skilled workforce makes it easier to adopt and implement new technologies.[40] Empirical support exists for the positive link between educational/skill levels and technological activity. For instance, some studies show that educational/skill levels are positively related to technological change at the sectoral level.[41] Jess Benhabib and Mark Spiegel furthered this point in a cross-national study of productivity growth rates. They assume that a country's productivity growth is positively affected by the rate of adoption of existing innovations from more advanced economies, as well as by the rate of technological innovations on its own. They demonstrate that the stock of human capital determines a country's ability to learn and implement existing innovations from a leading economy and accounts for the country's rate of catch-up with the leader.[42] They postulate that the stock of human capital, rather than increases in the stock, explains part of productivity growth. This is in stark contrast to the view that it is the accumulation of human capital that determines productivity growth.[43]

There is a further route through which human capital affects TFP. This consists of contributions to technical progress by those workers engaged in innovation activities. As noted earlier, Solow's neoclassical growth accounting framework does not explain how technical progress takes place, leaving it as an exogenous factor. Development in this area came from researchers who studied the relationship between R&D and productivity. The most notable is Zvi Griliches, the late distinguished Harvard economist. In the 1960s, Griliches and Robert Evenson examined the relationship between the level of public expenditure on agricultural research and agricultural production in US regions.[44] According to their framework, productivity is expressed as the stock of knowledge accumulated over time. This stock of knowledge is assumed to be proportional to the resources invested in research over time, called 'research capital'. Thus, either the sum of research expenditures or the number of researchers over a period of time represents the amount of 'research capital'.[45] In his seminal 1986 and 1990 articles, Paul Romer extended the research capital model to a wider economy.[46] Focusing on the non-rival and non-exclusive nature of knowledge, Romer assumes the sharing of knowledge among scientists and engineers engaged in research at the economy level. Furthermore, he adds the assumption that R&D workers capitalize on the stock of knowledge in their research through the creation of new knowledge enhanced by their existing stock. Based on this, Romer arrives at the conclusion that the rate of technical progress is proportional to the number of scientists and engineers engaged in R&D. In other words, the stock of human capital devoted to R&D determines the growth rate of the technology component of TFP.

As discussed in Chapter 2, the scale effects of Romer's model do not conform to empirical evidence of the rapid growth of the R&D workforce in advanced economies (i.e. the R&D workforce growing while TFP growth rates not growing). This suggests a shortcoming in the assumption that R&D workers share the whole stock of knowledge at the economy level. We resolve this issue by seeing the entire R&D workforce as being divided into a large number of communities based on specialty. Although R&D workers share low- to medium-level knowledge across such communities, only those R&D workers within a particular community can contribute to advancing its frontier. Today's R&D workers face an increased demand for learning within each area of knowledge, while their capacity to absorb knowledge is limited. This forces R&D workers to narrow their expertise. Reflecting this specialization at the level of individual R&D workers, their knowledge community also becomes more specialized. At the same time, many of today's products are underpinned by a growing number of technologies. The value of such products is the sum of technologies created by a number of knowledge communities. The two forces – increased specialization of R&D workers and a widening technological base – determine the rate of TFP growth in such a way that it is caused by the accumulation of the whole R&D workforce and the average stock of R&D workers researching the same area of knowledge.[47]

We have reviewed two types of human capital – human capital in the production of goods and services and human capital devoted to innovation. Both types contribute to TFP in two ways. First, their accumulation causes TFP to grow.

1 An increase in human capital in the production process leads to an increase in the human capital component of TFP.
2 An increase in human capital devoted to innovation augments TFP's technology component, which derives primarily from a widening of the technological base of an industry.

Viewed differently, their stocks are indicators of levels of each respective TFP component:

1 Human capital in production shows the level of TFP's human capital component.
2 Human capital devoted to innovation provides an indication of TFP's technology-component level.

Second, stocks of the two types of human capital are also sources of growth in the technology component of TFP:

1 Human capital in the production process helps to assimilate new technologies in these processes and helps lagging economies catch up with their more advanced counterparts.

2. Human capital devoted to innovation within each knowledge community creates new knowledge and advances the community's level of technological progress.[48]

In short, by measuring the stocks of human capital in production and innovation, we can gain insights into both the TFP level and its growth rate. The dual contribution of human capital has a bearing on our model for analyzing a regional economy's TFP, and it is to this model we now turn.

Our model

Because of difficulties in estimating physical capital stocks for regions in a wide range of countries across the globe, we take an alternative route. We use a model of an economy's productivity and analyze a set of indicators primarily related to human capital. Although this does not provide an exact estimate of TFP for each region, it identifies each region's relative strengths in those elements considered crucial to TFP. The set of selected indicators are concerned with three aspects of TFP:

1. Stocks of human capital represent part of overall TFP level.
2. They are sources of TFP growth.
3. Investments in human capital formation underpin long-term sustainability of TFP.

Our model is presented in Figure 3.1. The model consists of two domains, both of which are underpinned by the stock of knowledge or technology. One domain (the top half in the figure) represents the production of goods and services. A standard set of production factors – physical capital, labor, and human capital – are combined with technology. The other domain (the bottom half) represents the production of new knowledge, which in turn gives rise to productivity growth. A key activity in this domain is the R&D conducted by firms. Unlike the production of goods and services, the production factors of R&D consist of physical capital and human capital only (as the hand-eye coordination of labor by definition does not count here). Another activity in this domain takes place within the science base, consisting of universities and government laboratories. The two activities, R&D at business firms and research at the science base, capitalize on the existing stock of knowledge and add new knowledge to it.

The two activities in the domain of new knowledge creation and the production of goods and services are linked to one another through various feedback loops.[49] For instance, while the production of goods and services uses technology created by scientists and engineers, it also feeds back into R&D knowledge gained through learning-by-doing. As for interactions among firms, as well as between firms and the science base, a growing body of studies, particularly studies of the 'innovation system', identifies various linking mechanisms and examines their behavior and impact.[50] Many of those institutional factors that are said to account

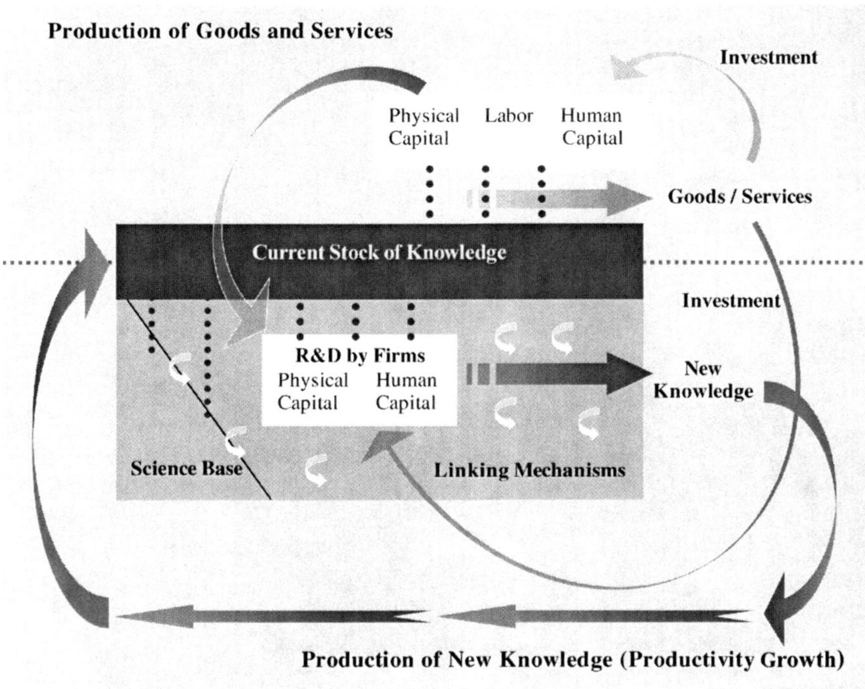

Figure 3.1 Productivity model.

for the 'Solow residual' fall into this category, including norms, routines, habits, conventions, as well as laws and standards. These factors influence how people relate to each other and learn. Lastly, part of the value created in the production of goods and services is invested in the factors in both domains. Such investment is crucial to the long-term sustainability of productivity.

Our analysis employs a set of 16 indicators which are presented in Figure 3.2. In the domain of new knowledge production, we choose the numbers of employees in five high-tech sectors as proxies for the human capital devoted to innovation. A number of studies attempt to classify sectors based on criteria of research and technology intensity.[51] We use Eurostat's (the European Commission's statistical office) scheme of industry classification, which was developed in collaboration with the OECD. In the classification of manufacturing industries, they use the ratio of R&D expenditure to value-added and the amount of R&D embodied in purchases of intermediate and capital goods.[52] As for service industries, there is no detailed data available for a similar calculation. As a result, Eurostat chooses those sectors that seem to have the closest links with the high-tech manufacturing industries.[53] We classify into five groups those sectors considered by Eurostat as 'higher tech manufacturing sectors', 'medium-high tech manufacturing sectors', and 'high-tech service sectors'. The five groups are:

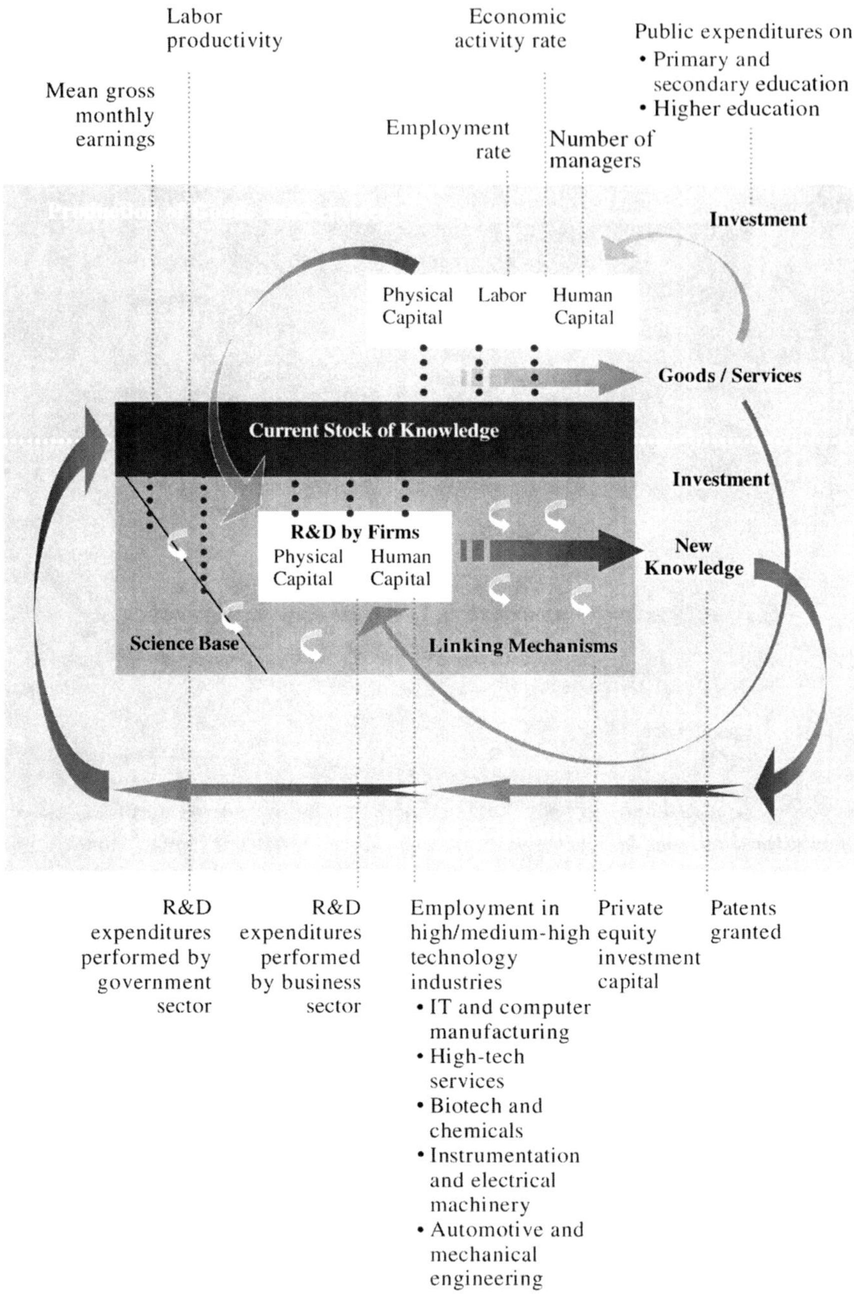

Figure 3.2 The 16 variables employed by the model.

1 IT and computer manufacturing;
2 high-tech services;
3 biotechnology and chemicals;
4 instrumentation and electrical machinery;
5 automotive and mechanical engineering.[54]

Other technology-input measures include R&D expenditures incurred by the business and government sectors. Compared with corporate R&D, the impact of public sector R&D is less direct in its route of both diffusion and timing. Nonetheless, there is evidence that spillovers from public sector R&D raise an economy's productivity.[55] Due to issues of data availability, R&D expenditures incurred by the government sector are used as an indicator of public sector R&D. As for technology-output measures, we use the number of patents granted.[56] As discussed in Chapter 2, the propensity to patent is known to vary widely across industries. Some industries conduct much R&D without seeking protection for their research outputs through patents, while others do the reverse.[57] Also, many patents turn out to be worthless, while a few are extremely valuable. Yet, patent statistics are the most widely available data of research outputs.[58] Furthermore, there is some evidence that suggests a close association between patents and other productivity-based measures at the national and regional level.[59] With regard to linking mechanisms, we use private equity investment capital as a proxy of the availability of funds for technology-based, start-up firms.[60] Private equity funding is often concentrated in small or medium-sized firms. It includes venture capital and start-up investments, which tend to be in knowledge-based activities.

In the production of goods and services domain, we include the number of managers as a proxy of human capital.[61] Though this is hardly a perfect indicator of human capital, a similar indicator is used in international studies of the labor market. The wages of managers are generally higher than those of other occupations, reflecting the greater amount of investment made in education and training.[62] We also include the employment rate (defined as one minus the unemployment rate) and the economic activity rate (defined by the ratio of the labor force to the working-age population) in our analysis. While these indicators show an economy's capacity to draw and develop a greater amount of human capital out of its population, higher rates also tend to suppress the average productivity level, with there being an increasing proportion of low-wage, low-productivity jobs. This is based on the observation that in many advanced economies, particularly the US, low-skill, low-wage jobs are a major source of job creation when absorbing a greater amount of labor from the working-age population. In the face of the global challenge from low-cost producers, some industries compete by improving their productivity. However, those industries where productivity remains low compete by primarily using low-cost and low-skilled labor. Low-productivity sectors have recently acquired a new prominence due to their relative propensity for job creation. By definition, low-productivity sectors produce more jobs per unit of turnover than high-productivity sectors. This phenomenon is particularly evident in those countries with deregulated labor markets, which generally show a greater capacity to use a larger part of the labor pool.[63] Such flexible labor markets tend to show high levels of economic participation and employment.

For indicators of the long-term sustainability of productivity, we include public expenditures on primary and secondary education and higher education.[64] There is a sequential interaction between a region's education and training system and its stock of high-skilled workers. The rate of enrolment in education is influenced by a region's employment and career prospects, as well as the socio-economic background of pupils and the quality of schooling. Enrolment in turn determines the region's workforce skills, productivity, and economic performance. Economic performance is itself then a determinant of the volume and occupational mix of inward migrant workers into the region. Economic growth also provides employers with great incentives to undertake worker training. A shift in the occupational mix toward skilled workers will have beneficial effects on the region's human capital formation. Skilled workers are often keen to invest in education for their children, while an improved economy also provides better employment opportunities and induces individuals to seek education and training.[65] Public investment in education plays an important role in this sequential cycle, particularly improving the quality of local schooling over time.

Lastly, we adopt labor productivity and mean gross monthly earnings as partial indicators of TFP. We have already shown how labor productivity differs from TFP, whereby the former does not explain the contributions of physical capital. Similarly, mean gross monthly earnings act as a proxy for the average value-added of each worker, though they do not account for differences in TFP caused by differences in the ratio of labor to capital.

To remove effects of the size of each region analyzed, we take per capita figures for the following variables: employment in the five high or medium-high tech industries, R&D expenditures incurred by business sector and government sector, patents granted, private equity investment capital, number of managers, and public expenditure on primary and secondary education, and higher education.

The variables selected in our analysis overlap one another (i.e. are inter-correlated). For instance, variations across regions in public expenditure on primary and secondary education and higher education are closely associated, since the income level largely determines the level of both expenditures. If we simply add the two indicators, it fails to distinguish the overlapping part of information from the non-overlapping part, which is likely to confuse the final assessment.[66] To separate the overlapping part of information as an underlying dimension and simplify a complex set of data, we adopt a data reduction method called 'factor analysis'. This particular technique reduces an original set of indicators into a smaller number of composite indicators called 'factors'. Each factor is a dimension underlying the original set of indicators, presented as a condensed statement of the relationships between them.[67]

A point to bear in mind is that factor analysis does not tell us the relative importance of a factor to others in accounting for TFP, that is, it does not show which individual factors matter more than others. Therefore, we have no theoretical foundation for constructing a single composite indicator of TFP from the factors identified. In a similar vein, we cannot tell whether taking an average of factor scores actually gives us a TFP estimate. In fact, it is most likely that an average of the factor scores does not represent TFP accurately. This is not only because we do not have information about the relative importance of factors identified, but also because there is no way telling that adding up scores of all factors identified would exhaust the entire sources of TFP.[68] Nonetheless, even if we do not know which factor matters more than others, we can calculate a region's position in each of the dimensions (i.e. factors) identified and analyze its relative strengths. In addition, we can see the key dimensions within the set of selected variables, each of which is assumed to have an association with the level, growth, or long-term sustainability of TFP.

Why Silcon Valley is the Hollywood of innovation

We compare the metropolitan statistical area San Jose–Sunnyvale–Santa Clara, known as Silicon Valley, with other 113 leading regions across the globe. The list of 114 regions is found in Appendix 1.[69] These regions are chosen from each of the selected major countries on the basis of GDP per capita during a recent period. Of the 114 regions, 55 are from North America, 44 from Europe, and 15 from Asia and Oceania.[70] Source years of the 16 variables are found in Appendix 2. Factor analysis identifies five factors from the 16 variables. Table 3.1 shows each factor's correlation (whose score is called a factor loading) with the 16 variables.[71]

Factor 1 represents the concentration of IT-related employment in both manufacturing and services. It correlates highly with employment in IT and computer manufacturing and employment in high-tech services, the latter of which includes computer and related services and telecommunication services, as well as R&D services. This factor also correlates highly with patents granted, as an indicator of new technical knowledge output. Factor 2 has a high loading for the two medium-high tech industries, but a low loading for patents granted. A high patent grants loading for factor 1 suggests either a higher rate of knowledge creation or a greater use of patents as a means of knowledge protection in the IT-related industries, compared with the medium-high tech industries. Factor 1 also loads highly on private equity investment capital, whereas factor 2 shows no correlation with private equity investment. This suggests a greater use of venture capital in the IT-related industries.[72] On the whole, factor 1 can be seen as a complex of IT-related knowledge creation. Factor 1 shows the contribution of IT-related knowledge creation to TFP levels and growth rates, the latter of which is likely to be higher than those industries in factor 2 for reasons discussed later.

By contrast, factor 2 loads highly on employment in instrumentation and electrical machinery and in automotive and mechanical engineering. As well as not showing a high loading for either patents granted or private equity investment capital, it also loads negatively for public expenditure on higher education,

Table 3.1 Factor matrix obtained

	Factor				
	1	*2*	*3*	*4*	*5*
Employment in IT and computer manufacturing	0.64	0.24	0.03	–0.07	–0.03
Employment in high-tech services	0.57	–0.04	0.32	0.02	0.09
Employment in biotech and chemicals	0.02	0.32	0.07	–0.04	–0.07
Employment in instrumentation and electrical machinery	0.28	0.74	–0.12	–0.10	–0.05
Employment in automotive and mechanical engineering	–0.05	0.63	–0.22	–0.07	–0.05
R&D expenditures performed by business sector	0.40	0.25	–0.11	0.58	–0.00
R&D expenditures performed by government sector	0.25	–0.35	–0.01	0.34	0.14
Number of patents granted	0.52	–0.21	–0.32	0.48	–0.01
Private equity investment capital	0.62	–0.00	0.11	0.30	0.19
Number of managers	0.14	–0.03	0.73	–0.25	0.00
Economic activity rate	0.10	–0.20	0.62	0.30	–0.30
Employment rate	–0.07	0.12	0.11	0.11	–0.34
Public expenditures on primary and secondary education	–0.02	–0.09	–0.03	0.94	–0.06
Public expenditures on higher education	–0.01	–0.38	0.08	0.72	0.09
Labor productivity	0.07	–0.13	0.06	0.50	0.85
Mean gross monthly earnings	0.43	–0.37	–0.11	0.63	0.36

mean gross monthly earnings, and R&D expenditures incurred by the public sector. This factor can be viewed as an indicator of human capital in medium-high tech industries. It indicates the particular human capital contributions to TFP levels and growth rates.

Factor 3 represents the concentration of workers in managerial positions. It also loads highly for the economic activity rate indicator. While the number of workers in managerial positions is related to the location of high-order corporate functions (e.g. headquarters), it is also likely that the number of managerial positions is associated with the number of employees they have to manage. This factor can be considered as an indicator of the particular human capital contributions to TFP levels and growth rates.

Factor 4 has a high loading for public expenditure on primary and secondary education and higher education. It also loads highly for mean gross monthly earnings, which is the source of wealth underpinning public investment in education. This factor is primarily an indicator of the long-term sustainability of human capital underpinning TFP.

Finally, factor 5 represents labor productivity as a partial indicator of TFP. The factor negatively correlates with employment rate and economic activity rate, although loadings are modest, confirming the association between low-productivity industries and job creation. Furthermore, this factor does not load highly on any indicators of the human capital devoted to innovation and technology inputs and outputs. Labor productivity fails to represent these human capital contributions to TFP accurately because it does not account for differences in the physical capital employed in production. This factor stands as a partial measure of TFP levels.

Following the analysis, we calculate each region's position in relation to each of the five factors. The scores, called factor scores, have a mean of zero and a standard deviation of one. In other words, scores range from negative values to positive values. The average deviation of scores from the mean is the same for all the five factors, making comparisons across factors meaningful. Table 3.2 shows the top five regions and the score of San Jose–Sunnyvale–Santa Clara metropolitan statistical area (aka Silicon Valley) for each of the five factors. Silicon Valley tops the rankings for factor 1 with a score of 6.27, which is significantly higher than the other regions. As noted earlier, factor 1 represents a complex of IT-related knowledge creation. It loads highly for employment in IT and computer manufacturing and high-tech services, patents granted, and private equity investment capital. The combination of the variables in factor 1 is in stark contrast to factor 2, which correlates more with traditional manufacturing industries alone.

The two groups of industries loaded on factors 1 and 2 are in fact two generations of key industries representing the twentieth century. Based on Nikolai Kondratieff's work on the cycle of major economic crises at approximately half-century intervals, Joseph Schumpeter wrote that each of the 'long waves' of economic development started with a new bunch of innovations, which resulted in the creation of new industries.[73] According to this long wave theory, the first

Table 3.2 Factor scores of top five regions and San Jose–Sunnyvale–Santa Clara MSA (aka Silicon Valley)

	Rank	*Region*	*Factor score*
Factor 1	1	San Jose–Sunnyvale–Santa Clara, US	6.27
	2	Tokyo, Japan	3.93
	3	San Francisco–Oakland–Fremont, US	2.87
	4	Boston–Cambridge–Quincy, US	2.22
	5	Washington–Arlington–Alexandria, US	1.26
Factor 2	1	Baden-Württemberg, Germany	2.73
	2	Shiga, Japan	2.29
	3	Shizuoka, Japan	2.27
	4	Switzerland	2.18
	5	Bayern, Germany	2.01
	19	San Jose–Sunnyvale–Santa Clara, US	1.10
Factor 3	1	Zuid-Nederland, Netherlands	2.40
	2	South East, UK	2.19
	3	Bratislavsky, Slovak Republic	1.86
	4	Norway	1.85
	5	Alberta, Canada	1.84
	19	San Jose–Sunnyvale–Santa Clara, US	0.91
Factor 4	1	Hartford–West Hartford–East Hartford, US	2.76
	2	Seattle–Tacoma–Bellevue, US	2.43
	3	New York–Northern New Jersey–Long Island, US	2.24
	4	Rochester, US	1.94
	5	Buffalo–Niagara Falls, US	1.88
	20	San Jose–Sunnyvale–Santa Clara, US	0.97
Factor 5	1	Brussels, Belgium	6.79
	2	Hamburg, Germany	2.64
	3	Hartford–West Hartford–East Hartford, US	2.34
	4	Bremen, Germany	2.01
	5	London, UK	1.77
	13	San Jose–Sunnyvale–Santa Clara, US	0.99

Kondratieff wave was based on iron and cotton industries, spanning the period 1785–1842. This is followed by a second wave (1843–97) with steel, machine tools, and ships as its key industries. The twentieth century includes two waves: the third wave (1896–1947) based on automotive, electrical engineering, and chemicals, and the fourth wave (1948–2003) whose growth has been propelled by electronics, computers, communications, aerospace, and producer services.[74] The leading and high score obtained by Silicon Valley for factor 1 is nothing short of a manifestation of its central position in the fourth wave. The close association identified between employment in the industries of the fourth wave and private equity investment capital signifies the role of venture capitalists, the new financial institutions that have experienced phenomenal growth during the last two decades. Furthermore, the factor's association with patents granted, an indicator of technical outputs, confirms Silicon Valley's role as the global center of technological innovation in the fourth wave.[75]

We can also draw another finding from the analysis: Silicon Valley is the best all-round region in terms of scores for the five factors. When compared with its stunning score for factor 1, Silicon Valley's position for the other four factors appears rather modest: it ranks 19th, 19th, 20th, and 13th for factors 2–5 respectively. However, these positions do tell us something about the uniqueness of Silicon Valley. Apart from Silicon Valley, no other regions rank in the top 20 for all of the five factors. If we look at top 20 regions based on an average of the five factor scores, all regions except for Silicon Valley has a score of lower than 0.50 for at least one of the five factors. Furthermore, with the exception of Silicon Valley and two others, all regions examined in this analysis have a negative score for at least one of the five factors.[76] Whether this all-roundness means anything to the level, growth, and long-term sustainability of a region's TFP is open to discussion. It might suggest a region's potential resilience to external shocks, though there is no strong theoretical foundation for such a claim. Nonetheless, there is little doubt that Silicon Valley holds a unique position across the globe with exceptional strength in the fourth wave's complex.

Conclusion

Silicon Valley is also known for another strength – the active networking that takes place across its corporate boundaries. In this chapter, we have attempted to analyze an economy's knowledge-based capacity. Due to the lack of robust definitions and reliable statistics at the regional level, we do not analyze institutional factors other than the availability of venture capital. Among such institutional factors, AnnaLee Saxenian shed much light upon those facilitating networking across corporate boundaries in her 1994 book, *Regional Advantage*, comparing Silicon Valley with Boston's Route 128 area.[77] Her study has made the subject of networks one of the most intensively discussed in the field of economic development. It is to a discussion of such networks, and the means by which they enable knowledge to flow across firm boundaries, that we now turn.

4 Networks and clusters

Introduction

Firms and organizations build or enter networks with other firms or organizations for numerous reasons, such as to find and maintain customers, suppliers, collaborators and partners, personal relationships, or even as a means of providing a platform to exploit a yet unarticulated future opportunity. As knowledge becomes the most important competitive asset of firms, the need to acquire and create it is a key factor why firms engage in networks.[1] Kevin Kelly, the founding editor of *Wired* magazine, argues that communication and networks 'are the economy' since 'communication is the foundation of society, of our culture, of our humanity, of our own individual identity, and of all economic systems. This is why networks are such a big deal.'[2]

In recent years, the concepts of both social capital and clusters have become a key means of understanding the fundamental and most effective assets required to move knowledge from one actor to another. Popularized by James Coleman and Robert Putnam, social capital broadly consists of the value derived from networks based on socialization and sociability.[3] Don Tapscott and his colleagues refer to these networks as social communities that foster conviviality for its own sake.[4] Social capital results from the social obligations and trust upon which these communities are built.[5] Social capital has proved to be a popular and powerful mechanism for analyzing how knowledge, in particular its tacit form, can be moved both within and across organizations.[6] The popularization of the cluster concept is largely the result of the work of Michael Porter, who defines clusters as geographically proximate groups of interconnected companies and associated institutions.[7]

This chapter analyzes the role of networks, social capital, and clusters in achieving knowledge competitiveness, as well as introducing the new and complementary concept of *network capital.* Network capital is defined as the perceived value inherent in networks and relationships strategically developed and maintained by firms to provide benefits that meet their objectives. The value of network capital is attached to the ability of firms to mobilize resources within these networks and relationships. While social capital can explain the value of networks that facilitate the acquisition and creation of knowledge based on sociability and socialization, usually on a communal basis, it does not explain the value of networks created and sustained by more economy-related expectations. With their own specific goals and strategies in mind, firms seek, create, and develop relationships with customers, suppliers, collaborators, partners, and the like. Although these networks might accommodate the public welfare considerations of a particular community, their development is inherently calculative and individualistic. If successful, their development allows firms to better mobilize resources (e.g. knowledge) within these networks. In other words, investment in their development bears fruit in the form of the creation of a relational asset, that is, network capital.

We highlight a range of features that distinguish network capital and social capital. We argue that while network capital can be strategically managed, particularly to influence knowledge flow, the nature of social capital is such that it is very difficult to manage. As others have found, social capital, and the trust upon which it is built, is much more related to the 'emotional skills' of individuals and the 'emotional direction' of firms.[8] This distinction between strategic and emotional influences on firms is important, given that firms increasingly require a highly strategic approach to their knowledge network building activities.[9] The chapter begins by analyzing some of the key issues relating to knowledge and the role of networks.

Networks

As Peter Drucker argues, management essentially concerns an understanding of the new knowledge required to make the best use of existing knowledge.[10] Drucker also provides us with one of the best available definitions of knowledge, viewing it as information that changes something or somebody, either by becoming grounds for action or by making an individual or an institution capable of different or more effective actions.[11] Knowledge, unlike simple information, is about action and is a function of a particular stance.[12] Knowledge is often described as a public good, where use by one actor does not preclude its use by others. In reality, it is no longer possible to think of knowledge as a truly public good that can be easily reproduced and diffused, but at best a quasi-public good where reproduction and diffusion cannot be taken for granted.[13] John Seely Brown and Paul Duguid distinguish between 'sticky' and 'leaky' knowledge, with sticky knowledge being that which is difficult to move, while leaky knowledge refers to the undesirable flow of knowledge to external parties.[14] The potential problem for firms is that knowledge may flow more easily out of them rather than move productively within them.[15]

With this risk in mind, the question can be asked – why would firms engage in knowledge networks rather than control their knowledge flows through the marketplace? Fundamentally, the answer is that knowledge markets are rare. They are difficult to create due to inherent asymmetry in the existing knowledge base of buyers and sellers. The buyer is often unable to convey specifically to the seller the knowledge he is seeking, and vice-versa. If the seller is able to effectively convey the knowledge he is selling, the buyer will in effect have acquired it for free.[16] Most markets of this type are actually for information rather than knowledge: for example, books, newspapers, and other 'fact-supplying' media. This means that knowledge must often be sought through other means, and while firms may seek to internalize knowledge sources to overcome market failure, networks are vital vehicles through which firms obtain access to knowledge.

Networks concern interactions, relationships, and ties between actors. Networks between firms consist of both the networks held by the firm itself (such as contractual partnerships and joint ventures) and the aggregate of the external networks of those individuals operating within the firm (i.e. the interactions, relationships, and ties these individuals have with actors outside the firm). Knowledge networks are often manifested in the form of strategic alliances between firms, such as formalized collaboration and joint ventures, and other 'contracted' relationships that result in frequent and repeated interaction. Firms gain competitive advantage from alliances by accessing the resources of their alliance partners.[17]

Converse to alliances, contact networks consist of non-formalized interaction and relationships between firms. The structure of these networks is often more dynamic, as firms continually update and change their contacts. Contact networks may involve acquaintances that individuals within a firm possess, as well as membership of informal networks such as chambers of commerce, trade associations, business clubs, and the like. Firms possessing larger networks tend to have more non-redundant contacts in the form of network members that do not possess the same or similar knowledge.[18] Non-redundant ties in knowledge contact networks may be of high value to firms that require regular replenishing of their sources of new knowledge in order to gain a competitive advantage.

Knowledge networks become redundant once there is knowledge equivalence between firms due to similarities in knowledge profiles.[19] As firms become increasingly familiar with each other's knowledge, negative network effects may emerge, locking firms into the network and stifling the creation of new knowledge and innovation.[20] Firms, therefore, need to monitor the emergence of this redundancy and lock-in and take appropriate action in the form of reconstituting their knowledge networks. Networks in knowledge-intensive sectors and markets are highly heterogeneous, requiring additional network management resources in order to convey complex ideas.[21]

A key feature of network development in the traditional economy has focused on 'repeated', 'enduring' or 'sustained' interactions or relationships.[22] In the knowledge economy, the focus is more on the dynamic nature of networks and their changeability, often being based on indirect or performative ties that are episodic.[23] The knowledge economy requires the continued reconstitution and dynamism of networks. Although more stable networks reduce the transaction costs of information and knowledge exchange, it is likely that such information and knowledge will become increasingly homogenous, and therefore less useful, across the network members. In other words, the preponderance of strong static ties may lead to firms operating inefficient networks. For instance, relatively static contact networks such as business clubs and local industry groups are often not best suited for improving the innovation and learning capabilities of members. A better choice may be networks that are more temporary in nature and geared toward achieving specific outcomes, such as benchmarking, best practice, and management development networks.[24] This reflects the possibility of an inverse relationship between the stability of networks and their capability to transfer knowledge that has a relatively high value for network members.

The emphasis upon sustained relationships in the traditional economy equates with Robert Axelrod's analysis of the prisoner's dilemma game (PDG). In PDG, a pair of accomplices are held incommunicado, with each being told that if he alone implicates his partner he will escape scot-free, but if he remains silent while his partner confesses he will be punished especially severely.[25] There is a difference between 'one-off' games between players, where there is little trust, and 'iterated' games, where the 'shadow of the future' influences the decision-making of players as more games are played.[26] This iterated PDG is analogous to the repeated exchanges for goods and services that occur in the traditional economy, where players bargain with a stable pool of players. By contrast, in the knowledge economy, players tend to move from one one-off game to another involving different players, as they continually search for new knowledge.[27] In her book *The Knowledge Evolution*, Verna Allee refers to knowledge networks as systems constantly in flux, which assemble and disassemble to meet required needs.[28]

The work of the theoretical biologist, Stuart Kauffman, on complexity theory provides important insights into the balance and evolution of stable and dynamic networks.[29] As Kauffman explains, the organization of a network is determined by both the number and strength of connections. If the number of connections is low, there is more likelihood of network stability. If the numbers are very high, there is possibility of network 'chaos'. However, another scenario is an intermediate state between stability and instability, or what is known as the *edge of chaos*. It is at this edge of chaos state, or one of stable instability, that knowledge networks are most effective in generating innovation, as network members are able to acquire and create knowledge at high speed.[30] Stan Davis and Christopher Meyer refer to this phenomenon as *blur*, which is the product of the speed by which networks are able to connect people to knowledge.[31]

Networks and company size

Within the knowledge economy, we are witnessing the reversal of the traditional control of large firms over small ones within value and supply chains, as small firms with relatively few employees are producing higher levels of value-added than their larger counterparts. Reputation gained specifically through firm size is becoming less realizable, particularly as small firms are able to leverage reputational assets through the Internet and e-business technology.[32] However, when compared with large firms, small firms have their own network management issues.

Small firms are faced with a need to manage complex systems of external interaction. Small firms are often diverse in their activities, while their knowledge creation capacity is more limited and specialized. This diversity, coupled with their specialized knowledge creation capacity, means that they require diverse flows of knowledge from an equally diverse range of sources. While the internal knowledge management of large firms is likely to be far more complex than smaller ones, the higher dependency of smaller firms on external sources of knowledge means that the management of knowledge networks across a number of firms and organizations is also likely to be highly complex. Also, if the cost of formal knowledge searches is proportionately higher for small firms, the relative and potential importance to them of non-market and non-internal sources of knowledge are greater than for large firms.[33]

In general, the requirement for small firms is access to 'non-standardized' and highly specific forms of knowledge, which results in them developing complex systems of external interaction. Large firms tend to reduce the diversity of knowledge sourcing and induce network inertia through the use of common knowledge network sources, such as the major management consultancies.[34] By contrast, the 'pre-packaged' knowledge available from knowledge providers such as consultants is often of less use to small firms. While the interaction undertaken by large firms is often regulated by a range of contractual agreements, there is far less regulation for small firms, resulting in higher flexibility and mobility of network partners. The lower survival rates of small firms also means that relative network stability for small firms is gained through participation in networks with multiple members, rather than dyadic networks and the bilateral alliances that are more commonly a feature of large firm networks.

However, small firms may form part of dyadic networks with large firms. Such small-large firm networks are generally seen to emerge as a result of the complementary assets of both. If small firms are required to access and capture external knowledge as much, if not more so, than their larger counterparts, it suggests a need for small firms to have equal opportunity concerning the flow of knowledge through inter-firm relations. However, there is evidence that asymmetrical relationships are highly prevalent in knowledge-based business environments.[35] Such relationships include the bilateral networks that exist in the biotechnology sector, where new small firms compete and collaborate with existing large pharmaceutical companies. Other examples include the multilateral relations within the IT sector, where large firms supply platform products which small firms must utilize in order to produce their own products or software, as well as the automotive sector, where components and parts manufacturers supply large-scale original equipment manufacturers.

Furthermore, small firms often cannot afford to adopt some of the network management tools utilized by larger firms. For example, strategic coordination and management are often better achieved through the use of knowledge gatekeepers who moderate the flow of knowledge both into and from the firm and translate this into a form that is meaningful within the firm as well as to other network members.[36] Knowledge gatekeepers are important to processes of knowledge absorption, particularly in relation to R&D functions. While a significant proportion of large firms have established such positions and possess a number of specialist gatekeepers, smaller firms are much less likely to possess such a capacity, limiting their ability to moderate the flow of knowledge. In sum, small firms have different network management requirements than their larger counterparts, and often suffer from limited in-house resource availability for such network management. Against this backdrop, social capital has emerged as a complementary asset for network management that is seen as being especially important to small firms.

Social capital

The concept of social capital has increasingly been utilized and applied to understand the capital resource associated with knowledge networks.[37] In his seminal work, James Coleman defines social capital as consisting of obligations and expectations, which are dependent on the trustworthiness of the social environment, the information flow capabilities of social structure, and norms accompanied by sanctions.[38] Coleman argues that social capital is defined by its function, and as with the cases he highlights, this common function is the creation of localized trust. Coleman's work is important because it locates tensions within the social concept, particularly relating to what are actually two distinct forms of capital. He describes social capital as being a public good, while at times he also states that it is contained within closed networks only benefiting its members. In recent years, social capital research has moved distinctively within these two directions.

First, the school of social capitalism focusing on the public good form of social capital emphasizes its benefits and negativities stretching beyond direct participation in its formation. The most important aspect here concerns the development of civil society and civic participation that improves the overall well-being of society. This has been most prominently advocated by Robert Putnam, who sees social capital as akin to a 'favor bank' in which people invest by undertaking a favor for others in the expectation that the favor will be returned at some point.[39] In contrast, the second school of social capitalism focuses on its captured variety, within which social capital investment is viewed as a private asset held by a group primarily to enhance its economic position.

Social capital principally concerns the ability of actors to secure benefits by virtue of membership to social networks or similar social structures.[40] Such social structure basically consists of relationships between individuals, with social capital acting as a resource that can be effective for furthering an individual's interests through such relationships.[41] As a result, social capital can arise and decline as a by-product of activities engaged in for reasons other than the accumulation of social capital.[42]

One of the most important contributions linking the role of social capital to knowledge networks is that of Janine Nahapiet and Sumantra Ghoshal, which focuses on the importance of social capital within the firm and the organizational advantages and intellectual capital creation it facilitates.[43] Nahapiet and Ghoshal point to social capital as consisting of friendships and obligations within organizations: 'Although it has value in use, social capital cannot be easily traded. Friendships and obligations do not readily pass from one person to another.'[44]

Nahapiet and Ghoshal's work is particularly useful because it makes the link between intra-organizational networks, knowledge, and social capital, focusing on the combination and exchange of knowledge in relation to factors such as access, motivation, capability, and anticipation of value. However, it has not gone without criticism. It has been argued that there is a potential loss of strategic objectivity in linking business and social relationships, since such objectivity requires information to be given to those who need it, without regard to whether or not they are your friends.[45] Edwin Locke states that

> The discoverers of knowledge should proactively build intellectual networks of people who can understand and see the value of what has been discovered. Furthermore, organizational leaders should encourage such networks. Whether personal friendships grow out of such networks should be irrelevant.[46]

Tiziana Casciaro and Miguel Sousa Lobo find that in reality, within an intra-organizational environment, network members tend to be chosen not on the basis of their ability but on the basis of being liked or not.[47] Locke, Casciaro and Lobo draw attention to the lack of strategic decision-making in the mobilization of social capital to the formation and role of knowledge networks.

There are also a number of theoretical issues, with the notion of social capital seemingly being applied to virtually all ties, relationships, and interactions between economic actors, even when there is little evidence of the social obligation and goodwill or blind trust implicitly associated with the concept. If they are all viewed as social, and therefore possessing social capital, the actual value of social capital as a distinguishing concept becomes instantly redundant. For instance, it is difficult to conclude that many strategic alliances and joint ventures between large multinational corporations involve significant levels of social capital when most of the interaction is usually highly rehearsed, stage-managed, and undertaken in a very formalized and bureaucratic manner. As has been found in the biotechnology sector, 'even tacit knowledge exchange is often hemmed-in by confidentiality clauses and the cash nexus'.[48]

The mere existence of *connectedness* in business and organizational interactions and exchanges does not imply that social capital is present, that is, connectedness does not equate to social capital. Most business and organizational interactions and relationships are not normally undertaken for reasons of sociability but are part of the strategic operation and decision-making of the firm or organizational environment within which they are predominantly set. Also, most investment in social networks is undertaken not for economic returns and favors, but for the creation of trust and friendships fulfilling more psychological and emotional needs. More precisely, it is often not social capital but the investment made in the formation of entrepreneurial and firm networks that facilitates transactions and exchanges beyond the market or within the firm.

These relationships require a form of trust, but rather than the blind trust associated with social capital's environment of obligation, it takes the form of 'reflective trust' which is more rational, studied, and tentative.[49] In the context of trust, there is also the issue of the role of place. Many knowledge networks are now operating at a global, rather than a local level, utilizing the Internet and other telecommunications technologies, which do not lend themselves to the type of localized trust present in social capital. This does not imply that relational resources are not present within virtual communities, but that such resources are not generally consistent with social capital. As Putnam states, 'building trust and goodwill is not easy in cyberspace'.[50]

Indeed, the conundrum Putnam's thesis leaves us with is that although communities, especially business communities, are more networked, they actually possess less social capital. As Putnam again states, this means that 'in some ways social capital may be economically counterproductive'.[51]

Network capital

In contrast to social networks, calculative networks, based on actions motivated by expected economic returns, often provide greater resource availability.[52] Therefore, such networks are likely to be highly significant to firms as they seek to create and acquire knowledge. While social networks usually possess or produce social capital, calculative networks possess or produce a different form of capital that is not necessarily dependent on the obligations and expectations associated with social capital. An appropriate label for this type of network resource is simply *network capital*.[53]

Network capital consists of the value inherent in networks and relationships generated through interactions motivated by business or professional expectations.[54] Distinguishing between network capital and social capital located in networks is a means of understanding their characteristics, function, and potential for management, particularly in relation to knowledge flows and transfer. Table 4.1 highlights some of the network capital and social capital characteristics of networks. A key feature is the difference in the rationality and motivation for network participation. Typically, a network will possess and allow actors to build network capital when the rationale for interaction and participation is based on expected economic returns, while networks will possess and allow actors to build social capital if the rationale of actors is more social in its expectations.

Network capital is associated more with calculative networks, and social capital with social networks. However, it is important to acknowledge two issues in this regard. First, rationality, network type, and capital type are not necessarily distinct and will often overlap. For instance, the rationality to participate in a network may be a crossover between economic and social expectations, resulting in networks with both calculative and social elements.

Table 4.1 Network capital and social capital characteristics of knowledge networks

Characteristics	*Network capital*	*Social capital*
Rationality	Economic	Social/normative
Network type	Calculative networks, although social networks and social capital may emerge as a by-product	Social networks, although calculative networks and network capital may emerge as a by-product
Nature of interaction	Based on a logic of business and professional expectations	Based on a logic of sociability and social expectations
Firm size of network actors	Large and growing firms	Small and new firms
Network investment	Network capital can be invested in by the firm	Difficult for social capital to be invested in by the firm
Network management	Can be strategically managed	Difficult to strategically manage
Network stability	Mix of dynamic and stable networks	Mainly stable networks
Trust	Reflective	Blind
Spatial proximity of networks	Network actors not necessarily spatially proximate	Higher propensity of proximity to other network actors
Knowledge network type	Knowledge alliance and contact networks	Primarily knowledge contact networks
Knowledge flow	Both knowledge acquisition and knowledge creation	
Type of knowledge	Both tacit and codified knowledge	

Source: Huggins, 'Network capital, social capital, and knowledge networks'.

As a result, the network may possess and build both network capital and social capital. Second, these processes are evolutionary rather than static. A network initially based on interactions concerning a logic of sociability and social expectations, and therefore social capital, may over time create network capital if the concerns of the network broaden or change to interactions based on a logic of business and professional expectations. Similarly, a calculative network with network capital may also create social capital if the concerns of the network widen to include social expectations. Therefore, networks with either network or social capital may produce the other capital form as a by-product.

This evolutionary aspect also applies to the network actors. New and small firms are more likely to be dependent on social capital, with networks consisting of the social networks of the entrepreneurs or owners of the firm (e.g. the relatives and friends of the owners). As firms grow, their dependency will typically shift toward network capital, as networks become calculative (e.g. suppliers, customers, collaborators, and partners become more important) and less reliant on the social networks of the owners. While it is difficult for firms to invest in or strategically manage social capital in networks, there is more opportunity to do so with network capital. For example, employees leaving a firm take their social networks with them, causing a loss of social capital regardless of the firm's strategy. However, relationships they have built with other businesses often stay with the firm. A firm can decide to create or deplete network capital with other firms as its interests and requirements change. As a result, networks with network capital may fluctuate more between stability and dynamism according to changes in the firm's strategy. Social capital is often built in an environment where actors are in relative proximity. This is not necessarily the case with network capital, as a firm strategically searches the most appropriate network actors for its needs. It is this strategic management aspect of network capital that is crucial in facilitating a firm to make the most effective use of networks that enhances its competitiveness and economic performance. Networks primarily based on network capital will contain a reflective form of trust, whereby a firm only trusts other network actors once it is clear that their actions and interactions are not potentially harmful to the firm. The more blind trust associated with social capital is based on an implicit assumption that network actors will all commit to a common good.

In general, networks predicated on either network or social capital may facilitate a firm either in the knowledge acquisition process or in the knowledge creation process. Both network capital and social capital are also able to facilitate the flow of tacit and codified knowledge. However, network capital investments will take more account of a firm's requirement to continually replenish and develop knowledge stocks utilizing the best available sources. Network capital may be equally apparent in either knowledge alliance or knowledge contact networks. By contrast, it is unlikely that social capital will be highly apparent in knowledge alliance networks, given that such collaboration is usually highly contractual and formalized. Furthermore, the balance between a firm's stock of network capital and social capital will necessarily vary according to the firm's overall strategy. A firm's capability to influence this balance, however, will be determined primarily by its ability to manage its network capital investments.

Clusters

While the focus on knowledge-based economics is indicative of the source of modern economic growth, clusters are often the physical manifestations of the source's centers. Network capital, as well as social capital, represents the realization that the human connectivity between economic agents, both within and beyond clusters, is the glue mobilizing the knowledge upon which competitiveness is centered. The importance of clusters can be traced back to the work of the French philosopher Michel Foucault, who stated that:

> geography must necessarily lie at the heart of my concerns . . . once knowledge can be analysed in terms of region, domain, implantation, displacement, transposition, one is able to capture the processes by which knowledge functions as a form of power and disseminates the effects of power.[55]

In current parlance, Foucault's analysis can be interpreted to contend that knowledge is a capital asset (form of power). It is how this knowledge capital is distributed and transferred that is of crucial interest within the global knowledge economy of today. Clusters are often a seedbed for infant industries, whereby a new product's frameworks have not yet matured into a specific identifiable technological trajectory. The need for additional technological developments before the product's full commercialization requires high levels of openness for new ideas and combinations of businesses to create them. This results in an innate network capital requirement, since network capital facilitates such combinations of innovative businesses. Accordingly, high-technology activity and network capital formation are closely associated at early phases of an industry.[56]

The concept of clusters, as developed by Michael Porter, has rapidly become the focus of competitiveness theory. The underlying tenet of this theory is that national competitiveness is determined by the strength of key concentrations of specific industries within the nation. Porter defines a cluster as a geographically proximate group of interconnected companies and associated institutions in a particular field, linked by commonalities and complementarities.[57] These clusters possess a socio-economic business culture linking certain fundamental conditions that are the drivers of economic growth within nations. These conditions are grouped by Porter into four distinct determinants of competitive advantage:

1 factor conditions – the amount and quality of production factors, such as the skills of the workforce and infrastructural capacity necessary to compete in a given industry;
2 demand conditions – nature of home-market demand;
3 related and supporting industries – the presence or absence of suppliers and other related industries that are internationally competitive;
4 firm strategy, structure, and rivalry – conditions governing how companies are created, organized, and managed, as well as the nature of domestic rivalry.[58]

Clusters offer a means for creating higher value-added by tapping into and distributing the potential of *local strengths* as a whole, rather than as a series of fragmented companies.[59] In particular, clusters can positively influence economic growth in three core ways:

1 by increasing the productivity of companies based in an area;
2 by driving the direction and pace of innovation, underpinning future productivity growth;

3 by stimulating the formation of new businesses, expanding and strengthening the cluster itself (Figure 4.1).

A cluster allows an individual business to benefit as if it had greater scale or as if it had joined with others formally, without requiring it to sacrifice its flexibility. Adam Brandenburger and Barry Nalebuff refer to these benefits as *co-opetition*, whereby firms utilize *complementors*, which are usually other firms that produce goods and services to add value to their own goods and services.[60]

Within economic systems such as clusters, there are some core historical patterns that can be deduced from the organization of each system at a particular time. Allen Scott usefully breaks these systems down into five basic tiers of activity, which form the basis of analysis for an economic system as a whole: an evolving technological system; a framework of industrial organization; the regime of labor relations and managerial norms; the forms of competition and market demand; the institutions of collective economic order and regulation at sector, regional, national, and international levels.[61] In the knowledge economy, the speed of change of all these areas of activity has become so rapid that regions and nations failing to embrace such changes may become economically disconnected.

The role of government in embracing these changes must be carried out with due care and caution, with overly active government intervention and public policy potentially counterproductive or harmful to the long-term developments. As Ross DeVol of the Milken Institute argues, such economic development:

> is an eclectic experience. The process of establishing a high-tech economy is complex and multifaceted. Its evolution is totally dynamic and, in many aspects, self-guiding. Developing a regional culture that is amenable to

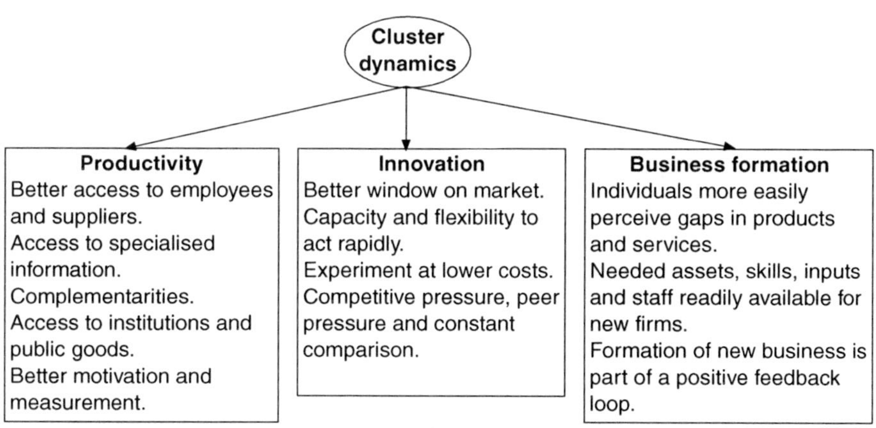

Figure 4.1 Mechanisms for economic growth through cluster development (source: adapted from Porter, *On Competition*).

> change and growth and building a society that is open to new ideas are probably the best strategies and principles government can have in both attracting and expanding high-tech industries.[62]

This emphasis on regional culture indicates the increasing importance of particular spaces and geographic areas below state or national level as the setting within which new economic systems are emerging. In the mid-1980s, Manuel Castells proposed the emergence of a new space of production, as knowledge-based activities became the engine of new economic growth and as new technologies permeated other economic activities.[63] Castells draws a five-point model outlining the characteristics required to make a given space attractive for such activities:

1 close connection to major universities and research institutes, and a large pool of technical and scientific labor;
2 integration into defense and space programs and government markets;
3 a non-unionized industrial tradition;
4 the existence of localized venture capital;
5 a good communications network.[64]

Although the majority of Castells's characteristics are still relevant today, it is clear that knowledge-based growth centers have far outgrown a reliance on government contracts. Also, the existence of non-unionized labor has increasingly become the norm rather than the exception.

Knowledge clusters

Innovation and its applications are at the heart of competitive advantage attainment, rapidly changing the eco-geographic landscape as knowledge clusters act as key drivers of the prosperity of nations. These clusters are focused on the intellectual and knowledge capital residing within and exchanged between both firms and individuals. Silicon Valley is by far the world's largest and best example of a functioning cluster based on knowledge-intensive economic activity, while San Francisco's Multimedia Gulch is an example of a new breed of smaller clusters engaged in knowledge-based activity. Other examples from North America of knowledge cluster locations include Boston (the Route 128 cluster), Seattle, Los Angeles (Hollywood), San Diego, Austin, and Ottawa in Canada. Examples from Europe include Helsinki in Finland, Munich and Stuttgart in Germany, Paris and Rhone-Alpes in France, Stockholm in Sweden, and Oxford and Cambridge in the United Kingdom. In Asia, knowledge clusters can be found in Tokyo in Japan, as well as newer but rapidly growing knowledge clusters in Beijing and Shanghai in China and Bangalore in India. These clusters consist of high densities of firms generally engaged in one or more of IT manufacturing, biotechnology, medical instrumentation, automotive, and other high-technology industrial manufacturing, or knowledge-intensive service activities, such as information and communication technologies and other high-end professional business services.

In these knowledge clusters, network capital mobilizes and fully develops the human capital residing within knowledge-based companies.[65] In an attempt to unpack the complexity of the network systems underlying clusters, Michael Porter argues that four strategic resources are crucial to their formation: (1) highly qualified human resources; (2) technological infrastructure (research institutes, laboratories, etc.); (3) knowledge resources (patents, intellectual property, etc.); and (4) financial capital.[66] Although these resources are the key tangibles of knowledge-based development, we have to take account of the functional resources facilitating the exchange and access to these more structural capital forms.[67] It is the availability and operation of network capital that provides the glue necessary to maximize the effectiveness and development of other capital endowments, as illustrated in Figure 4.2.

The dynamism of knowledge clusters is such that there is an ever-changing balance in the relative importance of the conditions leading from the genesis of a cluster to its growth and sustainability.[68] A study of Silicon Valley and other knowledge clusters finds that the network factors underlying the genesis of a knowledge cluster differ markedly from the networks sustaining an established cluster.[69] In particular, there is a shift from a socio-economic business culture that is initially localized to one that is more externalized and global, as the cluster acts as a magnet for attracting other high-value companies.[70] It is this evolving business culture rich in network capital that provides a knowledge cluster with feedback loops rapid enough to ensure the cluster's position at the head of the innovation race.

The effect of the knowledge revolution is such that knowledge workers are the core agents of the knowledge economy.[71] With the emergence of a *cluster culture*, these knowledge workers possess the ability to transfer and exchange knowledge through what Paul Romer describes as effective mechanisms for supporting collective interests and producing new ideas.[72] Swedish academics Jonas

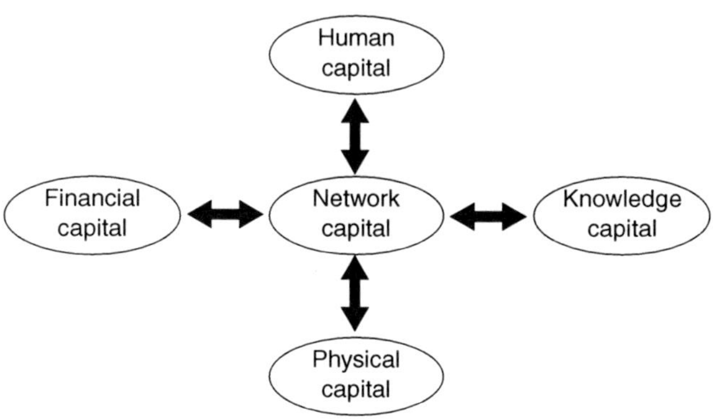

Figure 4.2 Capital formation of knowledge clusters.

Ridderstråle and Kjell Nordström use the metaphor of *funky business* to understand the knowledge economy, arguing that 'talent makes capital dance' in today's economy.[73] The requirement for knowledge transfer and exchange suggests that in Ridderstråle and Nordström's world it is network capital that plays the tune.

Conclusion

Networks are a vital means by which firms acquire and create knowledge. Both network capital and social capital are key resources required to build and develop knowledge networks. Firms are often better placed to strategically manage and invest in network, rather than social, capital. Making a distinction between these two forms of capital contained in networks is relevant to decision-makers as they seek to manage their organization's networks. As a starting point, it provides a framework for assessing those networks that can and cannot be managed and invested in to meet organizational requirements. With regard to clusters, the nature of network capital required during the life cycle and evolution of a cluster will change over time. For instance, as clusters seek new knowledge from new and non-local sources, the onus will shift from a reliance on *local* network capital to *global* network capital. This evolution of knowledge clusters forms the focus of the following chapter.

5 Knowledge clusters and their evolution

Introduction

As economic and technological change occurs with ever-increasing speed, the question grappling the minds of corporate managers and public policymakers alike is how to achieve sustainable growth and competitiveness within the evolving and complex web of blurred socio-economic business activity. The emergence of the global knowledge economy is creating innovative systems and models of work, business interaction and production that are only just beginning to be understood. In recent years, those seeking to find such an understanding have had many of their beliefs and analyses shaken as a result of the economic downturn post-2000. This badly undermined the rapid growth of the knowledge-based and technology-led sectors in the mid and late 1990s. Now that the dust is settling on this bubble-bursting episode, it is important to reflect on developments and, in particular, the ongoing evolution of knowledge clusters and their networks.

By drawing on an analysis of key and emerging knowledge clusters in North America, Europe, and Asia, this chapter shows that the modus operandi of these clusters is shifting from one of internal reliance to models based on wider connectivity and consolidation. The evolution of knowledge clusters in Silicon Valley, San Francisco, Tokyo, Ottawa, Cambridge (United Kingdom), Helsinki, as well as developing new knowledge clusters in India and China is discussed and analyzed. It is suggested that knowledge is increasingly flowing across clusters, resulting in heightened global knowledge connectivity. It is these new patterns of connected clusters and broadened knowledge networks that policy-makers are also increasingly attempting to foster. We start by tracing the development of the world's archetypal knowledge cluster – Silicon Valley.

Silicon Valley

Just as products have life cycles, so do clusters. Therefore, it is important to recognize the changes marking the end of these cycles – as firms should do with their products – and move existing skills and capital resources into more value-added areas of the economy. Similarly, if a cluster is limited in its market scope and potential, it is likely to have a limited capacity to act as an economic growth center. Risk-wise, product life cycles may have an overarching effect on a cluster as a whole, particularly if the product range of the cluster is limited or over-concentrated in one area of economic activity. One example of this was the effect of the semiconductor crisis in the 1980s on Silicon Valley. At the time, network capital, in the form of integrative alliances among members of the US semiconductor industry, was able to negate this threat. While much of the semiconductor manufacture was relocated to overseas regions, Silicon Valley concentrated on renewing itself as the world center of information technology (IT) and computer applications activity. The resurgence of Silicon Valley during the 1980s and 1990s was built upon firms within the cluster seizing on technological breakthroughs, with firms operating within a system of regional innovation dynamics involving a range of research and knowledge-based actors. For instance, Michael Best chronicles the case of Silicon Valley's Intel, which although not possessing a stand-alone R&D lab of its own works closely with universities in the region for much of its state-of-the-art research.[1]

The growth of Silicon Valley during this period occurred as part of what Valley observer Doug Henton describes as the on-going evolution of the cluster from the 1950s, when it specialized in technology related to US defense activities, through to integrated circuits, personal computers and, more recently, the Internet.[2] By the end of the 1990s, Silicon Valley was not only the economic model everyone was seeking to emulate but almost single-handedly seen as the driver of US, and even global, economic growth. In a 1999 article in the *Harvard Business Review*, Gary Hamel highlighted the 41 initial public offerings (IPOs) that had taken place in Silicon Valley the previous year, which had a combined market capitalization of US$27 billion, to present a eulogy of the Silicon Valley model, arguing that 'the choice is yours – you can do your best to make sure you never put a dollar of capital at risk, or you can tap into the kind of wealth that's being created every day in Silicon Valley'.[3]

However, it was the inflated stock prices achieved by these IPOs – primarily on the National Association of Securities Dealers Automated Quotations (NASDAQ), the public stock market for technology companies in the US – that led to another wave of disruption to the Silicon Valley model, which came with the bursting of the so-called economic bubble in 2000. David Rosenberg describes the frenzy that occurred for Internet shares in 1999 as an abuse of NASDAQ's role in acting as an equitable funding mechanism for technology-related ventures.[4] The impact of the adjustment in stock prices in 2000 contributed to a loss of 25,000 jobs in Silicon Valley in 2001 (almost 2 percent of total employment) and more than 200,000 jobs by 2006. Venture capital investment in the Valley also fell from an all-time high of US$21 billion in 2000 to US$6 billion in 2001 and made no improvement between 2002 and 2006.

Ironically, although Hamel's *Harvard Business Review* article now reads at best shortsighted, or what some may consider foolhardy, his overall analysis of Silicon Valley's core business model is fundamentally correct. This model is based on attracting resource allocation – principally human and financial capital – that is willing to take the risk of nurturing the innovation produced within the cluster. In this instance, the initial value placed on Silicon Valley moving onto the next wave of innovation – primarily around Internet technology – was more than the markets could sustain. These markets consist of the financial markets as well as the consumer markets for Internet products and services, which at the time were necessarily embryonic.

The new concentration of activities related to Internet technology suggests that Silicon Valley may never fully regain the majority of the employment lost in recent years. A more weightless Silicon Valley has emerged. While the average employment size of the traditional hardware firm in the Valley was 200, the average size of its software firms is 27.[5] As the 2006 edition of the annual *Index of Silicon Valley* report indicates:

> The past few years have also clarified certain realities about Silicon Valley's changing economic role. Many companies have grown their revenues and achieved record productivity, but they haven't added to the region's job count – choosing in some cases, to outsource work to lower-cost locations.[6]

By 2005, however, the Valley was once again growing, in terms of jobs, income, and population, as well as accounting for more than 10 percent of US patent registration (rising from 5 percent in 1995).[7] This highlights the continuing evolution of the economic and industrial structure of the Valley. Over the last 20 years, only three of the top 40 Silicon Valley companies – Hewlett-Packard, National Semiconductor, and Intel – remain located in the cluster. The others have either failed, relocated, or have been replaced by new companies, many of which did not previously exist.[8]

In order to gain an insight into the longer-term evolution of the Valley, it is important to have an understanding of its roots. The origins of Silicon Valley can be traced to the founding in 1908 of Federal Telegraph in the region and its development of wireless technology, coupled with the importance of defense spending and the role of Stanford University.[9] These assets, and the relationships they fostered, provided the launchpad for a host of path-breaking entrepreneurs who located their activities in the region.[10] These entrepreneurs were, at the time, responsible for establishing some of the largest Silicon Valley firms, such as Eitel-McCullough (Eimac), Litton Industries, Varian Associates, Fairchild Semiconductor, and Intel, which came to dominate markets for advanced tubes and semiconductors, while also stimulating a whole host of related activity in the region.[11] One of the most important of these entrepreneurs was Robert Noyce, who was the cofounder of Fairchild Semiconductor and Intel and coinvented the integrated circuit.[12] Individuals such as Noyce were responsible for creating a community in Silicon Valley built upon innovation, within which the strategic exchange of knowledge was at the heart of its growth and success. The networks these entrepreneurs and their successors established helped create a genealogy illustrating their influence in shaping the evolution of the cluster.[13]

Although the initial trigger for cluster development is often viewed as a random act, this provides a particularly unsatisfactory explanation of the forces shaping the eco-geographic landscape. In particular, while some have argued that clustering processes in Silicon Valley were initially random, this overlooks the importance of the close relationships, and the network and social capital embedded within these relationships, which occurred in the 1930s between Stanford University professor Frederick Terman and many of his former students. Among these students were William Hewlett and David Packard who, under Terman's guidance, created the Hewlett-Packard company within what is now known as Silicon Valley. The garage where Hewlett and Packard started their business is now a standing landmark of the genesis of Silicon Valley.[14]

This initial act was not in fact random but the outcome of a series of relationships whereby network capital enabled intellectual capital to be mobilized into the creation of Hewlett-Packard. Further spin-out companies from Stanford University and Stanford Research Institute were inclined to remain in the vicinity due to the associated development, interestingly by Terman, of Stanford Industrial Park. The expansion of Silicon Valley was based on the externalities of technology spillovers, integrated supplier networks, and the existence of highly specialized workforce skills that were predicated on the existence and maintenance of networks. Also, and often overlooked, is the role of Stanford University as an attractor of investment from elsewhere, by seeking the satellite operations of established firms such as Lockheed.[15] In more recent years, this attraction role has been balanced by an increasing emphasis on creating new spin-out ventures.[16]

Within knowledge clusters, network capital is generated through the crossover of geographical and organizational proximity, which is able to produce processes of collective learning. This crossover primarily consists of factors relating not only to co-location but also, as AnnaLee Saxenian found, to the fuzzy and blurred boundaries often existing between firms. The close interrelationships between some companies are so blurred, given the high degree of joint projects and capital sharing – especially human capital – that it is often difficult to actually 'see' where one company ends and another begins.[17] This creates a system of embeddedness – or the overlap of social and economic considerations – facilitating institutionalized innovation through the high-value tacit learning attained through these cognitive interactions. The significance attached in Silicon Valley to network capital investment can be traced back to the 1970s and to the creation of a number of informal and loose social-computer clubs, such as the Home Brew Computer Club. The members of this club included Microsoft founder Bill Gates and the creators of Apple – Steve Jobs and Steve Wozniak. According to Saxenian, networks are the resource upon which Silicon Valley is sustained:

> Silicon Valley has a regional network-based industrial system that promotes collective learning and flexible adjustment among specialist producers of a complex of related technologies. The region's dense social networks and

> open labor markets encourage experimentation and entrepreneurship. Companies compete intensely while at the same time learning from one another about changing markets and technologies through informal communication and collaborative practices; and loosely linked team structures encourage horizontal communication among firm divisions and with outside suppliers and customers. The functional boundaries within firms are porous in a network system, as are the boundaries between firms themselves and between firms and local institutions such as trade associations and universities.[18]

The key feature here is the balance within the cluster of competitive rivalries and a network system where repeated interactions are built on shared identities and mutual trust. This gives firms within the cluster the ability to adapt to changing markets and technologies, through processes of collective technological learning – with Saxenian referring to the Valley as a 'Protean Place'.[19] Some commentators have suggested that Saxenian's analysis of Silicon Valley as protean is illusory or even imaginary. Rob Koepp argues that networks in the Valley are more pragmatically the by-product of innovative and entrepreneurial drives, with companies often electing to become intertwined because of advantages in integrating their supply chains.[20] Following Saxenian, other researchers attribute high levels of social capital to the vital role of networks in Silicon Valley's development.[21] However, social capital, measured by involvement in civic activities, is relatively poor in the region.[22] This suggests that it is strategic networking, rather than informal or ad-hoc networking, which plays the key role in building the relationships fuelling the region's innovation. As David Rosenberg puts it:

> Silicon Valley is a ferment not just of start-up companies, which attract the most attention, but of mergers and acquisitions, tactical and strategic alliances, continuously evolving business plans, venture capital financing, public offering and product rollouts – all operating at a pace many times faster than conventional industry.[23]

Clusters, in particular Silicon Valley, are the pressure cookers of the knowledge economy. Michael Lewis's chronicle of Netscape founder Jim Clark vividly illustrates the requirement for even the most successful knowledge entrepreneurs to constantly evolve their strategies and networks through which they both receive and transmit information and knowledge.[24]

Some of the main aspects of the networks existing in Silicon Valley include access to collective services that both spread risk and pool technical expertise through the provision of services including financial capital, intellectual property law, research, management development, technical education and training, and market information – particularly for new entrepreneurs. Although companies individually have little incentive to provide such services, the concentration of high-tech companies provides significant incentives for those companies specializing in the delivery of such services to locate in Silicon Valley – for instance, a large proportion of the venture capitalists within the United States are located in the Valley. Kleiner Perkins, one of the most powerful venture capitalists in the Valley, has actually created its own network of entrepreneurs and firms, which are encouraged to collaborate as closely as possible. The network is referred to as the *keiretsu*, after the Japanese corporate model of business networks and ownership, and is a very powerful force within the Valley.

In the 1980s, changing computer systems produced a necessary change in the economic make-up of the Valley. No longer were the actual producers of silicon chips at the core of the value-added within the semiconductor sector. It was those firms assembling and designing final systems that were the new center of the sector. Although there are still a small number of firms manufacturing silicon within the Valley, the majority of manufacturing is undertaken by plants in lower-cost regions. Within the Valley itself, a business morphology occurred, whereby companies such as Sun Microsystems and Silicon Graphics became world-leaders in developing computer systems. Their positioning within the cluster enabled them to steal a lead on any competition located elsewhere. Throughout the 1990s and into the new millennium, the evolution of Silicon Valley has continued apace, as the knowledge economy has come to dominate global competition. The Valley has continued to attract companies into its network, and new networks have developed between computer system companies and the explosion of new media firms involved in the Internet and interactive entertainment. Indeed, the creation of digital networks has come to define new modes of communication and interaction. From the 1990s onwards, many companies from Europe, the Far East, and India have located a site within the Valley, hoping to benefit from both the prestige of the location and to become members of the networks within the cluster.

Po Bronson, in his highly informative and entertaining study of contemporary Silicon Valley, points to the 'people network' as the underlying framework upon which business in the seemingly chaotic environment of the Valley is carried out so smoothly.[25] In particular, he highlights the value of not only 'who you know', but also 'who they know' – the three degrees of separation or indirect ties. Carol Kinsey Goman finds one of the key traits of Yahoo!, the Internet company based in the Valley, to be that it evaluates the 'spheres of influence' of potential employees – or who they know and who they can get to know.[26] The importance of indirect ties as a source of network capital in the Valley is highlighted by the operation of the majority of venture capitalists in the region, most of whom only fund projects referred through an intermediary party.[27] Indeed, it is the network capital existing between the venture capitalists and key companies upon which financially equipped entrepreneurship in the Valley has thrived.

Sabeer Bhatia, the founder of Hotmail, is a powerful indicator of the reliance of Silicon Valley's system of entrepreneurship on network capital. Through the building of his own networks within the Valley, Bhatia was able to cut through traditional finance routes, enabling him to quickly access the necessary funding for one of the Internet's most successful websites:

> any kid with a good idea can make it big – as long as he networks like crazy. The only kinds of people the network discriminates against are those who turn their noses up at networking. So it's a meritocracy but a perverted one, based more on the merit of how well you knock on doors than the merit of your Java code.[28]

Furthermore, Bronson illustrates the advantage of proximity to be vital to the functioning of the Valley – as he says the fact that everybody knows everybody else is essential – even a company such as Novell, which invented virtual corporate computer networks, understands the importance of being located in the Valley.[29]

Commentators such as Bennett Harrison have argued that the creation and evolution of Silicon Valley has been dominated mainly by large multinational electronic and computer-related corporations.[30] This appears to ignore the fact that it is precisely these corporations that grew from very small firms within the Silicon Valley cluster environment. Harrison concludes that 'whatever one's preferred characterization of Silicon Valley, one thing is certain, as we approach the end of the twentieth century, Silicon Valley as a region is in trouble'.[31] Similarly, Mike Hobday argued that the growth of Silicon Valley would be constrained precisely because of a lack of large enough corporations within the region.[32] These prophets of doom have proved to be misguided, underestimating the power of entrepreneurship, provided it is mixed with a potent dose of network capital. The cluster has evolved into a new self-sustaining milieu through the Internet and new media technologies, created out of the exchange of intellectual and knowledge capital within a collaborative-competitive culture.

A number of analysts have suggested that a lack of network capital within Silicon Valley can be proven by the increasing frequency with which firms within the cluster are bringing lawsuits against one another for alleged violation of intellectual property rights. Such a hypothesis ignores the complexities of clusters. Given the 'relaxed' legal infrastructure and the high levels of employee mobility, it is to be expected that the ratio of litigation may be higher compared to business environments not sharing the cluster dynamics of Silicon Valley. However, this does not disprove the existence of an ethos of collaboration and network building. In many ways, it would actually appear to prove the existence of network capital, since for such violations to occur there must have initially been a degree of interaction and purposeful communication – there are no divorces without marriages.

An important impact of the post-2000 economic environment is the increasing focus of regional economic policymakers on the wider Bay Area region of California, covering San Francisco and Oakland, as well as Silicon Valley.[33] In the past, Silicon Valley developed along a path that was culturally and economically distinct from the neighboring city of San Francisco, which was not seen as playing any significant role, financial or otherwise, in the operation of Silicon Valley.[34] Perhaps as a result of necessity within both camps, there is now an economic and political will to achieve greater integration and connectivity between Silicon Valley and San Francisco. A 2004 report funded by regional stakeholders discusses the common challenges and strengths of the Bay Area as a whole, rather than focusing just on Silicon Valley.[35] The report describes the enduring strength of the Bay Area, with it continuing to be the home of more than one half (54 percent) of all US biotechnology companies, as well as global IT players such as Hewlett-Packard, Intel, AMD, Sun Microsystems, Adobe, and Apple and the advanced research centers of IBM, Hitachi, Lockheed Martin, SRI, and Microsoft. The report highlights the offshoring and outsourcing of knowledge-based activities to locations outside the Bay Area as an important determinate of the future for the region. It finds that 80 percent of jobs advertised in the region for quality-assurance and test engineers (knowledge-based jobs that are typically the first to be offshored) were for work that would be located outside the Bay Area.[36]

The response to these new patterns in the globalization of the knowledge economy is one that seeks to improve the strength of the knowledge cluster through geographic consolidation and connectivity. As 2006 *Index of Silicon Valley* report makes clear:

> Like other regions, Silicon Valley must find a role to play in a global economy that has become a series of 'value chains' connecting product design, flexible production, marketing, and logistics functions. This is a complex process involving many partners across numerous locations throughout the world.[37]

If Silicon Valley is to compete with emerging, but demographically and economically vast, knowledge clusters in locations such as India and China, it appears that cluster size and maintaining a significant critical mass are becoming an important issue. Therefore, consolidation into a larger Bay Area regional knowledge cluster may be the first important outcome of strategic policymaking. However, the challenge this raises is how to transfer attempts to consolidate from the tables of policymakers to those of strategic decision-makers in companies within the region. Cultural differences between the working and living environments in Silicon Valley and San Francisco mean that it may not be easily achieved, although recent evidence suggests that cultural convergence is gradually emerging as San Francisco seeks to develop itself as a high-technology hotspot. It is further suggested that Silicon Valley's operating culture is permeating and defining the operation of the global knowledge economy as a whole.[38] In the following two sections we look first at the associated yet stuttering emergence of San Francisco as a knowledge cluster and then the role of Silicon Valley in determining a global web of knowledge clusters integrating regions from Asia, specifically India and China.

San Francisco

By the end of the 1990s, San Francisco was riding the crest of the new Internet economy wave. In his 1999 article, 'The Wired Loft', Mark Wolfe critiqued the rapid rise of the 'Multimedia Gulch' in San Francisco, describing a dynamic cluster of media and technological companies located in the formerly run-down South of Market area (SOMA) of the city.[39] In less than a decade, network and cluster building was attributed with transforming a depressed, high-unemployment, high-crime urban district without the massive physical infrastructure investment associated with most urban development projects elsewhere. Rather than hard planning development, Multimedia Gulch is credited with emerging out of a convergence of business and cultural factors, or what we call the socio-economic business culture.

During the early 1990s, young technologically minded entrepreneurs, who were aware of the emerging possibilities of overlapping technological provision with content provision through multimedia and interactive media, were attracted to SOMA by the small loft inhabiting artistic and creative community, which resided in the area primarily due to the cheap rental accommodation available. This triggered the development of a core of new firms involved in merging IT, graphic arts and design, film, video, sound, and print into a whole array of new products for PCs, the Internet, and film and video producers. By the end of the 1990s, there were approximately 2,000 multimedia, Internet, and other firms in the cluster employing an estimated 40,000 workers, bringing an estimated US$5.7 billion into the local economy, which is five times the amount estimated in 1995.[40] The cluster was one of the most rapidly growing hotbeds of technological and innovative activity in the world, as well as being one of the most 'trendiest'. The cheap lofts originally rented by the artists became much sought after residences by high-paid professionals, who dined at a new wave of chic restaurants that sprang up.

How did this economic and cultural transformation occur at such pace and without policy intervention? Wolfe points to four key factors that shaped Multimedia Gulch:

1 the pre-existence of a small network of firms servicing the printing and publishing requirements of the artistic and creative community;
2 the cache of the residing avant-garde community;
3 the glut of cheap derelict office space available for refurbishment;
4 the removal of entry barriers to the multimedia sector as a result of developments in PC-based desktop technology.

If seeking a specific trigger institution for the emergence of Multimedia Gulch, it is the preexistence of the residing group of avant-garde artists who provided the area with a significant degree of cultural capital.

According to Wolfe, the integration of high-technology, publishing and art was responsible for the creation of a dynamic and growing cluster out of a seemingly incoherent mix of actors and assets:

> By the early 1990s, all three industries had clustered in relative abundance in SOMA and had begun to form networks of business linkages with one another … these three seemingly disparate sociocommercial groups ended

> up in the same rundown industrial area at the same time and created a unitary, spatially defined industrial network.[41]

Also, Multimedia Gulch was seen as breaking the cultural and economic barriers existing between San Francisco and Silicon Valley. San Francisco was described as Silicon Valley's urban backyard and playground.[42]

Since the growth of Silicon Valley in the 1980s, San Francisco increasingly became a subsidiary of its more southern neighbor. The high-technology boom in San Francisco meant that it could now become a more integrated subsidiary.[43] However, the speed of development and sustainability of Multimedia Gulch was severely curtailed by the 2000 economic downturn. As this shock was closely related to the hyper growth occurring in the stock of new Internet and related listed firms, it necessarily had a high impact on San Francisco and Multimedia Gulch. Although Wolfe's reasoning for the growth of the area is at least partly true, the drying up of finance, especially the venture capital that had funded the explosive rate of development, led to the *San Francisco Business Times* soon describing the area as Multimedia Mulch, as many of the firms that had so quickly flourished just as quickly either became extinct or significantly scaled back their operations.[44] In a 2002 visit we made to the area, it was clearly in deep recession, possessing the air of a ghost town, which is not surprising given that property vacancy rates at the time were running at 44 percent.

San Francisco and Multimedia Gulch were far from alone in suffering such dramatic setbacks. In New York's Lower Manhattan, a parallel to the rise of Multimedia Gulch was occurring. The so-called Silicon Alley was New York's equivalent of the cluster of new start-ups operating in the digital economy that emerged in the 1990s. However, its post-2000 fate was even worse than that of Multimedia Gulch, with the cluster being totally wiped out during the economic crash. Michael Indergaard's detailed study of Silicon Alley points to two underlying reasons for the decimation of the area. First, many of the firms and entrepreneurs lacked marketable and sustainable applications for the new technologies they were operating. Second, Silicon Alley was largely a creation of those individuals and institutions with a vested stake in Lower Manhattan's real estate.[45] Indergaard's implication is that the property owners in the area were using the 'growth' of the new firms, which often had little in the way of commercializable products and services, to inflate the value of previously rundown and vacant areas of Lower Manhattan.

While Lower Manhattan was destined to face even more catastrophic problems with 9/11 terrorist attacks in 2001, Multimedia Gulch – like Silicon Valley – has begun a period of economic revival, with property vacancy rates falling to 20 percent by the end of 2005.[46] The cluster has consolidated and matured into a number of larger key players operating in the converging fields of communications, advertising, and media. One example of such a player is Macromedia Inc., which was acquired in 2005 by Adobe Systems for US$3.4 billion. Also, the area is gradually becoming the home for a number of ventures operating in the crossover between IT and biotechnology – as is also occurring in Silicon Valley.

Although beset by drawbacks, the emergence of Multimedia Gulch as a new knowledge cluster, and the improved connectivity between San Francisco and Silicon Valley, is real and most likely enduring. As Michael Indergaard indicates, this can be traced to the networks that developed as Multimedia Gulch's entrepreneurs drew on the expertise residing in Silicon Valley's computer industry.[47] Also, as indicated earlier, there is now increasing political will for the two regions to stand together economically and culturally.

Clusters and the new Asia

Much of the rise of Asia, especially China and India, has been attributed to the shift of traditional manufacturing and low value-added service sector activities from the West to locations in the East. Less attention has been paid to the emergence of these nations and their regions as knowledge-intensive locations or the patterns of knowledge-based growth that are emerging. However, recent evidence suggests that both China and India are rapidly becoming key locations of knowledge-based investment attracted from North America and Europe, when measured in the form of Foreign Direct Investment (FDI) focused on R&D activity.

Table 5.1 highlights the global patterns of R&D FDI between 2002 and 2005. It shows that North America has been the source of 50 percent of all investment, followed by the 'old' 15 members of the European Union (EU) (28 percent) and Asia Pacific (14 percent). Asia Pacific has been the overwhelming destination for most R&D FDI, accounting for 58 percent of all investment, followed by the members of the EU15 (22 percent) and North America (14 percent). Table 5.2 further highlights that between 2002 and 2005 the largest proportion of R&D investment projects have occurred in India (26 percent of all projects) and China (17 percent). These nations are followed by the United States and the United Kingdom. The key sectors for R&D FDI, by total investment between 2002 and 2005, are the knowledge-based sectors of IT and software (26 percent), semiconductors (21 percent), and pharmaceuticals (11 percent).[48]

These R&D facilities are forming part of global knowledge networks within the multinationals they represent, where more interdependent and vertical

Table 5.1 Source and destination of R&D foreign direct investment 2002–5 (US$ million)

	Source of investment	*Destination of investment*	*Net home investment*
North America	24,781	7,078	–17,703
Asia Pacific	7,011	28,560	21,549
European Union 15	13,807	11,001	–2,806
Other	3,746	2,705	–1,041
Total	49,345	49,345	–

Source: Huggins, Demirbag and Ratcheva, 'Global knowledge and R&D foreign direct investment flows'.

Table 5.2 Number of R&D foreign direct investment projects by destination, 2002–5

Destination	*Number of projects*	*Percentage of the total*
India	488	25.6
China	328	17.2
USA	120	6.3
UK	83	4.4
Singapore	73	3.8
France	57	3.0
Canada	51	2.7
Taiwan	49	2.6
Germany	45	2.4
Ireland	45	2.4
Australia	41	2.2
Russia	40	2.1
Spain	35	1.8
Japan	35	1.8
Malaysia	33	1.7
South Korea	32	1.7
Sweden	28	1.5
Czech Republic	23	1.2
Brazil	21	1.1
Poland	20	1.0
Others	259	13.6
Total	1,906	100.0

Source: Huggins, Demirbag and Ratcheva, 'Global knowledge and R&D foreign direct investment flows'.

investment and knowledge ties are developing. As part of this process, new knowledge clusters are quickly developing in a number of Asian cites and regions, for example, Bangalore, Hyderabad, and Mumbai in India, and Beijing, Guangzhou, Hangzhou, Nanjing, and Shanghai in China. These new knowledge clusters and networks are part of the development described by David Rosenberg as being a global web of such clusters, at the heart of which is Silicon Valley.[49] The changes taking place in the global economy has meant that many firms in Silicon Valley, as well as other knowledge-based locations in North America and Europe, have shifted and expanded their activities in Asia in order to improve and sustain competitiveness. For instance, Intel in Silicon Valley has been one of the United States's most active international R&D investors in recent years. Since 2002, Intel has established or expanded R&D facilities in China (Shanghai, Dalian, Guangzhoung, Beijing, Shengyang, and Shenzen) and India (Bangalore).

These investments are not only facilitating the development of the indigenous knowledge economy in these locations, but also the ability of Chinese and Indian knowledge entrepreneurs and workers located overseas to contribute to the development of their home countries and regions. Previously, these individuals were attracted to locations overseas, as they were the globe's only leading knowledge bases. In Silicon Valley, AnnaLee Saxenian finds that immigrants account for one-third of the region's engineering workforce, with two-thirds of the region's foreign-born engineers being from Asia. In total, Chinese and Indian immigrants account for almost three-quarters of the total Asian-born engineering workforce.[50] Saxenian further describes how these Asian engineers and entrepreneurs are creating and building networks between Silicon Valley and locations in China and India, which is transferring knowledge from the West to the East, accelerating the development of key regions such as Beijing, Shanghai, and Bangalore. At the same time, they are providing more cost-effective yet equally skilled production processes to their companies located in Silicon Valley.[51] Saxenian refers to these linkages as 'brain circulation', whereby the Asian knowledge entrepreneurs and workers act as network nodes connecting distant regional economies, and also contributing to cluster development in India and China.

These developments indicate that the knowledge possessed by leading global clusters is not only positioned within and across local actors and networks, but a more global set of networks and constituent actors. The present phase of global economic evolution suggests that there is a distinct hierarchy of global knowledge clusters, with Silicon Valley and other clusters in leading economies continuing to be at the apex.[52] However, the sheer size of the clusters emerging in Asia, particularly China, means that the balance of power is more than likely to shift in coming years. In 'Rice Bowl & Chips', Dennis Posadas describes how Asian clusters can learn from and adapt the Silicon Valley cluster model to their benefit.[53] The advantage for Asia is the potential scale and number of clusters being created there in a very short span of time.

One example is the Zhongguancun (ZGC) science and technology park in the north-western part of Beijing. This area has rapidly transformed from a quiet Beijing suburb to becoming the home of more than 12,000 new technology companies, as well as the location of a number of China's most prestigious universities and research institutes.[54] Many of the companies located in ZGC are linked into local knowledge networks with these universities, as well as global knowledge networks through co-operation with foreign companies. Whereas local networks are mainly utilized for new product design, the global networks allow the companies to tap into the initial ideas required to stimulate the innovation process.[55] The relationship between the local and foreign-owned firms is not only one of interdependency but also hierarchical, with the multinationals able to control the nature and scope of the interactions.[56]

Even more so than Beijing, Shanghai has risen to becoming a leading center of the global economy. Shanghai has benefited from not only being the largest city in China but also from the unprecedented growth in foreign investment and foreign trade.[57] This has allowed Shanghai to develop a number of knowledge clusters across a range of sectors, which have grown from the creation of global knowledge and production networks. For instance, Shanghai has established a new automotive cluster through linkage with a number of key German automotive firms. The relationships between these German companies and local producers and suppliers in Shanghai were initially problematic.[58] However, in the long-run adaptability by both parties has helped overcome these problems, with the German firms becoming integrated into the local innovation system.

One of the criticisms made of Chinese knowledge clusters, particularly by Chinese commentators, is that they have lacked the necessary level of institutional and political support to fully exploit their potential. The same can largely be said of India and especially its leading knowledge cluster, Bangalore, which David Rosenberg describes as emerging with government intervention consisting of sticks without carrots.[59] Given the relative lack of government finance, this is perhaps to be expected, but nevertheless has not stopped Bangalore becoming one of world's leading clusters for software development. Also, it should not be forgotten that public policy at least had a role in the initial stimulus for cluster development through the initiation in 1991 of 15 software technology parks, which were important for supporting and developing the early players.[60]

Bangalore has created a number of companies that are now established global players, such as Infosys and Wipro, and has significantly benefited from the trend of western companies to offshore IT-related activities to cheaper-cost locations overseas. Increasingly, Bangalore has become the preferred location for the new R&D activities of a host of international IT companies including Dell, Microsoft, IBM, Intel, Samsung, Motorola, and Alcatel. These companies have provided a vital contribution to the development of the Bangalore cluster through the diffusion of knowledge and the networks created with local firms and institutions.[61]

Given the nature of this foreign investment and the linkages created, Balaji Parthasarathy has asked if Bangalore is India's Silicon Valley or Silicon Valley's India?[62] According to Parathasarathy, the latter description is still the most appropriate, as the cluster continues to mainly develop software for global markets largely controlled by the foreign investors, rather than one which indigenously defines its own products and technologies. Overall, this confirms the hierarchy described above, but does not imply that the situation is static. These regions continue to catch up, and with this the opportunity to lead in new and possibly disruptive technology increases. As Chong-Moon Lee and his colleagues state in 'The Silicon Valley Edge', 'knowledge about what others are up to, at least in general, motivates everyone to keep innovating, because even a small lead can be decisive and a small lag fatal'.[63]

Tokyo's Bit Valley

Alongside the emerging and large-scale clusters in China and India, another Asian example of high-technology clustering resembling the urban-style developments in San Francisco is Bit Valley in the Shibuya district of Tokyo. The cluster consists of a group of Internet-related companies that has grown rapidly since 1999, within a national economy that was initially slow to embrace the Internet economy.[64] The institutional trigger behind the development of Bit Valley was in fact a weekly web magazine, *Shukan NetAge*, produced by

NetAge, a Shibuya-based company that aimed to act as an incubator for Internet ventures.

Bit Valley has quickly become the center for Internet business in Japan, fostering venture firms, attracting investment, and enhancing competition and information sharing simultaneously. A key part of creating the new knowledge cluster was the inauguration of informal networking events, which were modeled on the CyberSuds events established by the New York Media Association in the United States. The 'Bit Style' was christened, with attendances at individual events topping 2,000. This led to the development of the Bit Valley Association and the introduction of more manageable 'working groups'. The outcome of these developments is that 40 percent of the total number of Internet-related companies in the Tokyo region are located in Bit Valley. In total, 90 percent of IT-related firms in Japan operate in the Internet sector, indicating the strength it has developed alongside the dominance it possesses in the videogame industry.[65]

Similar to the Multimedia Gulch experience, Bit Valley is situated within an urban district that since the 1980s has become one of the most fashionable and trend-setting in Japan. The success of Bit Valley is being spotlighted in Japan as the catalyst for the development of a new socio-economic business culture for jump-starting its competitive fortunes. The key feature of this new culture is a change of perception by the economically active from wishing to be employed by a large corporation to creating their own new small companies and ventures based in the new media sector.

Part of the human capital mobilization associated with this development is Digital Hollywood, the biggest player in the Japanese computer graphics and the Internet education sector, which has opened a 'university' in Bit Valley. The university offers digital and Internet-related business courses emphasizing the entrepreneurial and management components of company formation and growth. This emphasis is vital, given the lack of management and entrepreneurship studies available in Japan.

Although Bit Valley represents the new spirit of entrepreneurship in Japan, a number of the new firms are in fact spin-offs from companies such as NEC and Fujitsu.[66] Also, the developments have not been totally without public sector intervention, with the government taking a role in supporting the development of the cluster through its broader science and technology policies. These policies are aimed at reflecting not only technological and market needs but also Japan's social needs.[67]

Ottawa

The Ottawa city-region is Canada's center of high-technology activity, with a knowledge cluster that expanded extensively during the 1990s and now consists of more than 1,000 companies. During this period, the balance of employment in the region swung from the public sector, which is buoyed by Ottawa being Canada's federal capital, toward high technology, and in particular ICT-related employment. Between 1981 and 1996, the share of employment in manufacturing involving high-technology activities rose from 29 percent to 50 percent, while employment in the government sector fell by 17 percent.[68] At the heart of the cluster are a number of global players in the fields of telecommunications equipment, microelectronics, and software, such as Nortel, JDS Uniphase, Alcatel Canada, Mitel, Compaq Computer, Cognos, and IBM Canada. Of these players, Nortel has been of vital strategic importance to the development of the cluster, accounting for approximately one-fifth of Canada's total industrial R&D expenditure (the cluster as a whole accounting for a similar proportion of Canada's total R&D expenditure).[69] Nortel also recruits around one-third of all postgraduates in electrical engineering and computer science from Canadian universities.[70] At its peak during the early part of the new millennium, the cluster totaled 70,000 employees and was dubbed *Silicon Valley North*. Such a tag is well deserved, given the rapid growth of companies such as Nortel and JDS Uniphase and the global advantage the cluster achieved in telecommunications, software, photonics and life sciences.[71]

The roots of the cluster can be traced to its more mature segment, telecommunications, and the establishment in the region of the National Research Council's (NRC) laboratories, the Communications Research Centre (CRC), and Bell Northern Research (BNR), with 90 percent of Canada's R&D in industrial telecommunications being conducted in the region.[72] Both the NRC and the CRC have been responsible for spinning-out a barrage of knowledge-based ventures in the region, beginning in 1950 with Computing Devices, now General Dynamics Canada. Coupled with Nortel's expansion during the 1970s and 1980s, a series of knowledge entrepreneurs created and grew a number of new telecommunications, microelectronics, and software companies. Chief among these was the Welsh-born Terry Matthews, who, along with Michael Cowpland, established the highly successful Mitel. Both Matthews and Cowpland were previously employees of Microsystems International, a Nortel spin-off. Matthews went on to establish Newbridge Networks in 1985, which was acquired 15 years later by Alcatel for US$7.1 billion in stock, while Cowpland created Corel, which became the largest software company in Canada. Other important knowledge entrepreneurs and the companies they created include Jozef Straus with JDS, Rod Bryden with Systemhouse, and Michael Potter of Cognos. These individuals set the stage for the establishment of Ottawa's knowledge cluster, which by the mid-1990s had one of the world's highest per capita percentage of owner-operated high-technology companies.[73]

In summary, the development of Ottawa's knowledge cluster is intrinsically linked to three key initial institutional catalysts. First, as highlighted above, the cluster has benefited from the location of the research facilities of the NRC and the CRC, as well as other government laboratories in Ottawa. Second, the spillovers and spin-outs emanating from Nortel and BNR facilities cemented the growth of the cluster. Third, the universities of Ottawa and Carleton have played an important role in creating a significant amount of the knowledge utilized by the cluster's business community.

Of these resources, a major overarching factor is undoubtedly Ottawa's federal R&D activities. Canada spends more than CAN$5 billion annually in federal science and technology activities, which include the NRC, CRC, and several other leading technological institutions situated in Ottawa. These institutions have been instrumental in spurring commercial innovation, while many local knowledge-based firms whose genealogies link them with government-developed innovations have contributed substantial private sector investment to Ottawa's R&D base. For government R&D to have an impact on the cluster, local entrepreneurs must be able to secure patent rights and their firms must have access to these rights. Significantly, the number of patents filed by companies in Ottawa has more than doubled in recent years. Human resource development has also been an important feature of development with the cluster being able to take advantage of eight colleges and universities, and numerous professional and business schools. These institutions have forged deep linkages with business and industry, and this resulted in them being attuned to the human resource requirements of industry. In particular, many science and engineering graduates find careers in Ottawa's high-technology sector through relationships between the universities and the private sector.

The development and evolution of the knowledge cluster as a whole is strategically driven forward by The Ottawa Partnership (TOP), which is a public-private partnership involving all the key local economic agents. Policies have been firmly based on creating focused economic generators within core sectors that form segments of the knowledge cluster. These sectors consist of telecommunications, software, microelectronics, photonics, life sciences, alongside professional services and tourism. Policies are largely facilitative and hands-off, consisting of various fiscal incentives such as tax credits to encourage both start-ups and indigenous growing firms. As far as possible, industry has been given a degree of autonomy to lead the development of new initiatives, which has proved to be crucial in ensuring a focused cluster approach model. As with all successful and functioning clusters, a major aspect of their operation is the social and network capital they possess. David Wolfe, an expert and longtime observer of the Ottawa cluster, has found there to be a high degree of strength tying together 'local institutions of collaboration'.[74] Of these institutions, the most prominent is the Ottawa Centre for Research and Innovation (OCRI), which is a not-for-profit organization supported by approximately 500 knowledge-based firms and organizations. The membership consists of large corporations – such as Bell Canada and Nortel Networks – as well as high-technology small and medium enterprises (SMEs), research laboratories, academic institutions, regional government, school boards, and other businesses serving Ottawa's knowledge cluster. The networks facilitated by OCRI have been favorably compared with those of California's Silicon Valley, both in terms of their effectiveness and importance to the regional economy.[75]

Until the early 2000s, Ottawa's was a runaway, high-technology, success story. However, the economic downturn was to bite the region and the knowledge cluster particularly hard. It is estimated that following its employment peak of almost 70,000 in early 2001, more than 20,000 jobs within the knowledge cluster were shed by 2003. Such a large reduction in the employment size of the cluster – almost one-third – was mainly due to the high number of layoffs at the largest corporations, in particular Nortel and JDS Uniphase, significantly denting the telecommunications and photonics segments of the cluster.[76] Somewhat fortunately, a large proportion of the unemployment was mopped up by the public sector, which took on an extra 13,000 employees, as well as ensuring a stream of public sector procurement contracts to local, knowledge-based companies. Other individuals laid-off were forced into necessity-based entrepreneurship, which ironically meant that even though the employment size of the cluster was much reduced, the number of firms increased, with an estimated 400 new knowledge-based ventures created.[77]

Despite the efforts of the government to limit the economic and social fallout of the downturn, it resulted in a major readjustment of Ottawa's knowledge cluster and its future trajectory. In the past, the vitality of the cluster was credited to the strong intra-regional networks and their effectiveness in transferring and commercializing locally created knowledge. More recently, increased emphasis has been given to the role and importance of knowledge networks with actors that are external to the region and the cluster. Although local networks continue to provide mechanisms for transferring knowledge within the cluster, it has been found that the most important sources of knowledge and innovation for Ottawa's SME community are global knowledge networks.[78] The development of global networks across Ottawa's knowledge cluster appears equally applicable to both SMEs and large firms. For example, there is evidence of substantial collaboration between Nortel and JDS Uniphase's facilities in Ottawa and other facilities owned by these companies around the world, through their own global knowledge networks.[79] As John de la Mothe argues, 'we have here evidence of a strong, and growing, distributed system of innovation and a strong flow of knowledge'.[80]

As an outcome of economic readjustment, policymakers in Ottawa and Canada as a whole are setting in place initiatives to globalize their national and regional knowledge economies. Since 2004, international cooperation agreements have been instigated between Canada and India to facilitate increased trade and business in the ICT sector. Also, the Canadian Advanced Technology Alliance and the China Chamber of International Commerce and the Shenzhen High-Technology Industrial Association (Shenzhen being the home of one of China's rapidly emerging ICT clusters) have entered into agreements to develop business relations in the high-technology field. These agreements and other related initiatives point to a realization in Canada of the emergence of the global knowledge economy and the necessity to become players in this economy's networks. In April 2005, Ottawa's knowledge cluster achieved its first IPO in six years. Under the chairmanship of Terry Matthews, March Networks was floated on the Toronto Stock Exchange, with its success attributed to its ability to compete in and conquer global, rather than local or national, markets. This outward orientation represents the next phase in the evolution of Ottawa's knowledge cluster, which itself is the result of many years of strategic and creative thinking. As Terry Matthews notes, 'just setting up a cluster in Timbuktu won't work … you have to build a nucleus around something deep-rooted'.[81]

Cambridge (UK)

In the UK, the most prominent knowledge clusters are based around the universities of Cambridge in Eastern England and Oxford in South East England. Overall, cluster development in Cambridge is more progressed than its Oxford counterpart, with network capital almost 50 percent higher in Cambridge.[82] Within Cambridge, it is largely informal channels and personal relationships that have shaped the formation of the cluster, in particular the links between Cambridge University and its spin-out companies. These businesses have emerged from the science base of the university, especially its core strength in the field of early diffusing technologies.[83] Also, while Oxford University has a policy of claiming Intellectual Property Rights (IPR) for the technology generated by staff and students, Cambridge University has adopted the more entrepreneurial policy of endowing originators with such rights.

The region of Cambridge is better endowed with network capital through its role as a center of both computer hardware and software, which is continuing to create the localized multiplier effects associated with clusterization – the so-called 'Cambridge Phenomenon'. In particular, the university provides important sociocultural preconditions for learning, firm spin-outs, inter-firm and organizational networks, and local scientific and managerial recruitment practices. As a result, Cambridge attracts approximately one-quarter of the United Kingdom's venture capital and has the United Kingdom's biggest concentration of venture capitalists outside of London.[84] In total, the Cambridge knowledge cluster consists of approximately 30,000 employees across 900 firms. The IT sector accounts for approximately one-third of employment in the cluster, with the main activities consisting of application software, electronic equipment and instruments. IT is also by far the most dominant player in terms of number of firms, accounting for more than 500 of the 900 firms within the knowledge cluster.[85]

A key player in the IT field is Advanced RISC Machines (ARM), which like a number of high-technology ventures in Cambridge emerged from the Acorn company and Cambridge's most prominent knowledge economy entrepreneur, Hermann Hauser. ARM is a leading global licensor of chip technology, which is now an industry standard.[86] ARM began as a spin-out from a collaborative venture between Acorn and Apple Computer in 1990 to create a new microprocessor standard. ARM is now ranked as the number one semiconductor IP supplier in the world. Another prominent IT company is Cambridge Silicon Radio (CSR), which was listed on the London Stock Exchange in 2004. CSR is a spin-out of Cambridge Consultants, a company that can be traced as the founding father of the Cambridge knowledge cluster. It was formed in 1960 by a group of former Cambridge University students and acquaintances to 'put the brains of Cambridge University at the disposal of the problems of British Industry'.[87] Through various changes in ownership, the company continues to be a central node in the development of the knowledge cluster, providing specialist research and commercialization expertise across the healthcare and drug delivery, telecoms, industrial and consumer products, automotive and aerospace sectors.[88]

Alongside IT, the life sciences sector is the second most important segment of the knowledge cluster, with more than 200 firms and approximately 5,000 employees. Within the sector, biotechnology is the key activity accounting for more than 100 firms and 4,000 employees. This makes Cambridge the leading center for biotechnology research and commercialization in the United Kingdom, followed by Oxfordshire, Surrey, and Central Scotland, and is the location for corporations such as GlaxoSmithKline, Wellcome, Merck, Rhone-Poulenc Rorer, and Hoechst.

More than three-quarters of knowledge-based firms in the Cambridge cluster possess close links and networks with other local companies.[89] Cambridge is renowned for possessing significant clusters around university sites such as the Cambridge Science Park and the St John's Innovation Centre, as well as possessing a significant number of internationally important R&D establishments. These consist of both publicly and private funded facilities, such as the laboratories of the Medical Research Council, Hitachi, Microsoft, AT&T, Schlumberger, and Toshiba. In 1998, the networking activities of the cluster became more formalized through the establishment of Cambridge Network Ltd, a company set up to make more visible the linkages between business and the research community, and connecting both sets of actors in a more systematic way.[90]

Many of the R&D investments, such as those emanating from corporations including AT&T, GlaxoSmithKline, Hitachi, Intel, Microsoft, Olivetti, Oracle, the Wellcome Trust, and Toshiba, have been made in Cambridge University, thus making it a leading center of industrial research. As an outcome of these investment patterns, the IT sector is more clustered in its activities than the biotechnology and bioscience sectors, with a large number of inter-linked businesses spinning out from the University.[91] It is no coincidence that many of these companies were founded by members of the computer science department, while the biotechnology sector does not possess the same dominance of scientists with direct links to the University.[92]

As with Silicon Valley and other knowledge clusters around the world, Cambridge felt the impact of the 2000 downturn with employment in the knowledge cluster falling by 5 percent between 2002 and 2004.[93] Although the scale of the impact was less than that witnessed in California, it still gave enough of a shock for a major re-evaluation of the cluster and its future development.[94] As part of this re-evaluation, there is now a greater recognition of the role and importance of non-local and more global networks across the cluster, which many companies report as being of greater significance to their operations than local networks.[95] Also, increased attention has been given to some of the problems now encountered as a result of being a relatively small market town located in a rural area, such as the lack of adequate infrastructure and increasing problems of congestion (similar to those that have also entered the agenda in Silicon Valley).

These issues have resulted in a number of the cluster's business networks extending their activities into the area of policy intervention.[96] One of the main arguments propelled by those seeking intervention is the perceived realization that Cambridge 'can never rival Silicon Valley. But combined with Oxford and the wide swathe between the two university towns it would no longer be a welter-weight'.[97] In response to these arguments, polices are being developed to expand and largely merge the existing knowledge clusters in Cambridge and Oxford. The Oxford-Cambridge Arc initiative has mapped out a geographic area for economic expansion that will link both university towns. The framework involves creating and attracting knowledge-based investments to newly-developed high-technology sites along the 90-mile corridor between Oxford and Cambridge. The vision is to 'create an "arc" of entrepreneurial activity that would rival Silicon Valley ... characterised by a spirit of innovation, scientific and technical achievement and entrepreneurship, dedicated to wealth creation through both indigenous growth and inward investment'.[98] At present, a significant drawback to the realization of the Oxford-Cambridge Arc is the poor infrastructure and transport links between the two towns. In response to a demand for improved and speedy access, a twice-daily air service between Oxford and Cambridge was launched in 2006. Such demand is an indication that the proposed Arc is not just a vision of policymakers but also a reality of increased cluster connectivity in a post-bubble world.

Helsinki

Finland has rapidly become one of the industrial world's leading powerhouses and in 2005 was ranked by the World Economic Forum as the globe's most competitive national economy.[99] The key condition underlying this competitive growth has undoubtedly been the exploitation of R&D activity that has occurred within the mobile telecommunications sector and the accelerated growth of Nokia and its partners. Nokia's strategy in the early 1990s to shed a diversified portfolio of activities to concentrate on competing in the expanding global mobile telecommunications market has been a vital factor underpinning not only the improved competitiveness of Finland as a whole, but also the development of the Helsinki knowledge cluster. Nokia employs 10,000 people in the Helsinki region (approximately 20 percent of its total global workforce) and has driven forward the development of a knowledge cluster rooted in ICT and related activities. It has also taken a lead role in creating linkages and networks with businesses and research establishments in the region.[100] This has resulted in the Helsinki region, called Uusimaa, becoming the core of Finland's knowledge economy. Nine out of the top ten Finnish companies are located in Uusimaa. This list is dominated by Nokia, with the combined R&D activities of all other top ten firms accounting for less than 20 percent of Nokia's total R&D operations.[101] Many of the components of the national innovation system are also located in the region, which houses 42 percent of the business R&D undertaken in Finland. The University of Helsinki accounts for approximately one-fifth of R&D activity undertaken by the nation's universities, with 35 percent of all universities' R&D spending in Finland occurring within the region.[102]

Uusimaa is one of Europe's and the world's most competitive regional economies. It is ranked second, only behind Brussels, on the regional *European Competitiveness Index* 2006 (although this is a drop on its top ranking position in 2004) and twentieth on the *World Knowledge Competitiveness Index* 2005 (which benchmarks 125 leading regions around the world) and is the highest ranked European region with the exception of Stockholm.[103] With a population of 1.2 million, Uusimaa incorporates the municipal cities of Helsinki, Espoo, Vantaa, and Kauniainen. Espoo is a key location of the knowledge cluster, accommodating the headquarters for Nokia and the Otaniemi Science and Technology Park, the biggest science park in the Nordic nations. The park includes Innopoli, which houses a dense concentration of small high-technology ventures.

In total, 80 percent of the country's wireless technology companies are located in the Helsinki region. This allows them to remain close to Nokia and other important players such as Sonera and Radiolinja. Both public and private R&D investment has supported the globalization strategy of Nokia, which has established a vertically-integrated and strongly specialized sector in the region.[104] This has been underpinned by an education system strong in both research and learning. In their study of Finland, Manuel Castells and Pekka Himanen highlight the roles of the nation's universities and the education system in helping to catalyze improved national competitiveness during the 1990s.[105]

During this period, Finland followed a different path from most other industrialized nations. While many nations experienced either stagnating or declining R&D funding, in Finland government funding for R&D increased by approximately 40 percent between 1995 and 1999. Central to public R&D funding is Tekes, the National Technology Agency, whose technology programs are an essential part of the Finnish innovation system and are characterized by co-operation between industry, universities, and research institutes. The allocation of Tekes funding in 2003 consisted of research institutes receiving approximately US$50 million and universities US$130 million. Of the money allocated to research institutes, the large majority (93 percent) was allocated to the Technical Research Centre of Finland (VTT). At the regional level, Uusimaa received 39 percent of Tekes' total funding.[106]

This R&D funding role clearly makes Tekes an important node in Finland's innovation system, empowering the position of research-led universities along with VTT. These institutions, along with Nokia and a small number of other corporations, the National Fund for Research and Development (Sitra), and the Academy of Sciences, form a tight-knit group of major players constituting Finland's national knowledge system.[107] The operation of this knowledge and innovation system is facilitated by a funding regime that promotes interaction between the scientific research community and other public institutions. As highlighted above, one of the main beneficiaries of this system is the Technical Research Centre, VTT, which aims to improve the technological competitiveness of indigenous industry and foster the creation of businesses based on technical innovations. With a staff of almost 3,000, VTT lies in the intermediate area between universities and industry and is engaged in combining contract R&D work with long-term strategic research and advanced testing. A negative aspect of the public sector-driven funding regime is a private venture capital system that remains underdeveloped, and which did not have the opportunity to adequately develop due to the post-bubble economic situation.

The Helsinki knowledge cluster forms the major segment of Finland's innovation system and its economy as a whole. However, the focus on knowledge and innovation spreads beyond economy to wider societal and cultural considerations. For many Finns, knowledge and know-how are not viewed as being restricted to high-technology activity, but as a means of improving welfare and inclusion across Finnish society as a whole. This perception also seeps through to the way they view the rapid improvement in their nation's economic fortunes. During a number of visits we have made to Finland in recent years, many of those we have spoken to – from both a private and public sector background – give us the impression that they consider Finland to have 'gotten lucky', with Nokia being at the cutting-edge of mobile telecommunications at the right time. Explanations based on luck or strategy compound many success stories, particularly in relation to cluster development. The perception of Finns toward their success fits with David Rosenberg's observation of Finnish people being modest to a fault.[108] However, this modesty has not stopped Finland, principally through Nokia, creating a system of commercial exploitation resulting in a huge global competitive advantage. As Dan Steinbock has chronicled, such was the level of success during the late 1990s and early 2000s; only the US, Japan, Switzerland, and Sweden generated more patents than Finland.[109]

From 2001 onwards, the economic landscape and long-term outlook for Finland has looked less assured, particularly with the slowing down of mobile telecommunication markets. The benefits Finland received through Nokia's first-mover advantage in the mobile telecommunications sector meant that the national economy has become increasingly dependent on the company and its operating sector. It is estimated that Nokia ultimately generates one-third of Finland's economic activity, either directly or through its supplier network.[110] It also accounts for almost three-quarters of the market capitalization of the Helsinki Stock Exchange, and one-fifth of Finland's top 20 innovative companies are part of the Nokia Group, including Nokia Mobile Phones, Nokia Telecommunications, Nokia Networks, and Nokia Corp.[111]

It is almost little exaggeration to say that Nokia is Finland in terms of innovation capability. The problem is clearly not Nokia's, but the result of a lack of players in the Finnish economy able to come near to Nokia's levels of innovation and global market penetration. Dan Steinbock, who has closely audited Nokia's activities, finds that almost three-quarters of Finland's stock of international patents in 2002 accrued to Nokia, a proportion that has increased from 40 percent in 1997.[112] The pervasiveness of Nokia is increasingly viewed by Finnish policy-makers as a negative feature of their economy, with there being a requirement for greater diversification, which integrates Nokia's success with a realization of the need for a wider scope of industrial activity beyond mobile telecommunications.

With a flattening of sales since 2000, Nokia's own strategy involves transforming the mobile phone into a pocket-sized PC.[113] In a sense, such policies are a reverse of the recent strategy pursued by Nokia, which was founded way back in 1865 and for most of its existence produced a highly diversified range of goods. While Nokia is now fully engaged in a globalization strategy that extends far beyond its base in Helsinki's knowledge cluster, with R&D centers in China, India, and the US, the remainder of the cluster is no longer the engine of growth it once was. The cluster and its specialization in ICT-related activity is depicted as introducing considerable vulnerability to the Finnish economy, particularly as the demand for mobile phone technology switches from original to replacement demand.[114] Therefore, the maturation of the sector is resulting in price erosion, which in turn is eroding the strength of the cluster.[115] As with other knowledge clusters, there have been attempts to complement ICT-related activities with increased biotechnology and pharmaceutical developments. However, the competitiveness of the sector is such that although new companies such as Biotie Therapies, Hormos Medical, and Juvantia Pharma have emerged, they have seen big cuts in their R&D budgets in recent years, which has again compounded the dependence on Nokia as Finland's innovation provider.[116]

Policymakers in the Helsinki region are now embarking on a more radical course of diversification and internationalization as a means of reinvigorating the knowledge cluster. Along with the proposed establishment of an international university in Helsinki, more support and promotion are to be given to knowledge-based service sector activities, as opposed to the current cluster bias towards technology-oriented manufacturing. Also, there is an ambitious plan to form a wider knowledge cluster with the city of Tallinn, the capital of Estonia, an ex-Soviet Union country that joined the EU in 2004.

Intervention towards the promotion of knowledge-based services is a recognition that Helsinki, compared with other capital regions, is under-represented in high-value business sector activities such as legal services, accounting, software, advertising, and other professional services. Collectively, these sectors are often described as knowledge-intensive business services (KIBs) and are a crucial part of the support structure of any knowledge cluster, often providing small high-technology ventures with the services they cannot undertake in-house. In 2003, 5.5 percent of employment in Finland was accounted for by KIBs, compared with almost 7.5 percent for the EU as a whole. As part of a process of increasing this proportion, Tekes is providing funding for the future development of the sector. This should further enhance the natural growth already occurring in the sector, with a growth of 20 percent in employment between 1999 and 2003. Within the Helsinki region, KIBs now account for approximately 15 percent of total employment.

The knowledge cluster development with Tallinn, which is situated at a short distance across the Gulf of Finland, is partly an effort to replicate the strategic alliance forged to connect the Copenhagen region in Denmark to the Skåne region (southern part of Sweden), including the cities of Malmö and Lund in Sweden, by linking their respective biotechnology clusters to form a joint venture known as Medicon Valley. As a result of the relative isolation of much of its industry and economic activity, with the exception of Nokia and its collaborators, Finnish policymakers have become steadily interested in the possibility of connecting existing clusters both within and beyond national boundaries. Some recent policymaking has been informed by the concept of the super cluster proposed by Harvard professor Clayton Christensen, and the process by which innovations can allow clusters to drift and eventually bind together.[117]

In the case of the Helsinki-Tallinn knowledge clustering, it is primarily the scientific research emanating from the universities in each region that is seen as representing the initial possibilities to create this drift, covering biomedicine and biotechnology, ICT, materials science and related new technologies. Estonia, and Tallinn in particular, has embraced the information society and has geared its economic and industrial policies toward the creation of a sustainable knowledge-based economy. An important feature of these policies is the commercialization of the rich output from its technology and science institutions, a positive legacy dating back to the Soviet era.

Known as the 'Twin City of Science' project, the proposed 'science region' aims to profit from the economic momentum of the whole Baltic Rim area, as well as from its location on the internal and external border of the EU. Like Oxford and Cambridge, regional policymakers consider that each region alone is too small to compete separately at the global level. Tallinn, like Helsinki, has a strong technical university plus a number of other research institutions, and a benchmarking of both regions indicates significant scope for complementary knowledge transfer, primarily in the areas of ICT and biotechnology.[118] At present, however, the level of transfer and collaboration is limited.[119] This suggests that very significant resources will be required to create a functioning, cross-regional knowledge cluster capable of producing a 'coherent area of science, education and high-tech business in the future'.[120] A potential drawback to connected cluster development is the unevenness of existing business relationships between companies in Helsinki and Tallinn, which are largely that of mother and daughter. Firms in Helsinki often use Tallinn businesses for subcontracting purposes, a process not always conducive to creating parity in knowledge flow.[121]

In general, the cluster initiative currently lacks corporate sector involvement, although Finland is the most significant foreign investor in Estonia, with Tallinn being the location for most investors. Investment has initially taken place to take advantage of the cost differential, especially labor costs, between Finland and Estonia. If these investors increase their embeddedness in the region, there is a possibility that they may act as catalysts of increased linkage. Also, potential long-term advantages of Helsinki-Tallinn cluster development are the historical ties between Finland and Estonia. There is a deep cultural and economic bond in the form of the closeness of languages, and trade between Estonia, Finland, and other Baltic and Scandinavian countries, which existed long before Estonia gained its independence from the former Soviet Union. Overall, Finland has played and will continue to play an integral role in the economic development of Estonia. Whether this extends to the connection of the knowledge economies of their capital regions remains to be seen.

The Helsinki-Tallinn Twin Science City project and Nokia's globalization strategy represent examples of both government policy and a firm-level strategy targeting the internationalization of Finland's knowledge-based activities. It is the successful integration of policy and strategy that will help ensure the nation's continued competitiveness. As Dan Steinbock comments:

> If the drift between public policies and firm-level strategies is allowed to widen, the old practices will remain, but firms will shift their value activities elsewhere. Globalization allows Finnish companies to learn how to generate unique goods, and to excel in world-class marketing.[122]

Knowledge cluster development

Our examination of the leading knowledge clusters across the globe points to two main observations. First, knowledge clusters undergo an evolutionary process of development in which a number of stages are identified. Second, there is increasing consolidation and connection across these knowledge clusters. In relation to the first point, as Michael Storper, one of the world's leading economic geographers, describes: 'in evolutionary economics, what we do is path-dependent, that is truly historical; it is not the result of a series of actions on spot markets, where the long-term can be disconnected'.[123] Regional knowledge clusters are not accidental market creations but the result of planned communities of knowledge production, as evidenced by the case of US knowledge clusters, such as Silicon Valley, which consist of research universities and their role at the heart of Cold War defense activity.[124] Knowledge-based development is the product of interdependent choices predicated by the existing systems of networks. It is the system of networks within knowledge clusters upon which technological spillovers and 'untraded interdependencies' – or the linkage reliance between cluster actors beyond the market – are channeled and communicated. This facilitates knowledge cluster actors to travel along what Storper refers to as 'superior technological trajectories'.[125] However, knowledge clusters, like products, can have a limited life cycle. Those clusters able to renew themselves and evolve through innovation develop a morphological capacity to remain comparatively competitive through periods of national or global recession. Clusters must subject themselves to innovation, dynamic change and evolving processes, in much the same way as products have to change if they are to diminish the risk having a short shelf life.[126]

Figure 5.1 shows a route map outlining the generic evolution of knowledge

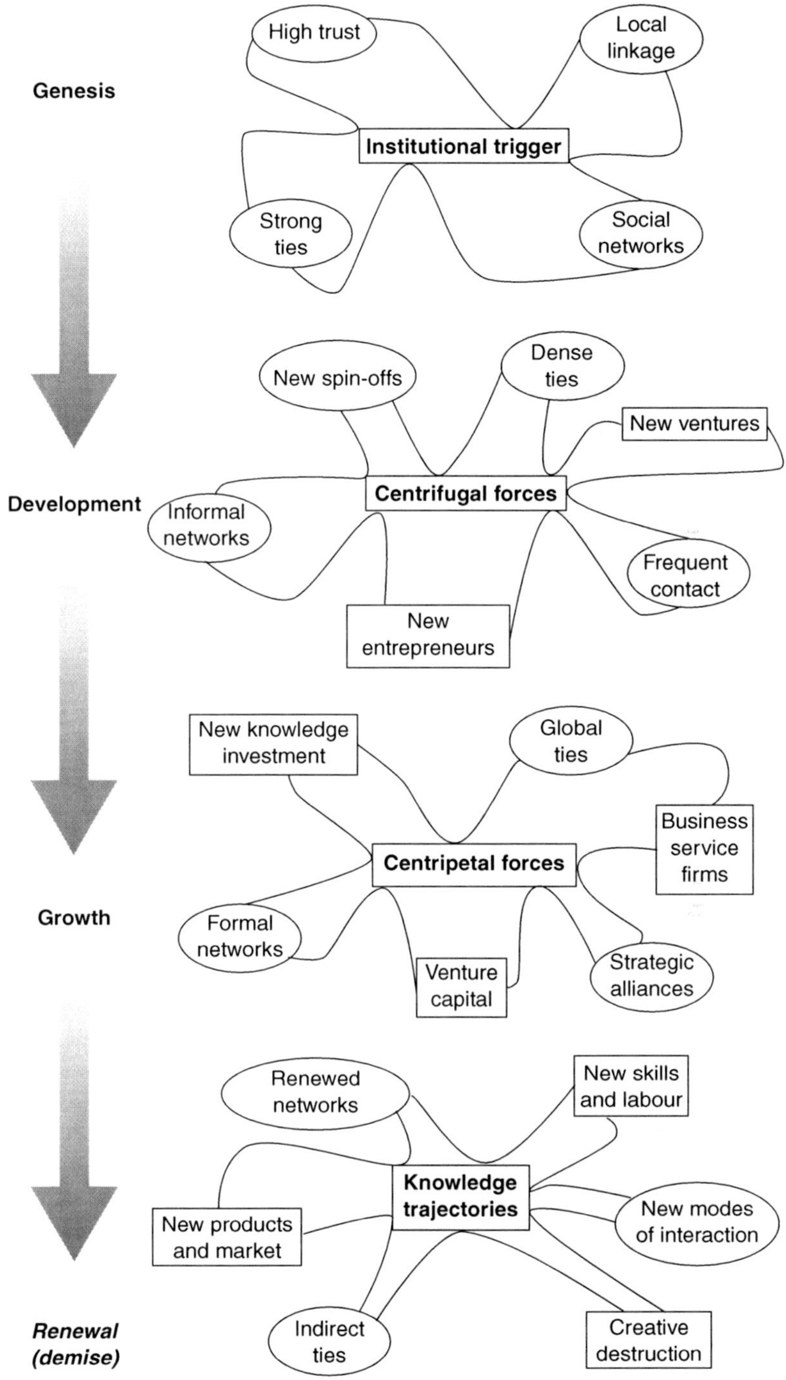

Figure 5.1 The evolution of knowledge clusters.

clusters. From this map, the key modes of chronological change can be summarized as follows:

Genesis – the creation of knowledge clusters is inevitably related to an institutional trigger. This may not necessarily be a singular institution, although there is a high degree of correlation with the existence of universities and research institutes, acting as an initial magnet organization for attracting talent.[127] Triggers are institutional in the sense that there is a set of pre-existing relationships or associations. The primary feature of institutional triggers consists of the existence of social networks, high trust, strong ties, and localized linkages.

Development – the initial developmental phase of a knowledge cluster is based on forces that spin-out knowledge from the institutional trigger, which remains localized. The existing relationships held by the institutional trigger – based on informal networks with frequent contact and dense ties – are proactively utilized to push-out new entrepreneurs and spin-out firms that create new relationships and collaborations between both themselves and the existing institutions.

Growth – knowledge clusters that successfully develop a critical mass act as a centripetal magnet for new capital inputs in the form of inward investing knowledge-based firms, venture capital organizations, and other firms specializing in specific business and professional service activities (such as those in the new Asian clusters). At this stage, the scope of existing relationships evolves with the creation of more formalized networks and strategic alliances, particularly through the generation of new ties beyond the cluster.

Renewal (Demise) – the final stage of a knowledge cluster's initial lifecycle is dependent upon the technological trajectory or path of its product and process base. Clusters able to adapt to disruptive knowledge shifts, through the creative destruction associated with new product and market development, will survive and grow, while those clusters that have become over path-dependent will eventually die. Perhaps the most important feature is the requirement for the continual development and mobilization of human capital. At the renewal stage, this is strongly related to the capacity to renew networks and create new modes of interaction, often with actors who are one step removed (indirect ties) from existing associations. This is the type of development now occurring in the knowledge clusters discussed above.

The second observation from our analysis of these knowledge clusters is their increased connection with each other as well as with other clusters at the global scale. In his seminal 1955 article, Francois Perroux argued that in the end, 'scale' and 'innovation' are the predictors of success, while Albert Hirschman recognized the role of interdependence and linkages across related sectors in stimulating economic growth.[128] The processes of consolidating and connecting knowledge clusters is a clear manifestation that these principles are reemerging as key tenets of change in today's global economy. In particular, there is evidence that some of the world's most visible knowledge clusters are operating networks that are geographically more open, as they seek new knowledge and the means to more efficiently exploit their existing knowledge base.[129] In Silicon Valley, it is found that cluster actors utilize the benefits of proximity to build and manage global-scale production networks.[130] In the UK, national and international networks are just as significant as their local counterparts for fostering innovation.[131]

In general, it appears that the constraining effect of distance on knowledge flow and transfer is gradually diminishing.[132] Figure 5.2 summarizes the complex local and global environment within which knowledge-based firms operate and melds the two schools of thought regarding proximity and knowledge. The first school argues that proximity is a significant mechanism for generating collaborative innovation. The second suggests that connectivity through global spaces is a more important stimulant of technological advancement. These two poles introduce an unnecessary divide of global and local forces, while the reality suggests that for firms in knowledge clusters both forces are operating in an overlapping manner. Successful connectivity in global spaces is often the outcome of an initial system of localized interaction, whereby it is the knowledge crossing hallways and streets – that is, at the local level – that initially catalyzes intellectual exchange and knowledge transfer across oceans and

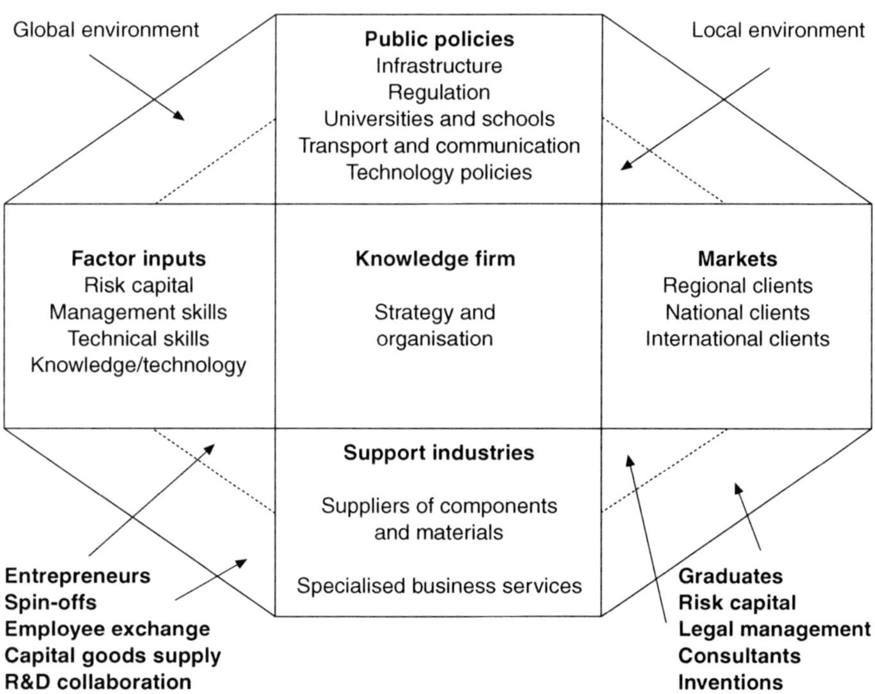

Figure 5.2 The knowledge firm and its environment (source: based on an initial typology of factors developed in F. Tödtling, 'Regional networks of high-technology firms: the case of the Greater Boston region', Technovation 14(5), 1994, 323–43).

continents. In other words, the accumulation of local network capital facilitates the building of global network capital.

The key aspect of increased global connection is that the knowledge base of the world's most advanced local and regional economies is no longer necessarily local but positioned within global knowledge networks, connecting clusters and their actors.[133] Bo Carlsson has suggested that national innovation systems are becoming more 'leaky' over time, whereby:

> The role of tacit knowledge and the spatial limits on knowledge spillovers have caused firms to locate R&D facilities where new knowledge is being created. As their absorptive capacity increases and they learn to transfer knowledge within their organizations and in the networks and alliances in which they participate, these firms become vehicles for internationalization of innovation systems.[134]

Our analysis of the globe's leading knowledge clusters also provides insights into the requirements for cluster development policy. Manuel Castells and Peter Hall refer to environments that integrate scientific and technical knowledge, relevant institutions, firms and skilled labor as furnaces of innovation.[135] Whilst it is undoubtedly impossible to replicate or clone furnaces such as Silicon Valley, or any other knowledge cluster for that matter, there are many lessons that can be learned as to how to go about improving the competitiveness of regions and localities and making them the centers of global growth. In particular, it is important to recognize that the challenges involved in the creation and sustainability of knowledge clusters are deeply set within factors relating to prevailing local and global forces. In such environments, network capital plays a crucial role.

For instance, the past failure of many science parks as policy response for generating high-technology activity can be strongly related to the fact that although they facilitated the co-location of companies, such policies ignored the processes through which this co-location could be activated into meaningful interaction and collaboration, particularly between industry and academia. It has long been argued that most science park developments are no more than high-tech fantasies which 'instead of contributing to increased links between industry and the academic world, may merely be removing one element of the social world of industry to lend it a little of the (fading) glamour of academe'.[136] The removal of firms from the social world of industry and their integration into the stylized environment of a science park hints at the actual destruction of network capital, facilitating a culture in which businesses are unconnected in spite of their mutual proximity.

In the post-bubble world there is an increasing recognition that knowledge clusters are susceptible to problems if there is little diversification in the type of knowledge the cluster is creating and seeking to commercialize.[137] As a result, knowledge cluster policymaking is quickly seeking to shift itself toward more open and connected systems. Yet, as with the initial policy movement toward localized systems, the evidence of policy playing an enabling role is often scant.

For example, a number of studies have shown that the networks and strategic alliances created as part of the Medicon Valley cluster initiative linking the life science cluster in the Øresund region of South Sweden and Copenhagen are weak in terms of their connectivity.[138] This may be a result of the infancy of the ties or the inability to integrate the strategic vision of policymakers with the decision-making strategies of the life science companies based either in South Sweden or Copenhagen, or the differing business and legislative environment operating in each region. However, part of the problem arises from the potential downside of knowledge clusters for firms, which may have a higher propensity to inadvertently transfer their knowledge through spillovers to competitor firms within the cluster. For instance, within a number of German high-technology clusters, many firms have attempted to counteract these spillovers and put in place knowledge protection strategies by moving to less concentrated locations, resulting in the spatial dispersion of the clusters.[139] While the existence of asymmetries in knowledge flow serves as the means by which firms are able to protect their knowledge from rivals, it is the minimization of such knowledge flow asymmetry that helps co-located firms develop a cluster culture.[140] The focus of cluster development policy should be set on the efforts to facilitate this process of minimizing knowledge flow asymmetry through the creation of 'soft' network infrastructure such as benchmarking, best practice, and management development networks.

Conclusions

Unfortunately, most knowledge cluster development policies across the globe have focused far too much on the structural products of development – especially infrastructure – to the detriment of the functional processes (e.g. the networks or value and supply-chains) underlying successful growth. It is not difficult to understand the reasoning for this, since it is far easier to 'see' and replicate structures than it is to understand and apply the lessons of functional activity, in particular networks and collaborations. However, replication is no guarantee for cluster success, as clusters vary across industries, location, and operating dimensions, meaning there is no one set of policies that will make all clusters successful.[141] For some, the problem is the result of policymakers becoming seduced by the concept of clusters without sufficient understanding of its fundamental underpinnings.[142] In some circumstances, this has led to cluster policies being no more than gimmicks attempting to justify badly conceived government interventions.[143] The ability to understand and implement functional processes is central to successfully developing business strategies and economic policies with the aim of nurturing new clusters of activity. Cluster policies inherently concern the development of relationships, exchange and interaction between groups of like-minded businesses, as well as their support bodies and agencies. The challenge is to stimulate the creation of processes facilitating the generation of these communication networks rather than putting the structural cart before the functional horse.

6 Nurturing and attracting talent

Within an increasingly knowledge-based global environment, the ability to compete on skills and talent will form the frontline for winning the race for productivity and profit. In his analysis of California's knowledge clusters, David Finegold argues that a key to creating what he refers to as self-sustaining, high-skill ecosystems is the provision of the nourishment and nutrients, in the form of talent, to sustain their growth.[1] In the knowledge economy, high skills are a prerequisite for high performance.[2] At the firm level, this is achieved through corporate strategies embracing talent and skills.[3] At the economic level, an ability to both nurture and attract skills and talent will create advantages for establishing accelerated and sustainable competitiveness.[4] The attraction of talent in the knowledge economy means that policies for securing overseas investment must be adapted to a new set of investor requirements that go beyond traditional subsidies in the form of land provision and tax discounts.[5]

This chapter draws on both firm and macroeconomic perspectives to analyze the role of human capital in the knowledge competitiveness equation. It initially outlines the skills economy approach we have developed to understand the linkage between the micro- and macro-level importance of human capital and its mobilization through skills development. It also assesses the changing role and modes of attracting and embedding foreign investment in a knowledge-based economy. We argue that locations, as well as corporations, require their own knowledge management strategies. Finally, it draws on empirical evidence to learn what policies are being implemented in some of the globe's most successful regions.

The skills economy

The emergence of the knowledge economy has placed education and training in a position of paramount importance throughout the world. From the discussions of growth theory in Chapter 3, it is clear that an under-investment in skills in the long run will result in deficient economic growth. A key challenge of the global competitiveness agenda is to develop and maintain a skilled workforce capable of adding value to an ever-changing portfolio of business, work, and occupational requirements. In fact, this challenge has become heightened by patterns of globalization and mobile capital location. By the mid-1990s, educationalists David Ashton and Francis Green were already stating that 'at no time in the history of capitalism has the education and training of the workforce assumed such widespread importance as at the present conjuncture'.[6] Whereas workers traditionally migrated to find better-paying work, work itself is increasingly migrating to find a workforce capable of adding value. Such processes will serve to raise the stock and effectiveness of these workforces.

Alongside the economic systems and forces that influence the location and development of workforces, societal and cultural factors also play a role in determining the shape, performance, and outlook of workforces across various landscapes, be they regions or nations. This interplay between the economic and the social factors is a key determinant of what we define as the *skills economy*.[7] The concept of the skills economy incorporates the means by which the expectations of employers, employees, and those outside the workforce influence the existing and potential skills-base of an economy. The skills economy reflects the linkage between skills and the performance of an economy, particularly in terms of its competitiveness. A skills economy analysis is subtly different from a labor market analysis, focused more on long-term factors in the shapes of skill deficiencies and gaps, rather than merely skill shortages. It aims to identify those skills that should be demanded, rather than merely those that are demanded, if an economy is to embed itself in a more productive and therefore wealthier environment. The conceptual framework underlying the skills economy approach is illustrated in Figure 6.1 and can be summarized as follows:

- External forces – forces exerted by changes in the global economy that act as a driver of skills requirements and variations in these requirements, with the global knowledge economy being the primary source of new sectors and new occupations.
- Capital requirements – characteristics of the capital required to achieve or sustain competitive or comparative advantages. Variations in human capital requirements result in the formation of skill gaps within the existing workforce.
- Existing resources – the existing skill resources residing within firms, whether indigenous or foreign-owned, are pushed by the demands of owners and managers as a result of their perception of the firm's requirements. This demand affects the supply of skills either in a positive or in a negative manner depending on whether the right skills are being demanded.
- Current skills base – the current skills base consists of the sum of the human capital residing within the existing workforce, as well as the unemployed and those not currently seeking employment. It is within this current skills base that new occupations will be developed and required.
- Potential skills base – the potential skills base consists of those individuals currently involved in education and training and refers to their ability to take up the new occupations created by new economic activities, sectors, and work practices.

- Internal forces – internal forces represent the socioeconomic, demographic, and cultural makeup of an economy and the influence this has on the collective aspirations, motivations, and opportunities of a population group as a driver of skills development.

It is difficult to establish comparative measures of the skills bases of economies beyond an assessment of formal education qualifications. A useful proxy measure of the current skills base is the level of employment in knowledge-based sectors, since these sectors are characterized by concentrations of high-end technology and intelligence.[8] Firms in such industries deploy a significantly higher proportion of their resources to research and development and often provide increased value-added in terms of generating wealth. Overall, these sectors have the most knowledge-intensive production processes, with the importance of innovation and the efficiency of production requiring an advanced skills base.

Table 6.1 shows the highest concentration of knowledge-based employment among the globe's leading knowledge economy regions. Unsurprisingly, at the head of the list is San Jose-Sunnyvale-Santa Clara MSA (metropolitan statistical area), the heart of Silicon Valley, followed by Baden-Württemberg – Germany's industrial powerhouse – and Tokyo. All the regions featuring in Table 6.1 have a very strong current skills base when measured by the proportion of employment in knowledge-based activities. There is a strong relationship between employment levels in these sectors and levels of innovation, which ultimately contribute to economic competitiveness.

A wider and longer-term indicator of the skills base is the economic activity or participation rate, which measures the ratio of labor force to working-age population. While a high level of economic participation tends to suppress the

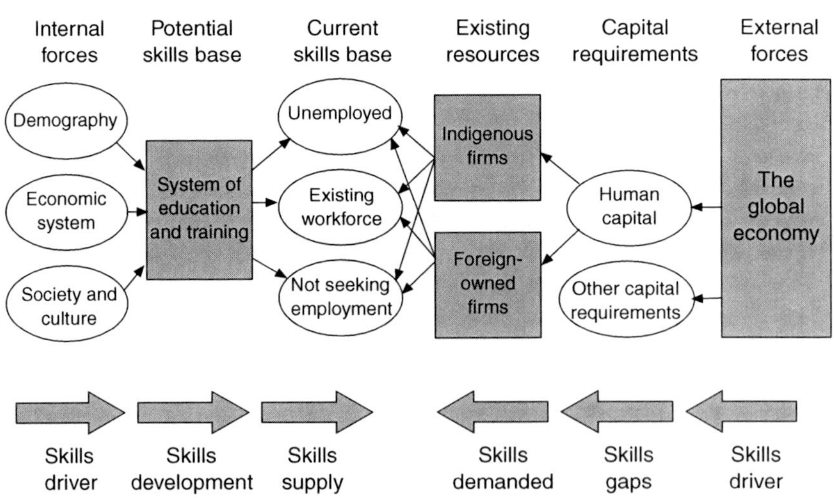

Figure 6.1 Skills economy model.

Table 6.1 Employees in knowledge-based sectors among the world's leading knowledge economy regions (employees per 1,000 inhabitants)

San Jose–Sunnyvale–Santa Clara, US	134.7
Baden-Württemberg, Germany	103.3
Tokyo, Japan	90.1
Bayern, Germany	84.6
Uusimaa, Finland	83.9
Shizuoka, Japan	82.9
Aichi, Japan	82.7
Shiga, Japan	77.0
Hessen, Germany	76.5
Tochigi, Japan	75.0
Bratislavia, Slovak Republic	72.3
Stockholm, Sweden	71.4
South East, UK	68.4
West, Sweden	68.0
Grand Rapids–Wyoming, US	65.1
Kanagawa, Japan	65.0
Eastern, UK	64.6
Osaka, Japan	63.1
Singapore	63.1
Lombardia, Italy	62.7

Source: Based on R. Huggins *et al.*, *World Knowledge Competitiveness Index 2005*, Pontypridd: Robert Huggins Associates, 2005

average productivity of businesses within an economy, it enlarges the economy's output and, therefore, the savings from which investments in education and training are made. Furthermore, a high economic participation rate potentially provides a greater proportion of the population the opportunity to undertake learning-by-doing and on-the-job training.[9] Conversely, a low level of activity suggests a lack of social and economic inclusion and a high burden of dependency across society as a whole. While demographic factors are particularly important, economic activity rates are also determined by the openness and flexibility of the labor market, the effects of the social security and welfare systems, and cultural factors. Open and flexible labor markets, coupled with provision of effective social, education, and training policies, provide individuals with freedom and the opportunity to be economically active. They also allow the economy to take full advantage of the demographic context within which it operates.

As shown in Table 6.2, at the top of the economic activity rankings among the world's leading knowledge economies are the Chinese regions of Pearl River Delta and Beijing, both of which have economic activity rates registered at over 75 percent of the working-age population. This illustrates the almost insatiable requirement for labor and human capital in these regions as they rapidly expand economically. However, a key feature of the expansion of Chinese city-regions is that it is propelling huge economic divides between urban and rural areas, with massive labor migration from the peripheral to the city-regions. In third

Table 6.2 Economic activity rates among the world's leading knowledge economy regions (labour force as a percentage of working age population)

Pearl River Delta, China	78.5
Beijing, China	77.1
Salt Lake City, US	75.6
Alberta, Canada	73.4
Norway	72.5
Minneapolis–St. Paul–Bloomington, US	71.3
Stockholm, Sweden	70.3
Milwaukee–Waukesha–West Allis, US	70.1
Charlotte–Gastonia–Concord, US	69.6
Washington–Arlington–Alexandria, US	69.2
Columbus, US	69.0
Manitoba, Canada	69.0
Indianapolis, US	68.5
San Jose–Sunnyvale–Santa Clara, US	68.5
Ontario, Canada	68.4
Saskatchewan, Canada	68.2
Cleveland–Elyria–Mentor, US	68.0
Switzerland	67.8
Boston–Cambridge–Quincy, US	67.0
Denver–Aurora, US	66.9

Source: Huggins *et al.*, *World Knowledge Competitiveness Index 2005*.

place is Salt Lake City, the first of ten US regions listed in the top 20. A number of Canadian regions also have high economic-activity rates, with Alberta leading the way in fourth.

As we have seen, new theories of economic growth are based on the importance of a skilled workforce that is able to adapt to and meet new business goals in an evolving economy. The potential skills base of an economy consists of the future human capital embodied within those individuals in the education and training system. Resources dedicated to education and training are an investment in knowledge, and sustained economic growth will depend on the quality of school and university graduates and their ability to produce, commercialize, and utilize knowledge. Much of the investment in education is set by national budgets, particularly for compulsory primary and secondary education, while higher-education investment is a reflection of the number and type of institutions within a region.

Table 6.3 highlights primary, secondary, and higher-education expenditure per capita for leading knowledge-based regions. US regions account for 15 of the top 20 rankings, which also includes Luxembourg, Switzerland, Denmark, Norway, and Brussels. The results of this investment are clear, with the US, Norway, Switzerland, Denmark, and Belgium being among those nations with the highest completion rates for higher secondary education and the highest proportions of tertiary level qualified individuals in the developed world.[10] Figure 6.2 also illustrates the strong relationship found between investment in higher

Table 6.3 Primary, secondary and higher education expenditure per capita among the world's leading knowledge economy regions (US$)

Seattle–Tacoma–Bellevue, US	2,576
New York–Northern New Jersey–Long Island, US	2,457
Rochester, US	2,319
Buffalo–Niagara Falls, US	2,319
Grand Rapids–Wyoming, US	2,212
Detroit–Warren–Livonia, US	2,212
Hartford–West Hartford–East Hartford, US	2,183
Luxembourg	2,127
Switzerland	2,101
Denmark	2,074
Milwaukee–Waukesha–West Allis, US	2,033
Norway	2,030
Brussels, Belgium	1,917
Minneapolis–St. Paul–Bloomington, US	1,916
Portland–Vancouver–Beaverton, US	1,910
San Diego–Carlsbad–San Marcos, US	1,875
San Francisco–Oakland–Fremont, US	1,875
Sacramento–Arden–Arcade–Roseville, US	1,875
Los Angeles–Long Beach–Santa Ana, US	1,875
Riverside–San Bernardino–Ontario, US	1,875

Source: Based on Huggins *et al.*, *World Knowledge Competitiveness Index 2005*.

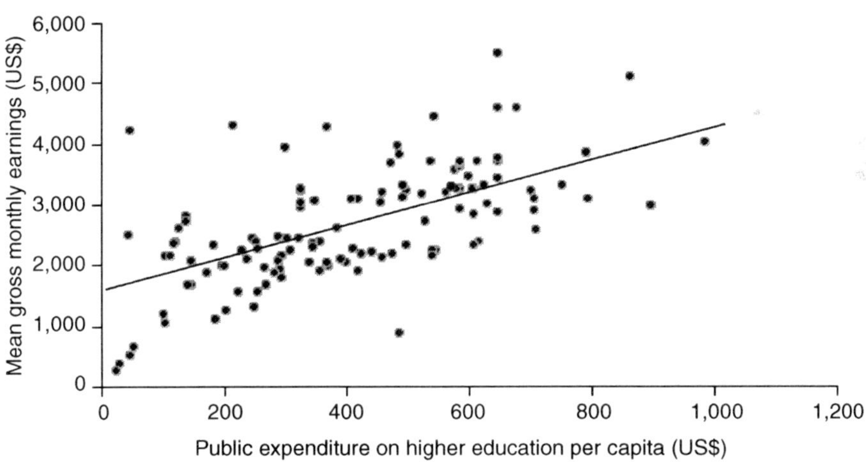

Figure 6.2 Relationship between public expenditure on higher education per capita and mean gross monthly earnings among the world's leading knowledge economy regions (source: Huggins *et al.*, *World Knowledge Competitiveness Index 2005*).

education and average workforce earnings among the world's leading knowledge economy regions.

In recent years, the on-going development of the skills base has become linked with the concept of lifelong or cradle-to-grave learning opportunities. Lifelong learning efforts have been taken up by policymakers across the globe in an attempt to build a culture of education extending beyond the traditional boundaries of schooling. However, in most instances this culture is still far from embedded and an understanding of how to create and participate in an integrated skills economy remains elusive. As business strategist Edward Gordon comments:

> Mention 'lifelong learning' to a typical group of managers and you will most likely hear a groan or see blank stares of disbelief. It's just too damn intellectual! Let's face it – many people still talk about the year they 'got out', not of prison, but of school. For most people schooling was not a very pleasant experience. It was a life phase to get through. Yet talk to these same people about systems and productivity applications, complex issues though they may be, and you will get all their attention.[11]

This epitomizes the challenges the lifelong learning agenda faces and the ongoing battle to convince employers that workforce development and training is an investment rather than a cost. A highly skilled society is not an inevitable feature of operating within a global knowledge-driven economy. It only occurs through the commitment of policymakers, employers, and employees, as well as the education system as a whole, to aspire to its creation.[12]

Skills investment

The failure to integrate lifelong learning into corporate strategy is linked to an on-going inability of managers and employers to see often long-term, hard-to-measure results from any investment in skills development. However, at a more macro-level the link between skills and competitiveness is more apparent. For instance, a study of engineering firms in the UK and the Netherlands found that lower levels of workforce skills in the UK companies resulted in productivity rates 25–30 percent lower than their Dutch counterparts.[13] Also, there is evidence of a strong connection between training and productivity across sectors, whereby a 5 percent increase in the proportion of the workforce undergoing training results in an increase in productivity of the order of 4 percent. Interestingly, this is more than twice as high as the respective increase in wages (1.6 percent).[14] Evidence from the US finds a link between the level of investment in training undertaken by stock exchange listed corporations in one year and their stock market performance the following year, with changes in training investment acting as predictor of future stock returns. Unfortunately for investors, very few corporations make training investment data publicly available, although there are calls in a number of nations for legislation requiring companies quoted on public capital markets to publish these figures.[15]

The benefits to employers of skills development training cannot be ignored, particularly if they are undertaken in tandem with other business competitiveness strategies. Other research has argued that a 1 percent increase in the proportion of workers with higher qualifications would raise annual output by between 0.42 and 0.63 percent.[16] As educationalist Mike Campbell argues, 'There are economic costs associated with being a low skill locality and considerable economic benefits associated with being a high skill locality. Skill rich localities are almost always rich localities'.[17] Such 'rich' economies sustain high levels of productivity, which continually catalyzes the creation of more highly skilled and better-paying jobs.

There is clearly an important link between productive performance and skill levels, with low productivity strongly related to a lack of long-term investment in education and training. Within current workforces, it is often those employed in SMEs that are not given the opportunity to participate in further education and training opportunities.[18] Leading analysts argue that the lack of investment in education and training can be attributed to market failure caused by a range of institutional factors, such as short-term financial markets, adversarial craft unions, and weak employer organizations. For instance, in the UK – which has one of the developed world's worst levels of skills inequality[19] – many companies have adopted lower skill strategies than their rivals in other national economies, suppressing demand for training and trapping the economy in a low-skill equilibrium with low levels of innovation.[20] The key feature of this low-skill equilibrium, or skills trap, is the lack of an overwhelming requirement for an effective education and training system. This has further led to growing wage differentials between skilled and unskilled workers.

Part of the skills economy approach is to distinguish between the existing human resources and skills demands of both indigenous and foreign-owned companies within an economy. Some evidence has found that training budgets are higher in foreign-owned companies when compared with their indigenous counterparts. Also, foreign-owned companies often have a more positive attitude to novel technology and process innovation, with the intensity and benefits of training greater for those employees involved in producing technological changes.[21] We are currently witnessing this process of multinationals taking a key role in workforce development in rapidly developing economies, especially China and India. In the longer-term, as these multinationals either become embedded in these economies or move elsewhere once again, China, India, and other developing nations will need to focus more on developing their indigenous corporate base, moving away from their traditional indigenous corporate strategy thinking where the prevailing culture allows little scope for initiative and talent. In such an environment, training acts as a positional good, more of which may threaten existing power relationships.[22]

Skill gaps

Skill gaps refer to the difference between the level of existing skills possessed by current employees in a company and the level required to meet its current and future business objectives. This cannot be defined in purely occupational or similar terms. Skill gaps do not describe the number of vacancies by occupation. For example, it is possible for a company not to be reporting any skill *shortages*, in the form of hard-to-fill vacancies, while simultaneously suffering skill gaps that are damaging its performance and competitiveness. In general, skill shortages make employers accept staff with sub-optimal skills. Skill gaps occur when a company has employees, or recruits new employees, that have sub-optimal skills for the role or occupation they undertake. Consequently, this results in companies adopting suboptimal working arrangements, enduring production cuts, lost orders, and dissatisfied customers. Whereas skill shortages are visible to managers and employers, in the form of hard-to-fill vacancies, skill gaps carry an additional risk – the possibility that the skill *problem* remains unidentified by the employer. Factors such as management's expectations of what skills are available and the continued adjustment of operational processes to match available skills often result in skill gaps going unnoticed. Interestingly, a survey of foreign-owned companies found that they consistently report higher levels of skill gaps than indigenous firms, precisely because they have more 'intelligent' human resource techniques.[23]

The measurement and identification of skill gaps is a major barrier preventing the development of solutions to their existence. The only real pointer to unidentified skill gaps comes in the form of productivity level comparisons. Where productivity levels are low, it is probable that hidden skill gaps are having a negative effect on the performance of the business. These hidden gaps are particularly prevalent among small firms, most of which tend not to have staff development plans or, if they do, are only focused upon developing lower level staff. Most SME owners and managers do not see themselves as the subject of staff development plans. In fact, the development of management skills to underpin the achievement of longer-term business goals appears to be countercultural to most SMEs, if the take-up of government-funded management training opportunities is used as a benchmark.[24]

Entrepreneurship and skills

The role of the skills economy in creating an entrepreneurial culture and building entrepreneurial capacity and sustainable growth is vital. There is no doubting the strong relationship between competitiveness, entrepreneurship, and skills. The most important international study of entrepreneurship is the annual Global Entrepreneurship Monitor (GEM) report.[25] The key objectives of GEM are to measure differences in the level of entrepreneurial activity between countries and to uncover factors determining the levels of entrepreneurial activity. GEM distinguishes between opportunity-based entrepreneurship, where an individual starts a new business due to an idea, innovation or perceived market gap they are aware, or in possession, of (i.e. knowledge-driven), and necessity-based entrepreneurship, where their motivation is due to the lack of better job alternatives. In this respect, true entrepreneurship can be said to be limited to those individuals motivated by knowledge-driven opportunities rather than by necessity. GEM produces a rank of opportunity-based entrepreneurship as a proportion of necessity-based within the countries it benchmarks, that is, those economies where entrepreneurship is most driven by opportunity. Figure 6.3 illustrates the association between this ranking and a composite ranking of the economic competitiveness of these nations.[26] It shows a significant relationship between the competitiveness of a nation and the proportion of opportunity-based entrepreneurship. Research at a regional level similarly shows a strong association between the level of new business start-ups and competitiveness.[27] In terms of skills and entrepreneurship, data from the UK indicates a very significant relationship between the current skill-bases of regions – based upon numbers of degree qualified individuals – and the creation of new business start-ups, as illustrated in Figure 6.4. The GEM research finds that countries exhibiting opportunity-driven entrepreneurship have a lower rate of early-stage business failures. This highlights that the focus of enterprise policy must be on nurturing long-term opportunity rather than short-term necessity.

Those individuals with the highest propensity and opportunity to establish a new business are often suitably qualified managers within existing corporations. However, whether or not a corporate manager will attempt to become an entrepreneur may be determined by the socio-economic business culture within which they are located. Primarily, it is the underlying cultural attitudes toward risk-taking that have the capacity to influence a would-be entrepreneur. Ongoing disparities between the economic competitiveness of Europe compared with

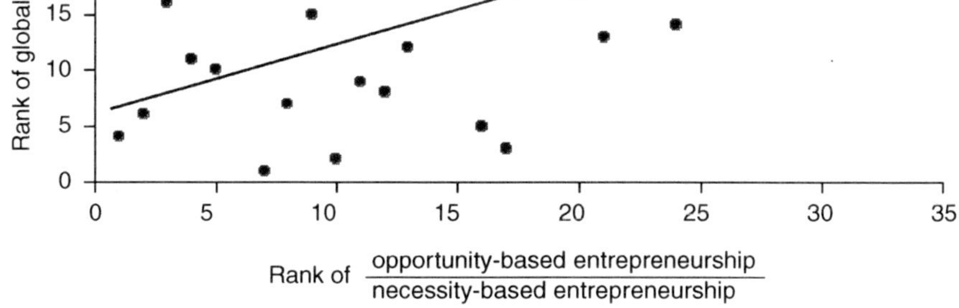

Figure 6.3 Relationship between national rank of opportunity- to necessity-based entrepreneurship and national competitiveness rank (source: based on Minniti *et al., Global Entrepreneurship Monitor*; Institute for Management Development, *The World Competitiveness Yearbook*; Porter *et al., Global Competitiveness Report* 2004–5).

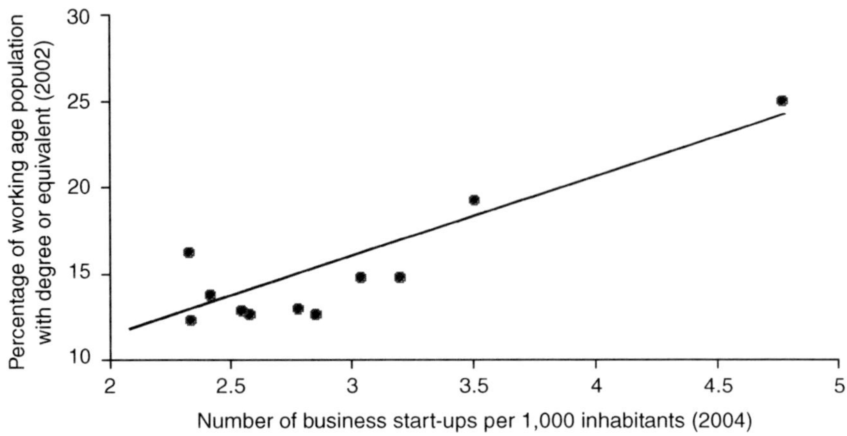

Figure 6.4 Relationship between new business start-ups per 1,000 inhabitants and the percentage of working age population with a degree or equivalent among regions in the UK (source: R. Huggins and J. Day, *UK Competitiveness Index 2006*, London: The Work Foundation, 2006).

North America are at least partly the result of the more risk-averse nature of European culture, which stifles entrepreneurial activity.[28] Also, the cultural esteem given to the possession and utilization of entrepreneurial skills is higher in North America resulting in a more proactive outlook to entrepreneurial engagement.

Figure 6.5 illustrates the results of a survey of new entrepreneurs and shows the relationship between an entrepreneur's characteristics and the early growth achieved by their firms.[29] In general, the more an entrepreneur is a change-driven networker and risk-taker, the greater the early growth rate of their company. It is also found that entrepreneurs who, in their self-judgment, consider themselves as possessing these characteristics are far more likely to develop their own managerial skills, as well as the skills of employees. Almost twice as many of the high-growth firms sought advice on skills and training development, compared with the average for all surveyed entrepreneurs. At a macro-level, these characteristics are manifested by a polarization of competitiveness between economies that have an entrepreneurial business culture and economies that do not. High-growth economies generally possess a stronger critical mass of entrepreneurially-minded individuals than their lower performing counterparts, with the skills of these entrepreneurs and their workforces developing along diverging competitive trajectories.

The most sustainable and profitable businesses are clearly based on elements of entrepreneurship such as business 'flair', leadership, and measured risk-taking. However, as highlighted above, many entrepreneurs, or would-be entrepreneurs, situated within under-performing economies may not consider that they possess these characteristics due to the underlying business and socio-

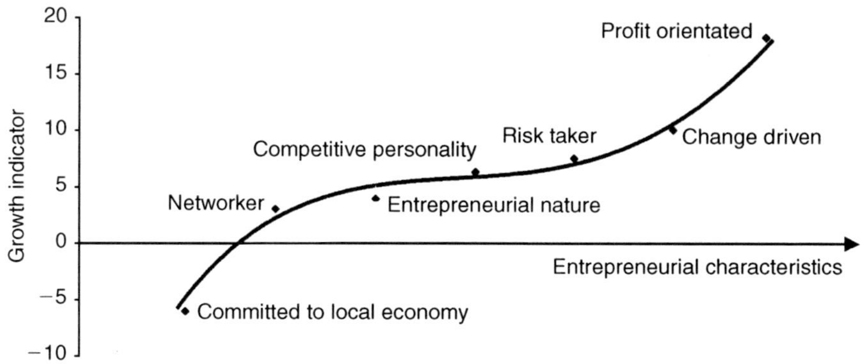

Figure 6.5 Relationship between the characteristics of entrepreneurs and the early growth of their firms (source: Huggins and Fido, 'Baseline tracking of new entrepreneurs').

economic culture. Public policy in these economies must address the creation of a cultural and attitudinal environment that is more receptive to entrepreneurship and business creation. Such entrepreneurial cultures and attitudes are far more difficult to stimulate and activate than policies relating to mainstream business support, requiring a velvet glove approach. Part of this approach should be to recognize, enhance, and develop the capabilities and confidence of potential entrepreneurs within the existing and future labor force. This consists of the identification and development of factors such as:

- Characteristics – an ability to take risks, be innovative, take the initiative, exploit business opportunities, create jobs;
- Attributes – to possess foresight, imagination, intelligence, decisiveness, alertness, and an aptitude for organization;
- Behavior – seek personal achievement, independence, self-realization, and creative activity.[30]

Corporate strategy and skills

The skills economy remains a sideshow for many corporate managers seeking to achieve both company competitiveness and personal prosperity. This would appear to be the case whatever the size of the business, but is most accentuated in smaller companies. Research carried out in the UK finds that the majority of employers in small companies do not provide any form of workforce development.[31] Many employers consider that such development is unlikely to generate benefits for their business. These views are most exacerbated in companies where the employer shows little ambition in terms of expanding markets, undertaking innovation as a competitiveness strategy, or extending their company in any shape or form.[32]

In many ways, we consider that the corporate strategies of many firms, in particular small firms, do not clearly account for or understand the skills base of the firm. It is the responsibility of the managers to establish the overall strategy of a firm, to set the context and environment for skills development, and to enhance the intensity of their utilization. They are in a position to stimulate an appetite for knowledge and, therefore, play the crucial role in creating either knowledge-rich or knowledge-poor workplaces. However, given the rapid evolution of the world of work, most managers cannot now be expected to have a full grasp of how to achieve these objectives.

Managers must redefine – or possibly define for the first time – their conceptualization of how their workplace addresses the needs and objectives of the business. Once there is a degree of clarity here, managers can explore the skill requirements necessary to meet these needs. From a knowledge-based perspective, the crucial factor in appropriately assessing these requirements is to differentiate and understand the types of work within the business. As shown in Figure 6.6, we distinguish between *mechanical* and *thinking* functions as the two key sources of work activities. Mechanical functions relate to workers who undertake activities dependent on process skills and one-off or periodical instances of learning. Typical activities are the repeated use of a particular piece of equipment or technology, whereby the nature of work changes only when there is a change or upgrade in the technology or plant utilized. The effectiveness of mechanical functions is dependent on both the reliability of the technology and its users. Effective users will be those who possess and further develop strong employability skills.

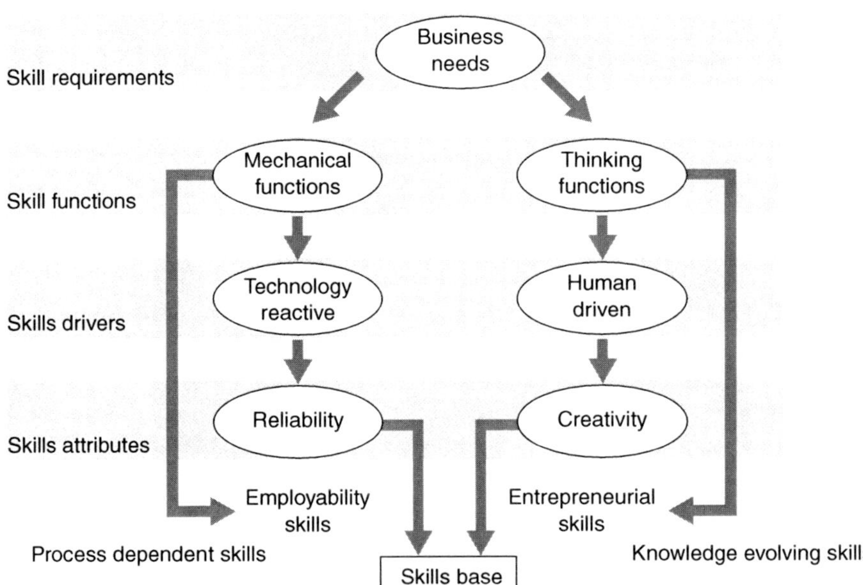

Figure 6.6 Skills in the knowledge-based company.

By contrast, thinking functions are driven by human enquiry and relate to workers who rely on continuous scanning of their environment, assessment of their situations, and the learning of new knowledge to undertake their role effectively. These functions are the premise of knowledge workers, whose own creativity is at the heart of their key skills and attributes. They operate in a dynamic manner through knowledge-building skills that are continually evolving. It is workers undertaking thinking, as opposed to mechanical, functions that possess the strongest propensity for possessing entrepreneurial skills. In other words, knowledge, creativity, and entrepreneurship go hand-in-hand as the factors upon which successful corporate strategies are formulated. In the evolving knowledge economy, skills requiring thinking functions are a key source of the competences that differentiate firm performance. As changes in skills requiring thinking functions continue to accelerate, management must give those workers responsible for these thinking functions the opportunity to keep pace with such changes.

Firms must create corporate and competitiveness strategies that identify and remedy gaps in thinking functions. Firms that do not invest sufficiently in such strategies may have little part to play in the knowledge economy of today or tomorrow. Too many businesses are continuing to operate with occupations and skills that are going to leave them stranded. Also, too many individuals are entering the labor market seeking careers that may soon be redundant. In sum, too many resources are being invested into economic activities that are quickly becoming obsolete, as customer expectations cannot and will not be as limited as they were in the past.

From a policy perspective, the knowledge economy demands structural changes in labor market policies. They must be based on foresight and future intelligence rather than being reactive to an already changed economic climate. An integral feature of the competitiveness agenda must be to ensure (as far as is possible within a world of uncertainties) that the managers of current and future workforces have an understanding of what skills they should be demanding and how ensuing gaps can be addressed. At a practical level, the development of new awareness and skills raising activities, encouraging both businesses and individuals to capitalize upon their latent skills capacity, is crucial to enhancing the skills economy. Within a broad sense, it is vital that these new activities incorporate the integration of a skills agenda within corporate strategy formulation.

Attracting talent

As the knowledge economy is prioritizing the nurturing of skills and talent, it is also changing how economies attract from overseas the type of investment creating high value-added. Global competition for such investment is increasing, requiring major shifts in policy and strategy. In particular, those economies that have traditionally attracted high shares of such investment now need to think more innovatively about how they attract and embed knowledge-based Foreign

Direct Investment (FDI). As we have already seen, in contrast to the traditional economy's requirement for capital and land, the knowledge economy relies upon less tangible inputs such as education, networks, and innovation infrastructure. The knowledge economy is radically altering the landscape of FDI and requires new thinking from those who wish to remain or become major players in the global knowledge investment and attraction race.

It is important to understand the different approaches required to attract and embed knowledge-based investment compared with more traditional sectors of activity. Traditional areas of inward investment, such as textile and other low value-added manufacturing, have declined within most OECD nations and are being replaced by knowledge-based activities such as financial services and pharmaceuticals. Also, the general size of initial FDI investments in developed economies has fallen in recent years, with a switch toward attracting smaller and growing knowledge-intensive businesses, as mainstream and large-scale manufacturing operations relocate to developing nations in Eastern Europe and Asia.[33] The requirement for most economies is to formulate the correct investment conditions both for retaining homegrown companies and for encouraging foreign investors to choose their nation or region as a home for knowledge-intensive industries.

In the past, the traditional rules of FDI attraction involved the provision of an adequate infrastructure, a relatively low-cost labor force and incentives – chiefly in the form of subsidized land and tax breaks.[34] The primary objective of the host location was job creation. In essence, many of the traditional methods of attracting FDI are cost-based, and this has been particularly relevant and effective where investments have been made in large-scale manufacturing. Under the new environment, the primary goal and means of FDI attraction is based more on the creation of knowledge spillovers, such as the transfer of new skills, science, and management techniques. Viewed by the host economy, such spillovers stimulate local competition and innovation.[35] When knowledge is the key competitive component of investment attraction, land or plant-based policy incentives become less relevant, replaced by opportunities for networking and technology transfer.

Until recently, businesses investing overseas have tended to keep the majority of high-technology and knowledge-intensive resources within their indigenous location. Under the new rules, there is a trend emerging whereby a research presence within the host location is seen to provide additional knowledge transfer benefits, especially access to new sources of technological, organizational, and marketing expertise, and to overseas innovation systems.[36] Knowledge spillovers are now viewed as moving more equitably between the home and host locations.

The arrival of FDI may signal an environment of increased competition, whereby local firms are 'forced' to improve efficiencies and undertake innovations if they wish to enter the supply chains and knowledge networks of the new investors. Indirect benefits in terms of innovation and productivity growth can, therefore, accrue as a result of increased FDI within a host economy. By attracting and embedding knowledge-based FDI, regions and nations can access these new benefit accruals, which help to create a sustainable and competitive economic environment.

The knowledge economy and FDI policy

In its traditional form, FDI policy followed a series of fairly well-trodden and rehearsed rules, encompassing the provision of pragmatic attractions such as financial incentives, ample land availability, and a sound infrastructure with competitively priced labor. In more recent times, FDI policy has become increasingly sophisticated, focusing on embeddedness, aftercare, and retention. Chiefly, this has come in the form of fostering local and global relationships and networks between indigenous businesses and inward investors.

The emergence of the knowledge economy means that the provision of tax incentives is no longer enough to secure inward investment. The emphasis is now shifting toward the requirements necessary for attracting knowledge entrepreneurs and workers. Knowledge-based economic activity does not always require large physical infrastructure or tax incentives. What it does require are the transformers and vehicles of knowledge – knowledge networks and knowledge workers.[37] As the American pop geographer Joel Kotkin has argued, a new social order is emerging wherein knowledge becomes the critical source of wealth generation.[38] Fundamentally different from the natural resource-based manufacturing economy that preceded it, Peter Drucker stated that the knowledge economy rests upon access to creativity, more so than physical capital or natural resources.[39] In the context of FDI, this is neatly summed up by the ex-Hewlett-Packard CEO Carly Fiorina who stated, 'keep your tax incentives and highway interchanges; we will go where the highly skilled people are'.[40]

As we stated at the beginning of this chapter, in the knowledge economy people do not follow jobs – jobs follow people. This alters the rules of FDI attraction. Within the traditional model, the firm is the key unit of attraction, whereby securing its presence leads to an influx of job opportunities and, in turn, labor. The new model puts people at the centre of attraction, with those locations enabling entrepreneurs and skilled labor to reap the benefits of the businesses they attract as well as the businesses they create and develop. Knowledge-based FDI attraction policies necessarily revolve around the movement and requirements of key knowledge entrepreneurs and workers. Knowledge workers spur knowledge networks, which subsequently leads to FDI attraction.

Some commentators have argued that the knowledge economy increasingly renders location insignificant.[41] They contend that the Internet and other telecommunication technologies make geography irrelevant, allowing knowledge workers to interact from wherever they may be in the globe. Although global communication channels do facilitate such interaction, we consider that location in the knowledge economy era is actually becoming more important. One need only look at London's financial district (now home to more American Banks than New York), or Silicon Valley, to understand that geography is alive and kicking. As Kotkin argues, 'if people, companies or industries can truly live anywhere, or at least choose from a multiplicity of places, the question of where to locate becomes increasingly contingent on the peculiar attributes of any given location'.[42] The choice of location has become more elastic, resulting in competition becoming more intense and, to quote Kotkin again, 'To them [the knowledge economy workers], the world is essentially a vast smorgasbord in which various locales compete for their affections and attention'.[43] According to Richard Florida, location decisions are increasingly a complex interplay of lifestyle interests, with these stretching beyond the cursory 'air quality' and other standard quality of life amenities.[44]

The attraction of knowledge workers is not solely concerned with 'techies' but also of high-level – and often like-minded – professional and managerial workers. This broader band of knowledge workers requires a strong mix of an appealing living and working environment – in cultural, physical, and business terms – as well as a cluster of stimulating people, businesses, and ideas across a broad cultural spectrum from art to high-technology endeavors. The successful places of the future will be those that build a creative economy attracting knowledge entrepreneurs and workers.

Knowledge workers are often inclined to prefer environments possessing cultural openness and diversity. There are a number of indices that track the link between knowledge-based regions and diversity, which highlight the existence of strong concentrations of social and cultural diversity in the most successful regions.[45] This indicates that not only are culturally diversified communities and regions the most productive and attractive, but that FDI policies should be formulated to create and market a socio-economic and cultural environment that is culturally diversified, transparent, and open.

Foreign direct investment policies across the globe have increasingly focused upon the importance of embedding firms within their host environment.[46] Many policymakers have taken considerable steps and encouraged training courses (often operated by the inward investors) to ensure that local suppliers match investor needs.[47] They have also established bespoke vocational training qualifications specifically designed to equip the local labor force to work with the inward investors. Such advances have been positive and innovative within the surroundings they have been set. However, a knowledge economy environment requires a deeper form of embedding, which helps knowledge entrepreneurs and workers access new opportunities for creative advancement. As well as linkages with suppliers, interaction with universities and other research establishments is a key feature of investor embeddedness in the knowledge economy.

Since an existing concentration of well-qualified workers is a crucial cog in the building of successful knowledge-based FDI policies, we consider that if the correct mix of skills is present, a knowledge-based company will gravitate toward a particular region, be it foreign or domestic, whether or not there are tax incentives on offer. By attracting knowledge workers, companies and investors will follow, allowing further start-up investment to be available and attraction activity and cluster development to occur.

We are not suggesting that the traditional cornerstones of FDI attraction policies are totally cast aside. Instead we are stressing that within the knowledge economy, location decisions made by individuals are subject to creative lifestyle issues, which were not always given priority within the formulation of more traditional FDI attraction policies. A sound economic development policy of high R&D and education investment, together with thoughtful planning in terms of cultural attraction, access to open spaces, and diversity of residential accommodation is playing a more substantial role in the attraction of FDI within the knowledge economy.

Attracting and embedding knowledge-based FDI

Knowledge-based FDI, as with all other types of FDI, hinges on the successful development and implementation of three core pillars: attraction; aftercare; and embedding. In addressing these components, Figure 6.7 is one perspective by which to view the long-term process of continuous attraction and retention of knowledge-based investment. The cornerstone of knowledge economy development lies with addressing the needs of knowledge workers, which includes supporting their ability to access knowledge and turn this knowledge into innovation, as well as the quality of place and environment in which they reside.[48] Therefore, the quality of available education is another key to the long-term sustainability of this policy. Attracting knowledge-based investment rests not upon excelling in one component but upon the ability to engage all facets.

Providing a positive living and cultural environment is a major requirement for attracting talented knowledge entrepreneurs and workers. Tax incentives, provision of infrastructure, and cost-effective labor may still apply, but alone these are insufficient as motivating mechanisms in attracting key wealth builders. Quality of life issues form the basis of a number of indices and rankings designed to compare the attractiveness of locations. Table 6.4 lists the top

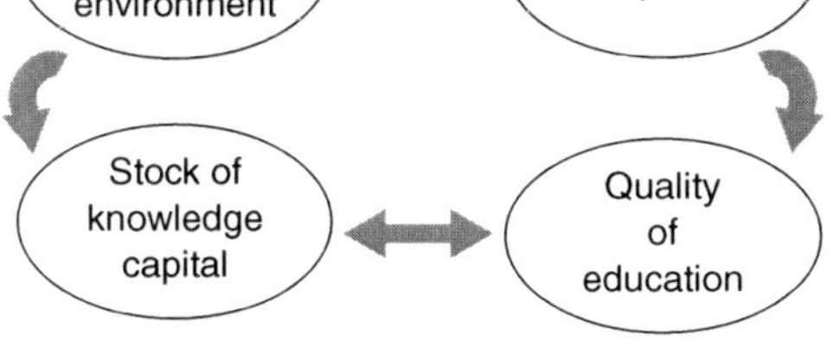

Figure 6.7 Attracting knowledge-based investment.

Table 6.4 Mercer top twenty city quality of living rankings 2005 and rankings on the *World Knowledge Competitiveness Index (WKCI)* 2005 for comparative regions

Rank	*City*	*WKCI Rank*	*WKCI Coverage*
1	Geneva (Switzerland)	44	Switzerland
1	Zurich (Switzerland)	44	Switzerland
3	Vancouver (Canada)	105	British Columbia
3	Vienna (Austria)	70	East Austria
5	Frankfurt (Germany)	67	Hessen
5	Munich (Germany)	65	Bayern
5	Dusseldorf (Germany)	94	Nordrhein-Westphalen
8	Auckland (New Zealand)	110	New Zealand
8	Bern (Switzerland)	44	Switzerland
8	Copenhagen (Denmark)	51	Denmark
8	Sydney (Australia)	91	New South Wales
12	Amsterdam (Netherlands)	77	West Netherlands
13	Brussels (Belgium)	45	Brussels
14	Melbourne (Australia)	88	Victoria
14	Berlin (Germany)	87	Berlin
14	Luxembourg	58	Luxembourg
14	Stockholm (Sweden)	8	Stockholm
14	Toronto (Canada)	66	Ontario
14	Wellington (New Zealand)	110	New Zealand
20	Ottawa (Canada)	66	Ontario

Sources: Mercer Human Resource Consulting (www.mercerHR.com); Huggins *et al.*, *World Knowledge Competitiveness Index 2005*.

20 cities around the world with the best quality of living, as ranked by Mercer Human Resource Consulting. Geneva and Zurich are followed by Vancouver, Vienna, and Frankfurt at the top of the rankings, with all the top 20 being covered by a concomitant geographic area in our *World Knowledge Competitiveness Index* rankings for 2005.

The commitment and integration of knowledge-based FDI in host economies is related to the ability of investors to develop networks and become key nodes in the skills economy and supply chains within the regions they are located. Traditional policy boundaries between FDI and indigenous development are becoming blurred. For instance, the retention and aftercare services offered by policymakers are often the same for both FDI and indigenous knowledge-based businesses, particularly if they are part of the same value-chain. This is a policy development occurring within the most knowledge progressive regions throughout the world. Poor trading conditions may render certain investors highly liable to make an exit from the host region or nation. Such investment may be repatriated to the country of origin in order to bolster local employment and income. This is less often the case with knowledge-based FDI, if it has become firmly rooted within the host economy. Such might be its dependency on the regional cluster in the host economy, knowledge-based FDI may be unable to relocate without an expense greater than the costs of continuing to operate within the host location.

Embedding knowledge-based investors is an area where policymakers must take a proactive approach. A systematic approach to aftercare and embedding is needed, together with a formal means of examining current and future investor requirements. Efforts must be made to understand the requirements of existing investors, ensuring that opportunities for further investment and expansion are not missed. Also, facilitating networks with local venture capitalists, universities, and knowledge entrepreneurs and workers will ensure that investors are fully aware of the range of advantages an economy has to offer. A commonly held belief is that the key strategic decisions of FDI are made in the home rather than host nation. In reality, there is often quite a substantial degree of local initiative, especially relating to reinvestment decisions. There is considerable opportunity and potential for policymakers to support and nurture this process through careful and strategic embedding activities.

The knowledge management of locations

If national, regional, and local policymakers are to take knowledge-based FDI seriously, they must work toward establishing a management strategy for knowledge attraction along the lines highlighted in Figure 6.8. The key features of such a strategy are:

- an understanding of the role for the strategic integration of locational development models between national, regional, and/or local players;
- an understanding of the role for strategic integration between the business community and knowledge actors, including universities and other public and private sector research establishments;
- an understanding of the importance of knowledge economy activities to the overall size and performance of national and regional economies.

Once the above factors are analyzed and understood, it is then possible to proceed toward the establishment of an integrated marketing strategy.

If Joel Kotkin is correct in his assertion that knowledge workers view the world as a 'vast smorgasbord' of choices,[49] then creating the most hospitable and appealing environment for such workers becomes imperative. The most successful and experienced FDI attractors combine proactive approaches with bottom-up approaches that stem from collaborating with educational planners in designing appropriate science and technology training courses and incentives for study and work for the best graduates.

Many of the leading regions on the *World Knowledge Competitiveness Index* score highly in terms of their quality of life attributes, as well as quality of the research institutes and science and technology networks they possess. These regions are not exclusive in their sectors of attraction and thrive in being homes to the knowledge economy as a whole. This knowledge cluster approach has

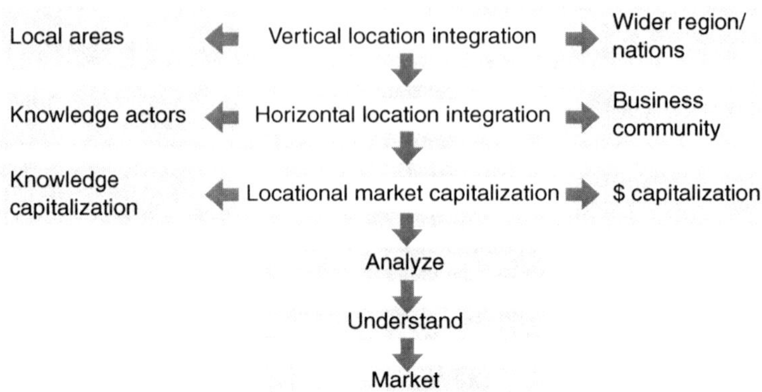

Figure 6.8 Key components of a management strategy for attracting knowledge-based investment.

resulted in plentiful opportunities for cross-sector networking and acts as a magnet to venture capitalists. Most importantly, these regions recognize the need for transparency in their approach to FDI and often adopt public-private partnerships in the design and implementation of FDI policy.

What are the best places doing?

As a means of further understanding what the most successful places and economies are doing right, we surveyed a selection of leading policymakers from the world's top-performing regional knowledge economies so they could explain their policies, practices, and success factors.[50] These policymakers told us that in recent years, particularly since 2000, they had established explicit regional strategies aimed at further developing their knowledge economies. These strategies mainly consist of support for areas of economic activity that have an increasing reliance on skills and knowledge in the production process and a more extensive use of specialist abilities and knowledge transfer. Knowledge economy strategies usually include a wide variety of actors and key participants and influencers, such as industry representatives, universities, research institutions, chambers of commerce, and economic development agencies. In almost all cases they are built upon public-private partnership.

The most significant objectives of a regional knowledge economy strategy are likely to be the improvement of R&D investment followed by education and workforce development-related goals. The foundations of these strategies are focused on investing in knowledge and the creation of the most appropriate environment for knowledge-based businesses and workers to flourish. Key components tend to focus on business and skills development assistance, the development of regional network and communication channels (especially between universities and businesses), and the provision of adequate venture finance, and training and consultancy services in entrepreneurship, leadership and management, highlighting the importance of creating the right business climate and framework.

When asked if and how knowledge economy strategies differ from previous or more mainstream development strategies, policymakers stated that it is the integration and increased focus on education, targeted business development, and cluster development that best define the key shifts in strategic decision-making. Other key examples of policy shifts highlighted include a change in public finance policy and fiscal incentives for knowledge economy businesses, the development of telecommunications infrastructure, deregulation and bureaucracy minimization, and the blending of public and private sector finance.

More than three-quarters of policymakers indicated that mechanisms for tackling social cohesion and inequalities emerged during the course of the knowledge economy strategy development. The most common mechanisms relate to retraining investment and welfare-to-work initiatives. We were also told that policies relating to sustainability and quality of place emerged in tandem with the development of the strategy. A range of policies and initiatives have been put in place, with most focusing upon improving the transportation system and the development of environmental policies and control, together with affordable housing and 'smart growth'.[51]

Since policymakers were operating at a regional level, we probed as to the influence and impact of national policies on the formulation and development of their regional strategies. As might be expected, a wide variety of factors were seen as having either a positive or negative impact. The key positive factors consist of the availability of tax credits, policy deregulation, and increased access to government-backed venture capital. Many of the negative factors mentioned are almost the reverse of the facilitating factors, consisting mainly of governmental cuts in R&D expenditure, an excessive tax burden, a lack of national coordination, and the slowness of the national government to react to rapidly changing future needs and commercialization efforts.

A suitable regulatory and financial framework is clearly vital when laying the foundations for stimulating a successful knowledge economy. Policymakers considered that regions must create an appropriate mix of financial incentives to draw knowledge-based businesses and a regulatory environment that encourages transparency and entrepreneurial spirit. Most policymakers had reviewed practices in other nations and regions as a means of shaping their own framework. The most commonly cited economies were Ireland, Canada, Germany, Sweden, Helsinki, Cambridge in the UK, and the US high-technology areas of Austin, Virginia, Boston, and of course Silicon Valley.

According to policymakers, indigenous SMEs are increasingly playing a crucial role in the development of their regional economies, particularly those involved in forging new routes for the commercialization of university research, helping to ensure regional sustainability and a high quality of life, and the development of networks, business associations, and regional strategic alliances through the utilization of their social and civic capital. Other factors include the willingness of local firms to employ local graduates and interns as a means of strengthening local research and graduate capability.

Policymakers were asked to rate the strength of their regional business culture in terms of a series of characteristics including entrepreneurship, innovation, risk-taking, and regional identity. From the results, we found a strong positive correlation between high levels of entrepreneurship and risk-taking within the regions. This might be expected, but it does confirm that these factors are mutually reinforcing and are a product of the regional business culture. They may also be influenced by regulatory and legal systems, such as tax credits for starting new businesses. In order to assess the perceptions of policymakers regarding key success factors in their regions, we asked them to rank the strength of various factors in relation to the evolution of their knowledge economy, such as research capability, presence of venture capital, and investment in infrastructure. The highest rated factor was the creation of a desirable location to both live and work, confirming the importance of cultural and environmental factors to knowledge-based economic development and emphasizing the role of high-quality living. High-quality living is seen by policymakers to come in a wide range of forms and guises including diversity, multicultural acceptance, low pollution, high levels of green space, and plentiful leisure activity – be this in the shape of night time entertainment or historic and cultural attractions.

Other key success factors consist of the research base and the creation and transfer of this research between universities, local businesses, and other research establishments, as well as workforce skills, telecommunications infrastructure, and the development of key business sectors. These factors are not seen as being mutually exclusive, with key business sectors likely to be developed in accordance with local research strengths. However, across the regions we analyzed, the variation in targeted sectors, within which further development is considered advantageous, is quite small. Life sciences/biotechnology, ICT, new media, and microelectronics appear on the lists of most policymakers, while others also list sectors such as machine tools, energy, and maritime activities as targets for development.

Finally, we asked policymakers to comment on those features they consider best distinguishes their knowledge economy. Paradoxically perhaps, most pointed to a similar range of features, the most prominent being partnership and collaboration, diversity and balance, and cluster development. The willingness of the education sector to partner with industry was stressed by most policymakers in these leading regions. Collaboration and joint working was viewed as a means of stimulating innovation and increasing the likelihood of commercialization activity. Top-level commitment and involvement by senior government officials and politicians was stated as a crucial factor in implementing new policy thinking. As one respondent stated, 'Local commitment among key community leaders has helped identify the need for diversifying the economy to carry it into the next century.'

A region where diversity is both accepted and encouraged is considered a key attraction to knowledge workers. Key clusters are highlighted by most policymakers, consisting not only of a concentration of similar businesses, but also of feeder services, appropriate infrastructure and suppliers, and access to financial and regulatory support. One policymaker told us: 'Our region's knowledge and innovation economy is distinguished by a concerted effort to leverage our region's strengths in manufacturing technologies into new product development and research that will keep our region prosperous.'

Conclusions

A key point of departure in attempting to think and act beyond the current conventions of economic and competitiveness policy is to acknowledge that it is no longer mainstream economic development practices, based on public sector pump priming of either structural or hard infrastructure projects, that are pushing forward growth in the global knowledge economy. New processes of what some practitioners term *economic gardening* are replacing traditional economic development models as the drivers of growth in those regions and nations that are successfully sustaining the growth of their economies.[52] The emphasis on *gardening*, as opposed to *development*, is a metaphor recognizing that new growth and improved competitiveness is best served by a policy environment allowing entrepreneurs and businesses to 'sow-seeds' that are nurtured over a significant period of time. The philosophy underlying economic gardening is an understanding that while many business development projects will not reach fruition, there will be a number of bloomers. These bloomers act as the catalysts for improved competitiveness through the distribution of new seeds ensuring longer-term growth. As we emphasize throughout this book, achieving success in the knowledge economy requires long-term commitment, as there are no quick-fix remedies.

7 Managing network capital and innovation

In his book *Open Innovation*, Henry Chesbrough sheds new light upon the importance of external knowledge sourcing and the shift from 'closed innovation' to 'open innovation'. In essence, Chesbrough discusses the management of what we term *network capital* and the means by which it can be utilized to acquire knowledge. The management of network capital is becoming increasingly important, as the locus of innovation in knowledge-based industries moves beyond the closed environment of the R&D laboratories of large corporations and spreads to small, technology-based start-ups, universities, and other players. Chesbrough sees this shift as arising from a number of factors, such as the increased supply of highly skilled workers who have received higher education, the growth of start-ups based on new ideas generated in universities and large corporations, and the mobility of highly skilled workers between start-ups, large corporations, and universities.[1] Large corporations have lost their ability to keep in-house knowledge by encircling their scientists and engineers, as opportunities for knowledge commercialization rapidly grow outside their R&D laboratories. This has resulted in large corporations developing an increased number of knowledge sources outside their R&D laboratories through collaborations and alliances with other parties. A symbolic event surrounding this shift is, as Chesbrough writes, Proctor & Gamble's decision in 1999 to extend internal R&D to the outside world through an initiative called 'Connect and Develop' and the creation of a position entitled Director of External Innovation.[2]

Knowledge sourcing from external sources has been recognized as important for some time.[3] While it has become increasingly relevant to large corporations, as discussed in Chapter 4, it is rather the norm for many small and medium-sized firms which cannot generate internally all the knowledge necessary for new product and process development.[4] By learning from external knowledge sources, small and medium-sized firms are more susceptible than large corporations to decisions and actions made by other firms and organizations. Yet, large variations exist among firms in how they manage their network capital, particularly in terms of the number of sources used, the frequency of contact, the types of sources, and the modes of sourcing. In this chapter, we examine three factors that determine how firms manage their network capital – geography, internal capacity, and industry life cycle. In particular, the impact of industry life cycle has implications for the management of innovation as a whole and, therefore, the management of its knowledge networks. For instance, a crucial determinant is how a firm manages the transition from a period of continuous, incremental change to a period of discontinuous, radical change. We look into the advantages of external knowledge sourcing through network capital building during a period of such transition and then consider the importance of nurturing a capacity for sourcing knowledge outside a firm's own expertise in advance of such discontinuities.

Clusters – to be in or not to be in?

In policy circles across advanced economies, there has been a frenzy of enthusiasm and interest in cluster development. We mentioned in earlier chapters that this explosion of interest owes a lot to the work of Michael Porter, particularly his influential book, *The Competitive Advantage of Nations*.[5] According to Porter, the location of a firm within a cluster enhances its productivity through superior or lower-cost access to specialized inputs. Sourcing from within the cluster reduces the need to maintain costly inventory. It also minimizes possible delays in delivery that are more likely to arise with shipments from distant locations. Furthermore, the cluster attracts labor with specialized skills and expertise that match the requirements of the businesses located within it. Such agglomeration of firms and labor gives rise to snowball effects. Once a cluster starts to form, it becomes easier to source specialized inputs and labor. The ease of sourcing gives businesses in a cluster comparative advantages over their competitors. This draws more firms and labor that are able to compete in an already specialized, competitive environment. As a result, clusters often gain a 'one-and-only' position in the national, and often global, market.[6] Another aspect that attracts the attention of scholars and policymakers alike is the common knowledge base shared by businesses within a cluster. In Porter's view, a cluster creates ample opportunity for interfirm collaboration, harnessing knowledge sharing and creation across corporate boundaries. The proximity to other firms and institutions within a cluster facilitates the development and utilization of a common knowledge base.

When other factors are equal, businesses are more likely to externally source knowledge if the sources are located in close proximity. As we discussed in Chapter 2, one aspect of the knowledge-based economy is the weightlessness of the commercial products traded. In fast-growing successful countries, greater value – as a proportion of gross domestic product (GDP) – resides in commodities that have little or no physical manifestation, such as microelectronic devices and financial services.[7] There is a close association between weightlessness and growth in information technology, which suggests that the latter has contributed positively to increasing weightlessness. Of such weightless commodities, a notable example are business services that provide firms with expert knowledge. Unlike manufactured goods, business services often transfer knowledge and carry little or no weight at all through the use of digital media, as well as old-fashioned face-to-face communication. Given the ease of delivery their weightless nature suggests, why does the proximity of knowledge sources matter?

Minimization of transport costs is a major concern to businesses, especially when they consider the location of offices and factories, as well as the logistics of the goods and services coming in and out of them. Any physical flow of commodities, whether knowledge-based or not, will incur two types of costs: (1) a direct transport cost, and (2) a transaction cost. Of these, the second is related to the number of man-hours involved in negotiating matters, such as price, quality, design specifications, and so on. The per-unit cost of delivering commodities tends to decrease as their flows either increase in size or become standardized in quality. Quantity discounts are usually available for transport costs. Also, standardization will cut transaction costs by simplifying ordering and reordering. Small businesses dealing with variable, non-standardized inputs and outputs are more sensitive to the proximity of sources than large corporations handling inputs and outputs in bulk. Furthermore, whereas transport costs have decreased over the last several decades owing to the development in transport technology, transaction costs on non-standardized goods and services have declined much less markedly.[8] As a result, the ratio of transaction costs to transport costs has risen in some product areas.

Business services, such as R&D, consulting, and IT services, are a typical example of services that incur small transport costs but require significant transaction costs. Normally, a business service transaction starts with a search for an appropriate vendor, which involves assessing the quality of services on offer. This often relies upon the second-hand reputation potential buyers can obtain from other users. Proximity to the vendor reduces the search costs, as information on the vendor's reputation is more readily available near the vendor's location. Once an appropriate vendor is identified, a prospective buyer enters negotiations. This involves clarification of needs and other specifics as well as the cost of services. Though the negotiations can take place over the phone, by email, or over the Internet, face-to-face meetings are a more satisfactory means to get to know each other and build trust, often an important ingredient for successful transactions involving knowledge-based business services. Furthermore, buyer requirements for business services more often than not vary from one occasion to another, making their planning and delivery hard to standardize. This often necessitates meetings between vendor and client on numerous occasions. As a result, proximity to business service providers reduces overall costs and encourages their use.

As we have seen, regions vary in the amount and quality of their knowledge sources. In general, the least competitive and most peripheral regions are usually less well-endowed with high-quality business service providers.[9] A study of business services – advertising, market research, graphic design, product design, and management consultancy – in UK regions shows that business services providers in London and the core Southeast region are characterized by higher productivity and greater export penetration, as well as faster growth and wider markets, than their counterparts in peripheral regions.[10] The more competitive characteristics of business services in London and the Southeast indicate a higher level of quality of their services. Businesses, especially small and medium-sized firms, located in peripheral regions are more likely to encounter the lack of a local pool of quality service providers. If they seek knowledge vendors outside their regions, they may face difficulties, such as (1) the low visibility of non-local vendors, (2) logistical difficulties stemming from the need for face-to-face meetings, and (3) the lack of reliable information regarding the skills of the vendors.[11] In other words, they experience difficulties in building the requisite network capital due to a lack of market knowledge.

For this reason, small businesses located in regions with low competitiveness face a catch-22 situation. The warranting of a pool of high-quality business services is unlikely to occur within regions until a core of progressive businesses using high-quality services appears. On the other hand, such progressive businesses may not emerge indigenously unless a sufficient number of high-quality service providers exist.[12] There is strong evidence that proximity to external knowledge sources facilitates their use and in turn improves the innovative performance of businesses. For instance, a series of studies concerning the technical linkages of small manufacturers in North America demonstrates that technical inputs from a blend of complementary external specialists significantly contribute to innovation performance.[13]

In this sense, advantages are derived from locating within clusters characterized by the active transfer and diffusion of technological and managerial expertise. This transfer and diffusion is provided by opportunities for inter-firm networking, as well as research and management staff recruitment from the local labor market. In addition, clusters endowed with a pool of technological and managerial expertise providers often give local firms access to wider global and national innovation networks, such as those discussed in Chapter 5.[14] This appears to place at a disadvantage firms, particularly small firms, in less-favored locations outside of such clusters. However, the lack of a pool of local knowledge sources is not as fatal as it appears.

Absorptive capacity and management style

Are those small businesses located in less-favored regions doomed to fail? Is proximity to a pool of knowledge sources the primary factor determining the success of knowledge sourcing? Resource-constrained small businesses in less-favored regions are disadvantaged in their access to external knowledge sources. Indeed, a study shows that less small business in peripheral regions – both manufacturing and services firms – are involved in collaborative arrangements with other organizations than their counterparts in core regions.[15] This leads some to argue that policy programs should be established to help develop sources of knowledge – such as public sector-based centers of advice, as well as universities and research institutes – in these less-favored regions. However, such supply-side policies alone do not solve the problem of under-achieving firms.

There is evidence that demand-side factors exert as much, if not more, influence upon external knowledge sourcing and network capital building. While fewer businesses are successful, small businesses in regions with low competitiveness as a whole overcome a variety of locational difficulties and compete with, and sometimes outperform, their counterparts in core regions by implementing compensatory innovation strategies. For instance, successful businesses in regions with low competitiveness often exhibit higher levels of R&D intensity, as measured by R&D staff as a percentage of total staff, than their counterparts in more competitive regions. Facing less favorable and competitive environments, they overcome locational constraints by making a greater R&D effort.[16] This suggests wide variations among businesses in their innovation behaviors and strategies including knowledge sourcing and networking activities.

External knowledge sourcing is not solely dependent on the availability of sources in close proximity but also on factors internal to firms. The most frequently discussed of such internal factors is the capability to assess and absorb knowledge.[17] In their seminal article, Wesley Cohen and Daniel Levinthal argue that the ability of a business to recognize the value of new, external knowledge, assimilate it, and apply it to commercial ends is critical to its innovation capabilities.[18] This ability, which Cohen and Levinthal call 'absorptive capacity', is history-dependent and reflects how much a business has invested in the area of expertise it specializes in. Absorptive capacity largely depends upon a firm's investment in innovation efforts.[19] Good in-house capabilities in R&D, design, and engineering help to capture and appropriate knowledge, both codified and tacit, in the process of learning from external sources.[20] Unlike the popular perception of technology adoption from an outside source as being a free riding exercise, adopting new technologies and knowledge is costly. For instance, there is evidence that for many processes the adoption costs for a single user (be it a firm or an individual) can be almost as large as the costs of invention.[21] A firm's existing degree of familiarity with the requisite knowledge not only helps to assess the value of knowledge available from outside sources but also reduces the costs incurred by its adoption.

The outcome of knowledge sourcing in turn feeds back into future decision-making patterns. Unsuccessful outcomes, combined with the 'not-invented-here' syndrome, suppress the firm's propensity to source knowledge externally and build new network capital. The mutual reinforcement of in-house commitment to innovation efforts and complementary commitment to external knowledge sourcing is particularly evident in technology-based sectors. In sectors such as biotechnology, successful businesses invest in their in-house capabilities while 'buying-in' more knowledge from external sources at the same time.[22]

The external orientation of a firm's management also affects knowledge sourcing. For instance, small businesses, particularly those managed by owner-managers engaged in local market and more traditional non-knowledge-intensive activities, are reluctant to engage in network capital building or the use of external knowledge sources. Holding responsibilities for many areas, managers of these types of small businesses often think that they lack the time to build effective network strategies for external knowledge sourcing. Furthermore, owner-managers of traditional firms often value their independence and are unwilling to seek knowledge from external partners, displaying what James Curran and Robert Blackburn call a 'fortress enterprise mentality'.[23] Small business owners consider the independence and freedom from control by others central to their entrepreneurship. Because of their motivational emphasis, they may show a reluctance to engage in any behavior that might lead to a dependence on others or even be seen as showing a need for support. They militate against networking activities beyond the minimum they consider is clearly demanded by their business needs.[24] As such a reluctance to engage in external knowledge sourcing may be engrained in the culture of their firms, a well-designed strategy and management commitment is required to change it. Indeed, the overriding strategy for these traditional sector firms is to make their activities more knowledge-intensive and knowledge-absorptive and adapt to the knowledge network and network capital building undertaken by more knowledge-based firms. It is precisely this lack of conversion that results in regions with low competitiveness being unable to improve their position even if they possess a number of star performers.

Industry life cycle

The industry life cycle phase within which a firm operates is another factor influencing its external knowledge sourcing activities. An industry's development is a cumulative process of adjustment within a set of *models* and *heuristics*.[25] Models refer to a product's basic artifacts, which firms in the product's industry seek to develop and improve. For example, what we see as a car today embodies a set of technological characteristics such as the internal combustion engine, the transmission shaft, the gear box, the chassis, and so on. These technological characteristics result in a commercial product within a range of prices consumers are willing to pay. On the other hand, heuristics describes methods to answer questions such as 'where do we go from here?' and 'what sorts of knowledge should we source?' They give rules of thumb about where to continue searching for solutions and which areas to avoid.[26] In the case of automobiles, when consumers preferred faster and more spacious cars, solutions were sought after in the area of constructing more powerful engines that could drive a larger body at a faster speed. After the oil shock hit developed economies in the 1970s, a new heuristic emerged and led automotive manufacturers to develop compact cars with fuel-efficient engines.

Industry life cycle theory views an industry's evolution as a process of establishing a de facto product design in response to market forces. James Utterback and William Abernathy divide this evolution into three phases – the fluid phase, the transitional phase, and the mature phase – while Michael Tushman and Lori Rosenkopf add another subsequent phase – the discontinuities phase.[27] In the fluid phase, the introduction of a product faces considerable uncertainty in two areas: user preferences and technological approaches. Normally, firms face uncertainty in one of the two areas after first coming across either a potential new market or a new technology. Some firms first identify a new market and then try to identify technological specifications to meet the new market demand. Others invent a new technology and then seek to commercialize the technology into a product consumers are willing to purchase. In the fluid phase, many firms, especially entrepreneurial start-ups, enter the market with different variants of the product. The number of major product innovations tends to reach a peak during this early growth period. Then, gradually, these product variations begin to converge around the most popular solution to an emerging configuration. This is called the 'dominant design' and marks the beginning of the transitional phase. The competitive emphasis shifts in the transitional phase from radical concept development to efforts targeted at improving a product's reliability, quality, and functionality.

When an industry shifts toward the mature phase, a change again takes place in its competitive focus. The efforts producers have made in the transitional phase gradually deplete opportunities to improve a product's quality and functionality. Producers begin to move to other forms of competition, which are normally related to the costs of a product. A new goal of cost reduction results in firms increasingly focusing on efficiency, rationalization, and scale economies. Producers that are unable to efficiently produce the dominant design exit the market, leading to a shake out in the number of producers. The depletion of opportunities to improve the product, the lock-in of the dominant design, and a shake out in the market creates pressure on profit margins and force producers to invest more in capital-intensive methods of production. As a result, R&D emphasis shifts from product innovation to process innovation in the mature phase.[28]

Finally, the introduction of a more advanced, next-generation technology renders obsolete the industry's existing technology during the discontinuities phase. Those innovations giving rise to a discontinuities phase are characterized as rare and unpredictable. They advance a relevant technological frontier by an order-of-magnitude and involve fundamentally different product or process designs. Such discontinuous product innovations command a decisive cost, performance, or quality advantage over prior product forms (e.g. integrated circuits, jet engines, and the Internet), while the advantages of discontinuous process innovations are reflected in order-of-magnitude improvements in the cost or quality of the product (e.g. just-in-time production systems, pharmaceuticals produced through genetic engineering).[29] Discontinuous innovations remove many previous entry barriers in an industry, attracting new entrants and making the market place volatile with active experimentation. With the conditions of the fluid phase restored, the industry again enters a new life cycle.

Industry structure and critical success factors change over an industry's life cycle. This exerts an influence on a firm's propensity to participate in network capital generation through joint ventures and alliances with other parties. Through life cycle case studies of Microsoft, Cisco, and Compaq, as well as the statistical analysis of industry data, Edward Roberts and Wenyun Liu suggest that firms are more inclined to form alliances as technology and knowledge becomes better defined and as competitive pressure increases during the transitional phase. The propensity to ally reaches a peak in the mature phase and then starts to decline when consolidation decreases the total number of firms in the industry.[30]

Aside from changes in competitive pressure and industry structure, there is another force at work that shifts the focus of innovation over an industry's life cycle. As noted above, different stages in the life cycle emphasize different aspects of innovation. In the early phases of industry life cycle, firms concentrate their R&D resources in product innovation to take a lead in turbulent environments. As an industry enters the mature phase, firms gradually shift their R&D resources from product innovation to process innovation. Efforts aimed at product innovation involve the laborious process of scanning for market opportunities and technological frontiers. In the fluid and transitional phases, the analysis of market trends and competitor behavior is essential for tracing competing product variations and catching a sign or glimpse of an emerging dominant design. Also, firms make efforts to scan technological frontiers in the science base (i.e. universities and public laboratories) to tap embryonic ideas for new technologies leading to new products. The orientation toward product innovation makes firms relatively network oriented. By contrast, process innovation typically depends on internal knowledge and capabilities, as it is often related to the identification of technical imbalances and bottlenecks through learning-by-doing. This identification enables firms to either specify or design new production methods and equipment that will improve productivity.[31]

Furthermore, while most technical efforts in the early phases are expended on the design of product architecture, the later application of technological energies shifts toward improving the performance and cost-effectiveness of individual components and subsystems. As the shift from architectural design to component-level improvement occurs, specialized groups are likely to be organized within a firm to focus on improving each component.[32] Patterns of communication are stabilized, reflecting the structure among specialized groups. Such stabilized communication patterns also occur with component suppliers, as the rise of a dominant design determines the types and specifications of required components, reducing the number of former varieties. Taken together, the shift in industry life cycle from the early phases to later phases comes with a reduction of external knowledge sourcing and in the number of sources used. The issue of communication also highlights the shifts that occur between external sourcing based on either network capital or social capital. During the fluid and early transitional phases, external sourcing is more likely to be based on network capital, as firms continually search for new knowledge that may lead to the dominant design, while in the later phases, relationships are stabilized and more likely to generate and be built upon social capital.

Our study of the UK electronics and automotive engineering industries confirms that small and medium-sized firms primarily target external knowledge sourcing at meeting their need for product innovations. For the great majority of the firms surveyed, process innovations are a secondary concern in the use of external knowledge sources. Many firms consider that the contribution of external knowledge sources to process innovations is unclear or non-existent. In general, three factors influence the number of external knowledge sources used by firms: the number of product innovations introduced by the firm during the last two years, the age of the firm, and its R&D intensity, measured by the ratio of technical staff to all employees. As a firm introduces a greater number of product innovations and has higher levels of R&D intensity, it uses a greater number of external knowledge sources. By contrast, the longer a firm has been in operation, the lower the number of its external knowledge sources. On the whole, automotive engineering firms produce a smaller number of product innovations and are older in age than electronics firms, indicating their position at a later phase in the industry life cycle. When the two groups are compared, automotive engineering firms use on average a smaller number of external knowledge sources.[33]

The innovation management challenge

A key challenge for those involved in innovation management is to develop a strategy to effectively handle the transition from the mature phase through the discontinuities phase and successfully enter a new industry life cycle.[34] The rise of a groundbreaking technology in the discontinuities phase is 'competence destroying', with radical technological developments shifting the basis of competition. This results in incumbent firms experiencing difficulties in adjusting their technical strengths and strategies to these developments.[35] Firms build their capabilities around a particular trajectory in a cumulative way. This is partly due to the inability of decision makers to consider the universe of options available to them. As a result, they tend to look to the firm's previous development decisions for guidance. Firms also concentrate their innovation efforts in areas of prior knowledge accumulation, aimed at providing consistent investments in personnel, intellectual property, inter-organizational relations, and tacit organizational knowledge.[36] Because of the path-dependent nature of their capabilities, firms, particularly those in the later phases of an industry life cycle, often find it hard to respond quickly to radical technological changes and move into a new cycle.

A solution to this challenge is to extend the boundary of external knowledge sourcing and form networks and alliances with partners in the areas into which they are seeking to move. As we discussed in Chapters 2 and 3, an important and underemphasized component of the dynamics of technological change is that the search for new knowledge is community-based. Firms and individuals in an industry search for new knowledge as members of a 'population' based on shared disciplines.[37] Such communities enhance productivity through sharing knowledge. However, they may also constrain the directions of technical progress and sometimes blind their members to developments taking place outside their knowledge community. Repeated interaction and the exchange of information between individuals within a community leads to a convergence of their norms, values, and behaviors through the creation of local languages (similar to the creation of social capital discussed in Chapter 4).[38] The maturation of an industry represents a case like this. After an industry undergoes early phases of creation, replication, and the selection of varieties in products and firms, it develops to a point where it consists of firms and individuals with similar mindsets.

There is a tension between efficiency and originality arising from the social, cultural, and technical homogeneity of firms and individuals in the mature phase.[39] Efficient and effective communication takes place most frequently between members who share common skills, backgrounds, and status. The evolution of local languages through iterative communication within an industry allows speedier and more accurate exchanges of information. Such efficiency is sought after in the mature phase when firms favor carefully planned stable growth based on incremental product and process development.[40] Yet, the homogeneity of firms and individuals within an industry may also stifle originality. A study of US federal R&D projects provides evidence that the intensity of interaction among a group of scientists and engineers with similar backgrounds shows no relation to their problem-solving performance. Fundamentally, it was found that more frequent meetings do not produce better ideas, which conforms to some of the concerns we have already raised regarding the social capital advantage thesis.[41]

Under such circumstances, alliances with partners outside a firm's own technological area represent possible strategies to bring about significant shifts in technological focus. In alliance formation, there is an inverted-U relationship between the degree of technological overlap between firms and the likelihood of their forming an alliance.[42] When firms have a lot of expertise in common, they are likely to be at mutually competing positions and have few incentives to enter into collaboration. On the other hand, if their technological positions are very distant from each other, alliances are also less likely to be formed. This is because the 'student' in an alliance must have considerable in-house expertise complementing the technology development activities of the alliance. For many firms, this is an onerous requirement.[43] In short, alliances are most likely to be formed when the technological positions of the partners are neither too close nor too distant. However, firms occasionally make use of alliances with technologically distant partners to make a jump in their technological focus. Toby Stuart and Joel Podolny demonstrate that such alliances allow firms to assimilate the developments of technologically distant partners and make considerable shifts in technological positions.[44]

In general, the decline in external knowledge sourcing in the mature phase poses a problem to the long-term sustainability of firms, particularly resource-constrained small and medium-sized firms. For large corporations, their large-scale resources allow them to use equity-based joint ventures and acquisitions to access technologies outside their specialized technological areas. They are able to mobilize these when faced with radical technological changes in the discontinuities phase and the need to access external expertise. Microsoft is a textbook case of a company surviving technological discontinuity through alliances and acquisitions. For example, the company neither pioneered the Internet nor reacted immediately to the technology's rise. The company's slow response placed it under threat in the market for software that subsequently became integrated with Internet technology. However, with a deep financial pocket and a strong customer base, the company held its dominant position through aggressive acquisitions and equity investments. From 1995 to 1999, it bought 15 companies and made 26 minority equity investments focusing on Internet-related technologies and application software.[45]

Such equity-based alliances are much less of an option for most small and medium-sized firms. Inevitably, they need to rely more on either contract-based alliances, such as licensing agreements, or more informal types of knowledge sourcing, such as seeking advice from contacts in outside sources, which we discussed in Chapter 4. Contract-based or informal types of inter-firm learning require specific skills to manage them, due to the information asymmetry between knowledge-seeker and knowledge-provider.[46]

The problems in transferring knowledge highlight its intangible, non-standardized, and inseparable nature. These particularities are actually shared by most services, as opposed to manufactured goods. To start with, services are unable to be seen, felt, or touched in the same manner as manufactured goods (i.e. intangibility). Also, a producer of services is unable to provide constant performance and quality, because services cannot be inventoried (i.e. non-standardization). Last but not least, while tangible goods are produced, sold, and then consumed, services are sold, and then produced and consumed simultaneously (i.e. inseparability).[47] These factors mean that users of knowledge-based services often lack the information required (due to the imbalances of information between knowledge-seeker and knowledge-provider) to effectively undertake knowledge transfer transactions.

The lack of information is particularly problematic when attempting to assess returns to knowledge both in advance and after its acquisition.[48] The fact that the production and consumption of services can occur simultaneously makes it difficult for a knowledge-seeker to evaluate services. This reiterates the problem of forming knowledge markets as discussed in Chapter 4. A knowledge-provider cannot fully disclose knowledge until it is purchased, because once it is disclosed, the provider loses some of the knowledge's property (i.e. a knowledge-seeker comes to know it without purchasing).

The difficulty of evaluating knowledge does not end here. The impacts of knowledge often pervade a wide range of activities, for which specific returns are difficult to measure. Returns may not immediately appear and may take a long time to emerge. To make matters worse, explicit contracts are often unfeasible, because required contingencies are either not observed or not measurable in a verifiable way, which is most often the case.[49] This forces a knowledge-seeker to rely on a provider's reputation, as well as process factors such as the visible quality of a provider's personal style (e.g. presentation, language) and other supplementary elements that the knowledge-seeker is competent to evaluate (e.g. location of office).[50]

Because of information gaps, small and medium-sized firms tend to seek advice from those well-worn contacts they come across in the course of ordinary business activities – predominantly customers, suppliers, banks, accountants, and solicitors.[51] A significant reduction in information gaps occurs through day-to-day interactions with these contacts. Day-to-day business communication helps both parties learn each other's vocabularies and smooth the way to understanding problems and needs a knowledge-seeker has. Also, knowledge of each other (e.g. activity, strengths and weaknesses, and history) may make the knowledge-provider's advice more effective. A knowledge-seeker will tend to take on board advice from traditional sources if business relationships with them are going well. However, the reliance upon 'worn-in, tried-and-true' sources is problematic when firms face radical changes in the discontinuities phase and seek to make shifts in their technological position. If they turn to their existing customers, these customers will most likely ask for more of what they have or merely better versions.[52] Location in a cluster may not help in this regard and could instead have adverse effects. As clusters build established positions in particular industries, movement of people homogenizes the knowledge pool within them.[53] As a result, firms within a cluster may become increasingly dependent upon a common path, rejecting knowledge that is irrelevant to its technological areas. This highlights the necessity for the more global approach to networking being undertaken by those knowledge clusters analyzed in Chapter 5.

Firms need to nurture their capacity to search knowledge outside their own technological area and manage relationships with unfamiliar, non-traditional sources. Such a capacity is distinct from the absorptive capacity we discussed earlier. Absorptive capacity in the traditional sense is underpinned by a firm's innovation efforts in its own area of expertise, since an accumulated stock of knowledge in the area allows the firm to assess the relevance and utility of new knowledge in relation to itself. In contrast, the search for knowledge outside a firm's own technological area relies on the capacity to keep its channels of information open to non-traditional sources through the creation of network capital. As described in Chapter 4, such a capacity is often possessed and exercised by 'gatekeepers' who are strongly connected to internal colleagues and linked to other firms and organizations. They are able to gather and understand external information and translate it into terms that are meaningful and useful to their more locally oriented colleagues. Also, they facilitate the external communication of their colleagues by training, directing, and socializing them.[54] The role of gatekeepers gained greater prominence when examples such as Proctor & Gamble's Director of External Innovation broke new ground in this area. Many firms now nurture the capacity of gatekeepers by selecting technically respected individuals and helping them develop internal and external linkages through unit/branch transfers and training.

Nurturing the cross-organizational, boundary-spanning capacity is an on-going, long-term process. As Joe Tidd, John Bessant, and Keith Pavitt write, 'new markets do not emerge in their full scale or with clearly identifiable needs but start out as messy, uncertain and risky places with small size and dubious growth prospects'.[55] Given this, the best way to catch such faint signals of emerging markets is to cast a wide net.[56] However, there is necessarily a limit to the net size firms can cast, since they operate under an inherent tension in resource allocation between the pursuit of efficiency in an existing market and the search for new markets. What matters more in our view, which is often neglected, is that the capacity to source knowledge from unfamiliar, non-traditional sources cannot always be built overnight. Our research on small and medium-sized firms suggests that they need a learning period when they embark on using unfamiliar external sources of knowledge. A great majority of firms take a cautious approach in the uncharted territory of knowledge sourcing, starting with a low-risk use approach. It is only when they grasp how knowledge sourcing operates with particular sources and network actors that they make full use of them.[57]

Firms need to build a portfolio of external sources of knowledge on a continuous basis, generating network capital and repeating the cycle of learning about new, unfamiliar sources outside its own technological area. Dorothy Leonard-Barton suggests that high performers keep up a consistent, continuous relationship with information sources of all types.[58] In this regard, the decline in external knowledge sourcing by small and medium-sized firms in the mature phase is a cause for concern. Compared with large firms, they may have difficulty in differentiating between strategic knowledge gathering roles and internal operational roles, and their organizational structure and procedures may not be geared to identifying key trends, changes, and events in their environment that might affect their functioning.[59] Given the narrow focus of their knowledge scanning, they may not respond to events or changes in the environment unless they appear as significant threats or opportunities.[60] As a result, their search for knowledge sources often takes place in a 'fire brigade' form, where solutions are sought to problems that have suddenly arisen.[61] The lack of resources small and medium-sized firms have at their disposal means they are less able to absorb the damage caused by a threat, making them more vulnerable than their larger counterparts.

Conclusion

In Chapter 2, we discussed the growth of knowledge communities, and in Chapter 4, the role of network capital in facilitating knowledge flows. As our knowledge becomes more advanced, our ability to create and learn new and state-of-the-art knowledge becomes more specialized. Such specialization, in turn, demands a greater role for drawing on and combining knowledge across communities of knowledge workers, situated both within and outside a firm.[62] This demand is particularly strong when firms begin to seek a new product architecture during the discontinuities phase. To prepare for such discontinuities, we need to engage in network capital building, enabling access to relevant external knowledge sources, well in advance.[63]

8 But what about the money?

Financing and commercializing knowledge

The commercialization of knowledge as a means of stimulating competitiveness and growth is becoming an increasingly important strategic instrument across the globe. A key element in the success of knowledge commercialization is necessarily the availability of suitable finance. There is increasing evidence that academic and research institutions, corporations, and individuals are facing significant problems in accessing finance to fund knowledge-based venturing. Such finance falls within the spectrum provided by venture capitalists through equity capital investments. However, barriers such as risk aversion, information asymmetry, and market failure have led to a decline in the number of venture capitalists investing in knowledge commercialization ventures, resulting in the emergence of an 'equity' or 'funding' gap.

These barriers are limiting the creation and growth potential of such ventures and the competitiveness of the economies within which they are located. This chapter examines the development of specific seed and early stage funds as a means of bridging the equity gap. It examines cases of seed fund development around the globe, drawing on empirical evidence from a study we have undertaken on the design and operation of these funds.[1] It also covers the findings of a case study of the knowledge commercialization activities of universities in London.[2]

Knowledge commercialization and finance

Knowledge commercialization is the process of transforming the raw outputs of science (natural, physical, and social) and technology, in their 'blue sky' or basic and pure research format, into a tradable commodity. As stated above, a key ingredient in this transformation is the availability of finance, with the financing beyond basic or pure research, most usually termed *seed* or *proof of concept* financing. Proof of concept or seed funding is required when a project has demonstrated its ability, within a research setting, to meet a well-defined challenge. At this point the project requires funding to demonstrate its commercial viability, that is, an ability to meet an identified market opportunity if produced at appropriate levels of cost and reliability.

Seed financing is a step upon the funding ladder and is designed to bridge a gap between pure research and the product development stage. Seed finance provides investigators and entrepreneurs with sufficient resources to develop their ideas to a stage where they can approach venture capitalists or other finance institutions for further funding. This further funding is then used to progress the opportunity to the next stage of development – the creation of marketable products and services. Therefore, a key stage in the research cycle consists of accessing seed finance in order to undertake detailed commercial feasibility work. If a researcher or research establishment is unable to raise these funds to invest in initial development, there is a high risk that the economic benefit of the research they have undertaken will not be accrued.

In terms of assessing the market scope of seed finance, it is useful to set it within the context of the venture capital industry as a whole. For example, within Europe, seed-stage investment accounts for only 0.6 percent of total venture capital investment. The investment stage receiving the largest share is buyouts (63.3 percent), followed by expansion (21.4 percent) and start-up stage (6.8 percent). In general, it is small specialist venture capitalists that are prepared to invest in seed and very early stage ventures.[3] This antipathy by venture capitalists toward seed financing is linked to the varying levels of risk associated with the different stages of venture capital investment. Gavin Reid and Julia Smith find that seed finance, followed by financing for the start-up and turnaround stages, are the three most risky potential investments from the perception of venture capital investors.[4] They argue that this perception of ventures requiring seed financing is due to a lack of evidence on the 'fitness' of the investee and high levels of 'agency risk'. Such agency risk refers to the incomplete alignment of investor and investee interests, which is often notable in the financing of knowledge-based ventures.[5]

For non-specialist investors, the area of seed-stage finance is seen as being fraught with 'chaotic uncertainty' and one that may build an insurmountable barrier between investee and investor.[6] As the venture capital industry evolves, it is expected to follow the investment-banking model, being operated chiefly by a few dominant players and supported by a small network of 'boutique' houses. This model compounds the issue of a funding gap, as the bigger players move away from seed-stage investment to a more passive, diversified portfolio strategy.

This gap, often described as the *valley of death*, embodies the particular challenges faced in the transition between basic research and commercial application, and where the lid becomes closed on a number of potentially profitable and commercial inventions. The valley of death constitutes market inefficiencies that create an imbalance between the demand and supply for particular amounts of finance. This inefficiency may result from increasing average investment levels, high risks and unproven returns, and inadequate deal flows.

Furthermore, the funding gap is the discrepancy that lies between the frames of reference of either the researcher or the investor. For example, research funds are often only available for 'blue sky' research and investment funds only for a validated business proposition. In between them, there are typically few finance sources available. Seed or early stage opportunities frequently go unconsidered by venture capitalists since the new project or company is not within their frame of reference. This issue is further compounded by the high-risk perception of seed-stage investments held by the traditional and institutional investors whose money actually constitutes venture capital funds.

This high-risk perception is often a product of the adverse experiences of investors in the market for seed-stage investment, as well as the imbalanced, asymmetrical relationship between researchers and investors. The researcher has a high degree of knowledge with regard to technology and feasibility, whilst the investor has knowledge of the market and is chiefly concerned with profitability. Investors that do take on seed-stage investments often find themselves faced with additional barriers in the form of lengthy lead times and extensive due diligence. For example, some pharmaceutical-based investments may take ten years or more to show a return on investment, and of course at a seed stage the financial risks are much higher. This is a particularly strong deterrent to venture capitalists who usually want to make a reasonably speedy exit with a 'sweet spot' of normally five to seven years. Due diligence is a crucial element of any funding decision and at the seed stage is often complex and extensive, since it is particularly difficult to anticipate the market for a product that as yet is unknown.

The role of government

The rapid growth of key knowledge-based companies in the US, such as Cisco Systems and Intel, has been partly due to the seed financing they received during their early development. However, there is evidence that many potentially promising start-ups are failing due to a lack of seed-stage finance. It has been argued that this is not a marginal case of market failure, but of private sector neglect of a major area of growth potential for a range of strategically important knowledge-based sectors.[7] In some ways this neglect is somewhat surprising, since it is only during the very early stages of a technology's life cycle that information asymmetries actually present investors with the opportunity to purchase intellectual property at a value lower than its potential economic worth.[8] However, venture capital investment is very much driven by macroeconomic conditions, growth cycles, and the overall global economic climate.

In the late 1990s, venture capital was booming, with investment extending into seed and very early stage ventures, particularly in the embryonic Internet sector. The dot.com crash that soon followed led to a rapid drying up of venture capital investment across the board, with the market for seed and early stage investment most drastically hit. This did not mean that there were fewer opportunities to invest in ventures requiring seed finance but that cash-strapped venture capitalists perceived a heightened risk to be associated with these ventures. The role of venture capitalists is to maximize the net return for investors in their fund, known as the internal rate of return (IRR). In general, ventures at a seed stage offer the opportunity for a very high IRR. However, in the aftermath of the dot.com crash, the high-risk perception led venture capitalists to turn more to lower-risk and lower-IRR investments, such as company expansions and buyouts.

This apparent private sector neglect and the funding gaps it causes have drawn government attention across the globe to the commercialization of knowledge. Knowledge commercialization policies have rapidly gained substantial government support in many areas of the world and are generally now seen as playing a pivotal role in the development of sustainable and prosperous regional and national economies. This commercialization emphasis has been accompanied by an increasing acknowledgement of the economic impact of small and start-up firms, with the importance of the two rising in tandem. Stimulating innovation and commercialization, particularly for small and start-up businesses, is seen by economic policymakers as crucial for improving and sustaining levels of competitiveness.

Knowledge commercialization policies have taken a number of forms, such as the provision of physical infrastructure in the shape of business incubators that act as hotbeds for the growth of knowledge-based projects and ventures, as well as more general business development support. Undoubtedly, the most innovative, as well as controversial, form of intervention has been the provision of seed finance, often in the form of equity capital, by governments or their agencies. One of the earliest movers in this field was Israel, now home to one of the most developed venture capital industries in the world. Much of this success is attributed to public sector intervention in the form of the Yozma fund, which was set up by the government in 1993. Credited as the first step in the expansion of Israel's venture capital industry, Yozma provides 40 percent of the capital for venture capital companies, and since its establishment has formed ten drop-down funds, each capitalized with over US$20 million. Its early success and subsequent privatization are indications of the potential for public sector-financed seed funds to stimulate the venture capital industry and ensure its sustainability. Our research has identified that more than 100 similar funds have now been created in many parts of the world at either a national or a regional level. Among such funds are Scotland's proof of concept fund, the US's Advanced Technology Program, and Australia's Pre-Seed Fund.

Scotland's proof of concept fund

Scottish Enterprise, Scotland's main regional development agency, established its proof of concept fund in 1999, with close ties to the region's cluster building strategies. It is primarily geared at increasing commercialization activity within Scottish universities as well as the National Health Service in the region. The fund supports only the commercialization of public sector and university-generated innovations, and due to public finance regulations is unable to attract co-investment from the private sector. Funded projects benefit from an average capital injection of usually between US$200,000 and US$275,000, with a clause that they do not engage with private sector financiers prior to completion of a 12–24 month commercialization process. In recent years, the fund has been committed to investing approximately US$20 million annually.

As the fund is tied to investment opportunities linked with the region's cluster strategy and its eligibility is restricted to one of the cluster streams, ventures with cross-platform technologies can be limited in their ability to apply for funding. These constraints prevent the fund from operating on similar terms to the private sector, and potentially profitable opportunities are perhaps lost as a result of the stringent regulations. The absence of private sector funding involvement during the funding period may also limit the ability to forge relationships with financiers who may want to invest in future funding rounds.

There is often the prevalence of an 'academic culture' toward the use of seed finance, and in Scotland some researchers use the finance for the continuation of a research project rather than specifically to work toward the commercialization of intellectual property, restricting the fund's ability to meet its commercial objectives. There have been some successes though; for example, Brinker Technologies is a spin-out company from Aberdeen University that has attracted serious American market interest for its pipe engineering products. The academic entrepreneur behind Brinker notes that it would have been difficult to commercialize the research without the support of the fund.

The United States' Advanced Technology Program

The Advanced Technology Program (ATP), part of the National Institute of Standards and Technology (NIST) in the US, was established in 1988 with the purpose of encouraging businesses that could potentially advance national economic benefit. The ATP is involved in commercialization activities from both public and private sector sources, not restricting the source of applications. Since 1990, the ATP has funded more than 600 projects, with a cumulative funding of US$3.5 billion. The funding method requires the use of both public and private sector funding. The ATP funds only the direct costs associated with an innovation, requiring all indirect costs to be paid by private sector sources. Applicants are therefore required to undertake considerable capital-raising activities themselves.

Placing such an onus on the applicant to raise a portion of the required capital encourages a commitment to the commercialization process. This is not always evident where only public sector sources provide the capital. The ATP has experienced considerable success and financed over 100 commercialized technologies, with some 60 percent of the program's small, single applicant companies doubling in size. The insistence on private sector financial involvement is aided by the fact that the ability to attract ATP funding is seen as providing credibility in a bid to secure future venture capital investment. Success stories include an estimated US$30 billion economic benefit gained from seven ATP-funded tissue engineering projects and two ATP-funded companies that are now featured in the Fortune Fastest Growing Companies List.

Australia's Pre-Seed Fund

Australia's Pre-Seed Fund is a public-private partnership initiative aimed at the earliest stages of commercialization, supporting projects from the public sector and universities. The overall Pre-Seed Program has been developed as part of Australia's wider innovation strategy and is demonstrative of the close relationship between public sector seed funds and wider economic development aims and objectives.

The fund consists of both public (approximately US$20 million) and private sector (US$55 million) finance, matching a portion of the public sector capital 'pot' with the private sector finance through four drop-down funds. It funds individual projects to a maximum limit of US$0.75 million. Each fund is administered by a private sector fund manager who, with a 'hands on' approach, provides both management and technical advice to investees. The managers are sourced globally, aiding the process of credibility building and lending a strong commercial focus to the fund. They also provide additional and wider networking opportunities that may open additional avenues of deal flow.

Of course, the fund is ultimately the responsibility of the state, and for this reason a number of regulations have been applied, including the need to invest at least 60 percent of the fund's capital within five years. Any public sector-based seed fund is, by necessity, subject to certain regulations governing the use of tax payers' money and must adopt an approach whose primary goal is to assist economic growth. However, this fund shows that such regulations can be structured in a way that builds flexibility into the system and allows for an operation to be as commercial in its approach as possible.

The design of seed funds

Of the public sector seed funds we have studied, the vast majority attempt to combine private sector expectations with a public policymaking requirement for stimulating broader economic benefit. The two key objectives are a need for returns on investment and economic benefits usually in the form of job creation. The establishment of a public sector seed fund is also a means of signaling the benefits of seed-stage investment to the private sector. Some public sector funds have a further objective of attempting to create a sustainable fund that will no longer require further injections of public money.

Most seed funds operate almost exclusively at this stage of development, with no plans to become involved in any subsequent rounds of funding. This suggests that seed-fund activity is significantly different from traditional stages of venture capital and requires specialist seed-stage staff and management. Some seed funds operate with a specific sector focus, with the life/medical sciences and IT being the most important sectors for the funds in our survey. The majority of funds (75 percent) source projects from both public and private sectors, with approximately one-half of funds combining investment received from both public and private sectors. Public sector funds without an input from private sector investors are usually limited by state regulations that do not permit the mixing and matching of public and private sector finance.

The key method of accessing and attracting suitable projects is networking and referral, which is most often associated with financial intermediaries, such as banks and accountancy firms. Some seed funds use venture scouting or *field engineers* to forge relationships with universities and other research establishments. These relationships play an important role in helping to reduce wariness and mistrust between researchers and fund managers. The operators of some seed funds recognize the danger of relying upon fund managers with traditional venture capital experience. They are viewed as having operated in a culture that is relatively risk averse and may be uncomfortable with the greater level of risk associated with seed-stage investments.

The majority of seed funds (76 percent in our survey) take some form of financial stake in the projects they invest in, normally in the form of an equity holding as per typical venture capital investments. This stake varies from anything between 20 percent and 80 percent and is dependent upon the sums invested and the involvement of any co-investors. Aside from an equity holding, many funds also take other stakes such as board membership, which provide fund managers with an additional element of control and security. The most common and significant criteria used by seed funds in assessing whether or not to fund a particular project are technical integrity and commercial potential. These are determined according to due diligence, especially competitor analysis and market forecasting, as well as issues relating to IP protection and ownership.

As part of this process, fund mangers identify the strength of the management team as the most significant factor when considering applications. It is considered vital that a strong management team is already in place, or at a minimum there is a willingness amongst project researchers and leaders to be flexible in their approach to 'bringing in' a strong management team. Alongside management, the market opportunity for commercial exploitation and the potential to attract later rounds of funding is a key issue for many fund managers. This is particularly important, as seed funds are based on the expectation of achieving a relatively early opportunity for exit, enabling ventures to progress further up the venture capital ladder. Finally, IP ownership is also rated highly by fund mangers. If IP cannot at least be partly obtained or negotiated, fund managers are often less inclined to provide financing.

The mean average number of investments made by the seed funds we surveyed is 8.5 per annum. The relatively small number of average investments is indicative of the time, risk, and extensive due diligence required to prepare a proof of concept investment for commercialization. Forty percent of funds in our study provide investment of between US$350,000 and US$1 million per venture, with a further one-quarter of funds providing investment of less than US$350,000. Twenty percent offer investment of between US$1 million and US$1.75 million per venture, with the remaining 13 percent offering funding beyond these limits.

Funding limits are tied to milestones of achievement, which are used to ensure that the seed fund does not stray out of the realms of 'seed stage' activity. As most funds have an underpinning economic development rationale, there is often a geographical aspect to eligibility, with funded ventures usually having to be located in the nation or region for which the policymakers responsible for fund implementation have jurisdiction. Alongside the actual financial investment in projects, most seed funds offer additional services such as business planning, IPR analysis, mentoring, and venture capital introduction schemes. These additional services are seen as a means of adding value to investments. The mean average IRR for the funds we surveyed is 18 percent, which is in line with the returns often achieved by venture capitalists on their early stage investments, although this is obviously subject to significant volatility and variance. According to the fund managers, maintaining quality deal flow and accessing quality projects are key future challenges to the sustainability and performance of their funds.

Universities and knowledge-based venturing

The focus of many public sector seed funds has been to stimulate the commercialization of the knowledge and research residing and undertaken in universities. This has occurred as universities have come to be viewed as an increasingly important stimulant of economic growth.[9] These developments have been coupled with notions of 'entrepreneurial universities' and 'academic entrepreneurs' that are closely involved in venturing and commercialization activities such as the establishment of spin-out firms and the exploitation of IPR through the licensing of technology and patent registration.[10] Such activities are typically seen as the key forms of knowledge and technology transfer from universities. However, it has been found that an inability to obtain finance results in many university knowledge-based ventures being abandoned, constraining the potential of universities to become key levers within the knowledge-based economy.[11]

Our research on the university sector in London finds that significant involvement in knowledge commercialization is still limited to a relatively small number of universities.[12] London is an interesting test bed since it is the location of one of the highest concentrations of universities in the world (39 in all, accounting for approximately 25 percent of the UK's total), as well as being one of the world's leading financial and business centers – approximately 75 percent of UK venture capitalists are located in London.[13] As shown in Table 8.1, London is the second highest ranked European region in terms of private equity investment on a per capita basis (private equity referring to finance provided in the form of venture capital and buyouts to companies that are not quoted on a stock market). Therefore, it is a key location both for the generation of knowledge and of the potential finance to commercialize it.

Many of the resources associated with successful knowledge commercialization are skewed toward London's larger and more prestigious universities. Substantial company spin-out activity is restricted to only a handful of universities,

Table 8.1 Private equity investment per capita among the world's leading knowledge economy regions (US$)

San Francisco–Oakland–Fremont, US	1,441
San Jose–Sunnyvale–Santa Clara, US	1,441
Boston–Cambridge–Quincy, US	639
Hartford, US	639
San Diego–Carlsbad–San Marcos, US	368
Denver–Aurora, US	363
Stockholm, Sweden	326
London, UK	268
Île de France, France	268
Baltimore–Towson, US	175
Washington–Arlington–Alexandria, US	175
Portland–Vancouver–Beaverton, US	168
Seattle–Tacoma–Bellevue, US	168
South East, UK	158
Uusimaa, Finland	155
Quebec, Canada	146
West, Sweden	143
Austin–Round Rock, US	139
Dallas–Fort Worth–Arlington, US	139
Houston–Sugar Land–Baytown, US	139

Source: Huggins *et al.*, *World Knowledge Competitiveness Index 2005*, Pontypridd: Robert Huggins Associates, 2005.

resulting in the existence of a large knowledge–commercialization divide across the region. This divide in knowledge commercialization performance can be summed up by a three-tier system: an upper-tier of universities that are intensively involved in knowledge commercialization processes – often at a global level – through licensing, patenting and spin-out activities, a middle-tier that is seeking to intensify their knowledge commercialization activities but are failing to fulfil their potential due to both internal and external restrictions, and a group of lower-tier universities that have not prioritized knowledge commercialization activities and do not view them as core to their overall strategic vision.

In general, the lower-tier universities lack awareness of the potential gains from such activities and have adopted few measures aimed at addressing commercialization barriers. In terms of the differing knowledge commercialization approaches adopted by universities across the three groups, one of the key differences is whether or not the university possesses a unit, office, or company dedicated to the management of knowledge-based venturing. Of the top-ranked universities, 80 percent have established a specific entity aimed at managing the commercialization of research, compared with only 25 percent of the bottom-ranked universities.

For the universities surveyed, the most significant problem to knowledge commercialization activities is the lack of time academics are able to contribute to such activities (68 percent of the respondents). This is followed by a lack of management acumen and skills to develop efficient and effective knowledge commercialization systems (64 percent), difficulties in accessing relevant finance and funding relating to proof of concept and early stage development (44 percent), accessibility of the appropriate space and physical infrastructure necessary to establish new spin-out firms (36 percent), and difficulties in undertaking relevant market research (36 percent).

It is useful to interpret the lack of time factor as a stated barrier to involvement in knowledge commercialization processes. We view this apparent lack of time to be a measure of the significance most universities and their academics currently place (or are able to place) on commercialization activities, compared to their more traditional pursuits. The value and rewards structure of the university system in the UK is still primarily geared toward traditional academic outputs, working against the adoption of knowledge commercialization activities, and to a large extent is reflective of the lack of development toward alleviating the key barriers highlighted above.

For the top-ranked knowledge commercializing universities, the most significant constraint on future development is the lack of appropriate management skills. These universities have the infrastructure requirements for knowledge commercialization in place and are in a position where human capital factors are the focus for continuing and improving their knowledge commercialization capabilities. The most significant barrier among the middle-ranked universities is the difficulty in accessing seed funding. This indicates that the middle-ranked universities are unable to compete with their top-ranked counterparts in obtaining a significant slice of the seed funding cake available to universities. Amongst the bottom-ranked universities, the most important barriers are the lack of time and management skills. Across the three tiers of universities, a key factor underpinning these perceived barriers is the lack of transparent and visible networks and communication channels linking the academic, financial, and business intermediary sectors. This results in information asymmetries among the parties involved and an inability of the university sector to externally access relevant resources.

Seed finance

The primary and secondary sources of seed financing accessed by universities are shown in Table 8.2. Seed finance is drawn from a variety of internal and external sources, with many institutions accessing funds from several different sources. The most important funding sources are specialist funds created and funded within universities. The University Challenge Fund (UCF) is the next most important source and the main source of funding for one-fifth of all universities. The UCF is the most important UK national policy development relating to the seed financing of university knowledge commercialization. The purpose of the UCF is to enable universities to establish seed funds for proof of concept and early stage knowledge-based venturing. The UCF has recently been incorporated within a wider Higher Education Innovation Fund (HEIF), aimed at supporting knowledge transfer from universities through a number of channels and to a range of communities.

Table 8.2 Sources of seed financing for London's universities (% of respondents)

Source of finance	*Main source*	*Secondary source*
Specialist funds created by the universities	36	48
University Challenge Funding	20	32
Higher Education Funding Council for England	12	44
Private sector seed or venture capital	8	36
Government grants or loans	4	44
EU programme funds or loans	0	20
Wellcome Trust	0	16
Other charity, trust or research foundation	0	8
Other	0	4

Source: Huggins, 'Universities and knowledge-based venturing'.

This public sector involvement underlines the further development of the 'triple helix' model of university–industry–government interactions in the field of innovation and commercialization, with government increasingly acting as a public entrepreneur and venture capitalist.[14] However, public sector seed funding has been skewed toward the top-ranked universities, all of which had accessed seed funding from at least two public sector funds at the time of the survey. Slightly less than two-thirds (63 percent) of the middle-ranked universities and only 33 percent of the bottom-ranked universities had accessed two or more funds. This suggests that London's triple helix does not fully intertwine the breadth of the region's university sector.

Private sector seed or venture sector capital is the primary source of finance for only 8 percent of the universities surveyed in our study and is a secondary source for a further 36 percent. Almost two-thirds (64 percent) have no experience of private sector involvement in gaining seed financing for their knowledge commercialization activities. Private sector involvement most commonly takes place through the provision of equity in return for seed financing. This again is most prevalent among the top-ranked universities, with 60 percent involved in seed financing through private equity stakes. However, only one institution has experience of gaining finance through corporate venturing, whereby established corporations directly provide equity capital in return for a stake in the development of a university-based venture or project. This is a very low number given the strength of the region's business sector.

Those universities gaining significant amounts of public funding are also more likely to access private funding, with a very high correlation between the two across institutions. The relationship between the two modes of financing substantiates the view provided by key actors in the region that public sector funding acts as a signal for private sector involvement. Although public sector financing could have the effect of crowding out private investment, a pan-European analysis shows similar evidence of public investment acting as a signal to private investors, primarily through the demonstration of legitimacy.[15]

In his review of the funding of new technology-based firms in the UK, Ray

Oakey argues for the better integration of public and private sector funding, which, as he says, should not be seen as 'oil' and 'water'.[16] In general, where such private sector investment is provided, it comes from either venture capitalists or business angels. Major banks are very unlikely to invest in university ventures and will only lend money once significant equity is in place. Alongside public sector money, the academic entrepreneur's own money or money from friends and family – so-called 'hurt money' – can also act as a signal for potential investors.

According to university fund managers interviewed by the study, potential private sector investors in university spin-outs rarely understand the technology underpinning a proposed venture and often make an incorrect judgment as to the level of risk involved. Conversely, members of the finance community consider that potential academic entrepreneurs are rarely able to effectively and fully demonstrate their ideas. Public sector financing is seen by both groups as playing an important role in alleviating these information asymmetries. It facilitates the effective demonstration of technology and ensures a realistic assessment of the risks involved.

Management resources

According to members of the finance community, an apparent lack of managerial skills within universities is a key deterrent to venture capitalists and business angels (i.e. high net-worth individual investors) investing in university knowledge-based ventures and, in particular, spin-out companies. As one fund manager put it: 'Forget the finance gap, there is a management chasm.' A leading banker added:

> A lot of scientists will have good ideas, but will have no business acumen at all. There is a big need for skills on the management side ... the quality of business plans is absolutely grotesque – below that of someone studying a business studies course.

One financier pointed out a critical divide between the UK and the US:

> Even basic financial management skills are often lacking amongst [UK] academics that seek to commercialize their ideas. There is still a staggering ignorance amongst intellectuals. For example, a lot of academics don't know what equity is. This is one cultural difference that exists between the US and the UK. Academics in the UK desperately need to be trained in the workings of the commercial world if they are to be successful in any commercialization of their work.

One of the key explanations for this UK–US differential is experience and accumulated knowledge, as the US has been involved in public sector knowledge transfer activities significantly longer than the UK.[17] A key deficiency lies in the relative quality and range of skills contained within the Technology Transfer Offices (TTOs) of UK universities compared with those in the US.[18] TTOs are seen to lack the degree of professionalism required when dealing with the private sector. In particular, the relative 'quality of personnel' is seen as leading to a structural failure of the commercialization process in many universities.

In the US, there is evidence that the compensation received by TTO personnel has an impact on the effectiveness of the office.[19] In many advanced regional and national economies, with a generally well-remunerated private business and financial sector, it is likely that university technology transfer officers will be less well remunerated than those undertaking a similar role in the private sector. It is also probable that the level and speed of engagement required by those operating in the financial and business sector is out of step with the more long-term process of engagement undertaken by many universities. Indeed, in the eyes of a number of our interviewees, there is often a wide cultural divide between universities and businesses which has led to 'deal breakdown'.

While there may be a deficiency of management skills in many universities, it is also important to recognize that there should not be a dilution of technical expertise by making academics concentrate their efforts upon managerial issues – as one business-university intermediary put it: 'We don't want to make the world's best scientists mediocre businessmen.' A solution to this is the transfer of strong management skills from the private sector. One business angel network manager stated that: 'Academics will not entirely change – a large proportion of academics never touch life outside academia. It is better to bring in managerial expertise rather than expect academics to change.'

'Surrogate' or 'interim' management not only gives a university venture the commercial acumen required to move it forward but also assists academics in their long-term approach to commercialization activities. Furthermore, interim management should have a degree of investment in the venture. This ensures that they have an incentive to make the venture successful and become involved with ventures that best suit their particular managerial skills and field of specialization.

There are a number of mechanisms available for developing interim management, such as 'parachuting' in managerial expertise or mentors, using managerial networks for academics seeking managerial skills to augment their commercialization activities, and utilizing business angels as a managerial resource. As stated above, these mechanisms are primarily based on building management teams through importing management skills from the private sector. However, there is often only fragmented knowledge of those managers and mentors who are available and best suited to working with the academic community on knowledge commercialization ventures. The relative success of knowledge commercialization activities in the US, particularly compared with most parts of Europe, has relied far more on the development of strong networks with the venture capital community, which are often facilitated through a rich infrastructure of intermediary organizations.[20]

In the US, a key role of these intermediary organizations is to make spin-outs and start-ups 'investment ready', that is, to have in place the managerial and technological framework and plans that allow them to negotiate with venture capitalists and business angels on a level playing field. In the UK, by contrast, there is evidence of significant deficiencies in the investment readiness of many knowledge-based ventures that are either tabled or have the potential to be tabled to financiers.[21]

Network capital

Networks play an important role in controlling access to finance, acting as the 'pipes and prisms of the market'.[22] From a venturing perspective, network capital is integral to securing resources and obtaining legitimacy. The ability to access external finance through networks is an important predictor of the performance of start-up ventures.[23] From our research in London, we found that networks between the academic and finance communities generally lack either visibility or transparency.[24] The following statements are indicative of the views of the key actors in the region:

> There is little connection between actors in London. There is confusion and the match-up [between potential investors and investees] is atrocious.

> London is a bit like a fog – the challenge for the region is to exploit the capacity and break down insularity … we need to increase [regional] institution to institution dealings.

These statements suggest that poor underlying network conditions make accessing finance problematic for those academics seeking to commercialize their research and knowledge. Other research similarly finds that poor network conditions, manifested by a lack of ties between entrepreneurs and venture financiers, result in the existence of information asymmetries between both parties.[25] The lack of effective interactions between universities and the finance community has a negative effect on the commercialization of knowledge not just in terms of financing, but also in terms of exchanging expertise and experience.

Rebecca Harding argues that the equity gap is itself a manifestation of the existence of information asymmetry.[26] Potential investees do not have access to the relevant networks and intelligence needed to make an effective case for financing and cannot, therefore, effectively demonstrate their ideas. This equates with evidence showing that new ventures founded by entrepreneurs that already have direct and indirect relationships with venture investors are more likely to receive venture funding and are less likely to fail.[27] Similarly, we found evidence of a number of university ventures that should have been able to attract private sector financing but were instead 'put-on-the-shelf' due to a lack of effective engagement with those financiers capable of making a significant investment.

To a large extent, the poor networkability of London is related to the sheer size and number of players within its financial community. This leads to networks between actors that are at best disjointed and at worst disconnected. An alarming finding from our survey is that most of our interviewees do not have a complete view of all the relevant actors, and that much of the network remains *uncharted*. For the most important players – both financial and academic – the reach of their networks is global with many venture capitalists dealing purely at an international level and leading universities establishing commercial alliances with other leading universities and multinationals around the world.

The international nature of London's venture capital community is somewhat contrary to those who argue that venture capital investments are usually made locally and are reliant on a network of local contacts.[28] More in line with our findings, there is evidence that while finance and knowledge-based activities are often spatially clustered, older and larger venture capital firms tend to make more non-local investments in more commercially advanced projects.[29] This is supported by Olav Sorenson and Toby Stuart who find that venture capitalists involved in axial positions with large scale syndicated projects are more likely to invest in spatially distant companies.[30] London's venture capitalists appear to conform to these wider spatial investment patterns.

International comparisons

In order to gain a better understanding of the variation in university involvement in knowledge commercialization, it is useful to compare outputs at an international level. Although there are currently few sources of comparable data, one survey has shown that while leading universities in the US annually spin out 2.8 new companies per institution, universities in the UK achieve an average of only 1.3 spin-outs per institution. The mean average licenses granted to the US universities is 23.2 per annum, compared with only 3.8 per annum in the UK, resulting in average annual license income of US$6.6 million per US institution and US$365,000 per UK institution. As for license income as a percentage of the total research expenditure, US universities generate 2.8 percent compared with 1.1 percent in the UK universities.[31] Although we must exercise some caution in the interpretation of this data – since the US sample is limited to 142 leading universities, while for the UK it covers all 164 institutions – it does highlight a significant difference in knowledge commercialization performance.

This gap is all the more interesting, given that existing evidence informs us that even in the US there is still a significant gap in the seed capital required by technology-based new ventures.[32] An increasingly popular bridge mechanism in the US is the formation of strategic alliances between embryonic ventures and larger firms or organizations through corporate venturing. As well as gaining access to seed capital, the alliances are used to access complementary tangible and intangible assets, such as embodied technologies, patents, know-how, and distribution networks.[33]

There is little evidence that such corporate venturing activity is permeating the European economy, which may in part be due to differences in the economic structure between Europe and the US. For instance, the US economy is driven to a greater degree by the actions and activities of its large corporations than is the case in Europe, which has a greater reliance on its SME base. In other words, Europe does not possess the same depth of large corporations with a capacity to become involved in activities related to this form of strategic alliance development and corporate venturing.

Brent Goldfarb and Magnus Henrekson have undertaken an interesting study of the US–Europe commercialization gap, arguing that despite the seeming success of Sweden's university system, the commercialization rate of academic results is low when compared with the US.[34] They conclude that this is at least partly due to top-down national policies in Sweden stifling and discouraging universities from actively commercializing their knowledge and research – a situation not dissimilar to that found in the UK.

The Swedish model, which in many respects is similar to that in the rest of Europe, creates strong disincentives toward academics to undertake knowledge transfer activities aimed at the commercial sector, especially the establishment of spin-out companies. Despite the implementation by the Swedish government of numerous technology-transfer initiatives aimed at universities, the key barometer of success for universities has continued to be academic results, with a lack of incentives for universities to become involved in the commercialization of their ideas. Therefore, there are little upside gains to be made and considerable downside risks in terms of the esteem which government funding bodies hold for particular institutions. Goldfard and Henrekson argue that the introduction of the Bayh-Dole Act in 1980 in the US, which gave universities – rather than individual researchers – title to innovations established in its confines, has created a more vibrant and decentralized system of knowledge transfer and commercialization.[35] The US system is more bottom-up due to the experimentation it has facilitated in the way university policy can best exploit IP.

The Bayh–Dole Act has furthered the role of US universities as drivers of their regional business communities, many of which have traditionally been key actors in forming part of knowledge clusters in the US. Indeed, the clusters of Silicon Valley in California, Route 128 in Boston, and the Research Triangle in North Carolina have evolved around the universities of Stanford, MIT, and Chapel Hill respectively.

Conclusions

In the knowledge economy, the world of finance needs to develop strong links across the public and private sectors. Unless this occurs, potential entrepreneurs may not have the opportunity to fully exploit their knowledge and ideas for the benefit of themselves and the economies they operate in. As Josh Lerner argues, there is a need for public officials to invest in building relationships with the finance and venture capital sector.[36] There is evidence of market failure in the provision of seed finance to knowledge-intensive business ventures. The extent of government interest in seed finance provision across the globe implies the inability of the private sector to satisfy the market.

Even in an economy as strong as London, substantial spin-out and other commercialization activities are restricted to only a small number of universities, highlighting the existence of a large knowledge-commercialization divide. However, government intervention will only succeed in its goals of catalyzing commercialization and economic development, if it is perceived as credible to both entrepreneurs and the venture capital community. A long-standing complaint with government initiatives is that they are constrained by politics and are unable to react as quickly as the private sector to changes in the market. Political procrastination is potentially the death knell of seed finance mechanisms. Furthermore, such funds should not be considered a panacea, since seed finance alone is not sufficient to stimulate successful knowledge-based entrepreneurship. As we have seen, it also requires strong accompanying amounts of human and network capital.

Policymakers must not compromise the integrity of seed financing policies to satisfy short-term political requirements. Expectations should be managed carefully, making it clear that such finance is just one tool in the pursuit of increased knowledge-based entrepreneurship. Importantly, there should be an avoidance of grant-based financing for commercialization activity. Grant-based funding encourages an artificial security in many nations and regions that are already overly dependent upon it and fails in its objective of signaling opportunity to the private sector. In short, offering such seemingly 'easy money' is counterproductive. Finally, funds of this nature are clearly, politically sensitive initiatives and will only be sustainable if they can show that they are making a difference, or as one fund manager told us: 'Bend the trend or don't bother.'

9 Conclusion

We have highlighted three processes in the knowledge-based economy: the increased importance of innovation to *growing* businesses and economies, the accumulated capacity of *creating* knowledge and its changing distribution across the globe, and the growing significance of *connecting* knowledge across organizations, places, and disciplines. First, the knowledge economy has fundamentally shifted the way in which the value of both firms and economies are measured. In the past, although sources of knowledge such as research and development were important for some sectors, labor and physical capital were largely the dominant resources upon which competitive advantage was achieved. Over the years, the playing field for accessing labor and physical capital has become more level across both firms and economies. It is now the ability to access and utilize knowledge that has become the core means of enhancing business and economic competitiveness. The first priority in the knowledge race is innovation. Second, with this change in priorities in the race, there has been a growing accumulation of human capital creating and utilizing knowledge. The development accompanying this is the changing global map of knowledge creation capacity. The distinguished economist Joseph Stiglitz argues that there are five core elements underpinning globalization: capital market liberalization, foreign direct investment, the movement of labor, trade, and knowledge.[1] According to Stiglitz,

> At the top of the list is globalization of knowledge, the free flow of ideas that has followed the lowering of communication costs and the closer integration of societies. The transfer of that knowledge, which globalization has facilitated, is likely to prove one of the strongest forces for growth in emerging markets in coming decades.[2]

As described throughout this book, the changing global map of knowledge creation capacity underlies the globalization of knowledge. Indeed, by the end of 2006, China had overtaken Japan in R&D spending, becoming the world's second highest national research spender. Recording a growth of 77 percent between 1995 and 2004, China now has the second largest number of researchers (926,000), just behind the United States (with more than 1.3 million).[3] Advanced economies are now facing competition from well-educated, yet still low-wage, entrepreneurs and workers in newly emerging economies like China and India.

Third, both firms and economies are trying to capitalize on the synergy and creativity arising from sharing and connecting knowledge. This is not only because of the *non-rival* and *non-excludable* characteristics of knowledge, but also because of the availability of new modes by which to transfer and network knowledge. One of the key thrusts of technical progress during the last few centuries is the growth of technology aimed at sharing knowledge. The invention of the printing press is a prime example of such technical progress, which made it possible to diffuse and share knowledge to a far greater number of people than before. Advances in telecommunications link previously stand-alone computers and allow people to transfer and share information at a faster speed across the globe. Furthermore, the economic systems of advanced nations and regions are increasingly geared toward knowledge sharing. As we saw in Chapter 8, advanced economies have introduced new mechanisms of financing ventures, primarily aimed at facilitating the further integration of universities with profit-seeking businesses. Knowledge clusters, the subject of Chapter 5, are an expression of maximized knowledge sharing through interactions both within and increasingly across clusters. Furthermore, our concept of network capital is a tool that signifies the importance of relational ties for knowledge sharing between organizations. Economies are able to sustain economic growth only through such technical progress and changes in their economic systems.

The corporate management of innovation

The focus of innovation management has radically shifted from the timing of entry into a new market to the creation of sustainable competencies and knowledge. In the past, a key issue concerned whether or not to develop a new product as a first-to-market entrant or to follow a pioneer by imitating their product. This assumed successive stages within the product/industry life cycle, with firms aiming to dominate a mass market at a late, mature stage. Protection of a leading market position through the creation of entry barriers was a key to survival, employing a number of defense mechanisms such as patents, brands, and standards. However, as product cycles have shortened and disruptive changes become more frequent, the domination of the market at a mature stage has become less relevant to a growing number of industries, particularly high-technology industries, since the relatively stable market conditions of the past are disappearing.

Along with the creation of sustainable competences, which first emerged in the 1990s as a means of successfully innovating under the new market conditions, there has been a growing trend for firms to *open up* the innovation process. An increasing number of products and services have become technologically more complex, consisting of a number of distinct technologies. For instance, Apple Inc's iPod contains a number of technologies including signal compression, DRAM cache, LCD display, lithium-ion battery, and micro hard drive. Without any of these, iPod would not take its current form. At the same time, each scientist and engineer involved in the development of the iPod and other technologically advanced products is faced with the need to master a growing amount of knowledge to keep abreast of leading edge developments. As we discussed in Chapter 2, this results in these scientists and engineers becoming increasingly specialized. When these two forces (distinct technologies and knowledge specialization) combine, firms – with the exception of a few very large corporations – will not have all the knowledge relevant to the goods and services under their control. At this point, firms realize the significance of opening up their innovation processes by searching for external knowledge sources, evaluating externally owned technologies, as well as undertaking and managing collaboration with external knowledge sources. Such opening up of the innovation process even extends to passing part of the innovation process to users and consumers.[4]

The major issue for innovation management is how to manage this opened-up innovation process and, in particular, how to exploit diversity within an external environment and translate it into a firm's internal competencies. Through both case studies and large-scale surveys, there is evidence of some success being achieved in managing knowledge diversity within the firm through the use of functional teams and concurrent engineering. As for external knowledge sourcing, there is a growing body of studies on different forms of strategic alliances and their management.[5] However, we have yet to see any conclusive evidence as to whether or not economies with a high degree of diversity in an industry or technology mix are more innovative.[6] While there is a possibility that the methodologies employed in these studies are not good enough to detect the causality, it is also possible that the majority of firms have not yet developed techniques to exploit diversity within an external environment. There is even a possibility that when exploiting diversity firms go beyond their immediate environment and scan external sources at a global scale.

The rise of Internet-based search engines is also transforming approaches to building knowledge at the individual level. Before search engines appeared, long periods of training were often required to learn a subject's (i.e. a particular discipline or type of knowledge) structure, which was used as the guiding tool in searching for relevant knowledge. This search process assumes, as Wesley Cohen and Daniel Levinthal suggest, the importance of accumulated learning efforts through which knowledge is evaluated and absorbed. By contrast, knowledge search using Internet search engines relies more on the underlying principle of networks. For instance, *Google* lists search results according to a set of criteria, such as the number of links to other sites, with the importance of these linked sites based again on the number of links they possess. The more linked a site is to others, the more important it is deemed. This evaluation does not assume learning of a subject's structure. Rather, it is the position of a knowledge source within a network, or whether the source is a node in a network or not, that decides its importance. In the Internet age, we build our knowledge by following links between popular nodes over the Internet's space.

At first sight, *Google* style knowledge search and building would seem more likely to make use of the diversity of users as a means of sparking creativity.

Yet, a herd mentality logic lies behind it. While *Google* drew upon the criteria for the evaluation of academic articles made by specialist groups (i.e. the more cited by others, the more important an academic article is deemed), it opens up the process of knowledge source evaluation to an anonymous mass of Internet users. When buying a good or service from the Internet, it is relatively easy to make comparisons of price, delivery time and the like before deciding on which website to purchase from. By contrast, when searching for knowledge, there is the increased risk of relying upon judgments made by others, who may or may not have the ability to correctly judge the authenticity and validity of the knowledge or its source. Given the growing significance of the Internet across disciplines, this emerges as an issue of importance for future knowledge building.

The policy management of competitiveness

For policymakers, improving competitiveness through economic development in the age of the knowledge-based economy represents a range of significant and difficult-to-achieve challenges. As we have seen, although more knowledge is being generated, meaningful innovations are harder to come by. Growth in the number of knowledge workers does not necessarily equate with the growth of knowledge productivity. The studies we have presented demonstrate the need for policy managers engaged in the competitiveness agenda to assist the development of a balanced set of competencies in their respective economy. A short-sighted focus upon the accumulation of a single type of capital or resource is unlikely to achieve a significant impact. For example, the recent policy emphasis upon clusters and networking is a case in point. Unless clusters and networks are able to create and transfer state-of-the-art knowledge, they will result in the sharing of mediocre expertise with little positive impact on competitiveness. Similarly, a lack of investment in the absorptive capacity of firms will result in a failure to put externally gained knowledge into practice. Policymakers and policy managers must encourage and assist firms to make balanced investments in the whole range of knowledge resources discussed throughout this book. Imitating or copying only one aspect of best performance will lead lagging nations and regions nowhere.

In this respect, it is impossible for us to conclude with specific policy recommendations as to how particular places should go about improving their competitiveness in the knowledge-based economy, as each nation or region has a unique combination of requirements. However, it is possible to highlight some broader strategic guidance as to how knowledge-based competitiveness policies should be configured. First, it is clear that a knowledge-rich environment and economy requires a strong supportive infrastructure. This consists of the ability to access the physical (including ICT) and financial capital to effectively create, transfer, and commercialize knowledge, but perhaps more importantly, the network capital that sustains these knowledge processes. We have discussed that while policymaking in recent years has tended to focus on building and utilizing social capital, it now needs to be strongly complemented by the generation of network capital, in the form of strategically managed – or *calculative* – links and interactions between firms and other knowledge-based organizations. While social capital is important in building local interactions and linkages, network capital is required to build and manage the more global knowledge networks, which are crucial to ensuring future competitiveness.

Second, once a supportive development infrastructure is in place, attention should be paid to creation of knowledge. If an economy is under-performing in terms of investment in knowledge through R&D, there is often little option other than government attempting to stimulate private sector investment by either increasing its own R&D expenditure or improving links between relevant sectors. In order to produce a positive R&D multiplier, it is vital that government itself creates networks with the private sector to enable the effective transfer of knowledge from government-funded R&D projects to firms, which are then catalyzed to undertake further R&D in a bid to commercialize the output of the initial investment. Such policies are already in place in many nations and regions, with increased public sector investment most usually being routed through the university and higher-education sector. However, given the broad remit of this sector, extending from education (i.e. the formation of next-generation human capital) to basic and applied research, it is often difficult for them to prioritize their R&D engagement with the private sector, specifically in the places they are located (e.g. top universities are often more likely to be collaborating with multinationals headquartered elsewhere). This suggests that investment is made in other areas, such as the funding of intermediary organizations that can transfer the outputs of academic research into the private sector in a form conducive to its utilization by firms (i.e. the translation of academic research outputs into a near-market form).

Third, entrepreneurship measures should make a departure from job creation to knowledge-based business formation as their core goal. Entrepreneurship is now established as a major pillar of most competitiveness and economic development strategies. However, the nature and type of entrepreneurship is often unexplored, resulting in an 'any new business will do' attitude being implicit in many policies. Clearly, more focus is required, and although it may sound simplistic, it should be stressed that an economy pursuing a knowledge-based policy approach should prioritize knowledge-driven entrepreneurship. Such prioritization should ensure that entrepreneurs with *sound* ideas and visions for creating high value-added businesses have access to the networks, skills, knowledge sources, working environments, and financial capital we have emphasized in this book.

The outcome of these support measures and interventions must be primarily geared toward developing an economy's tradability and external markets through the creation of innovative goods and services that are in high demand. As discussed throughout this book, securing and sustaining such demand in the knowledge economy is very much a long-term effort. Although we may see sprinters winning short-term gains, the nature of the global race is that of a marathon. Stakeholders at all levels – individuals, firms, regions, and nations –

must recognize the importance of innovative capacity building, shedding their doubts as well as the sense of *learned helplessness* they have acquired.[7] Overcoming an aversion to risks and uncertainties is the first essential step toward innovation and achieving sustained competitiveness and growth. Once such competitiveness is achieved, it creates a virtuous circle whereby human and knowledge capital are renewed through the generation of new wealth.

Clearly, the above guidance is far from ubiquitous in terms of its application, since strategies for creating a balanced set of competencies will need to be adjusted to account for national and regional environments. For example, although there are many similarities in their economic systems, Europe will require a different model of economic growth and knowledge accumulation when compared with that implemented in North America. The expansion of the knowledge-based economy in North America in recent years has mainly been based upon innovations by start-ups and spin-outs from large corporations and universities, catalyzed by a well-developed venture capital sector. Europe is different – it is an economy with a far larger proportion of small and medium sized businesses, resulting in long supply chains and the relative dispersion of knowledge-based activity. It also has an under-developed base of equity capital investment. Europe can best enhance its economy by pursuing a different route, such as the type of public sector funding to stimulate private sector R&D investment we highlighted above, as well as mitigating the fortress enterprise culture of many European small and medium-sized firms. Asia is far more economically heterogeneous than either North America or Europe. However, its overall destination within the global knowledge economy appears to be one where increased access to knowledge is facilitating massive catch-up, particularly compared with the less-competitive parts of North America and Europe. Indeed, many of Asia's best performing regional economies have already caught up with Europe in terms of R&D investment made by the private sector.

Redrawing the global knowledge map

In the recent past, clusters in North America and Europe dominated the global knowledge hierarchy and order. To a large extent, they still do, but they are changing the rules of the game through the creation of a global web of knowledge clusters. With more technologically advanced knowledge transfer processes than those occurring within regionally bounded innovation systems or clusters, they are linking and aligning themselves closely to emerging clusters in the developing world.[8] These knowledge cluster links, often involving multinational enterprises headquartered in advanced clusters, are clearly a major influence on processes of wider globalization. However, they also have the potential to create a new global knowledge order based on a network of knowledge locations across the globe, which are able to offer the most cost-effective access to the best knowledge and the best means of producing innovations. As highlighted in Chapter 5, both India and China are prime examples of nations that have taken advantage of large and growing numbers of technical university graduates, highly qualified engineers, and computer programmers, and public research institutes, as a means of attracting foreign investment, particularly in R&D activity. This investment is highly concentrated in only a small number of locations, such as Bangalore, Hyderabad, Shanghai, and Beijing. It is these locations that are forming part of the new order, while much of the rest of China and India remains adrift of the global knowledge economy.

A number of commentators argue that the cross-border supply and demand for knowledge inputs across nations is meshing previously independent national innovation systems into open, more inter-connected national innovation systems.[9] However, these linkages concern only a relatively small number of new knowledge centers in developing nations and existing knowledge clusters such as Silicon Valley. This suggests that we are witnessing more the creation of a new global network comprised of a small elite club of regional innovation systems and clusters, rather than the global connection of national innovation systems.

The redrawing of the global map of knowledge creation capacities and the newly emerging order and hierarchy of regions bring further challenges to policymakers in both the developed and the developing world. The challenges come in two main forms: cross-regional disparities in knowledge-based wealth creation in particular nations; and anxieties about the offshoring of knowledge-based tasks and jobs. In the developing world, the impact of growth is bringing pressures on both the continuing availability of quality human and physical capital. As we highlighted in Chapter 6, economic activity rates in places such as Beijing and Shanghai are now among the highest in the world. The concentration of knowledge-based activities in a small number of clusters in China and India is also creating disparities in wealth and potential conflict between those knowledge clusters and the rest of the country. In a BBC interview with ex-Infosys Chairman Narayana Murthy, the interviewer mentioned that a recent state election in India had been won by a campaign based on the premise that the urban elite in Bangalore had ‘too much of the cake, now the cake has to be redistributed to the poor’. ‘Yes’, Murthy replied, but ‘you saw the roads, you have been in Bangalore for the past couple of days so you must have seen that this is not really the best of anything’. He argued that Bangalore provides 60 percent of state taxes, and therefore it makes economic sense, for the region, to use some of that money to upgrade the physical and educational infrastructure on which that wealth has been built.[10] This clearly highlights the implications that success in the knowledge economy is having on the long-term formulation of policy in emerging nations.

By contrast, the issue troubling politicians and policymakers in North America and Europe is the extent to which the on-going shift in global patterns of production and consumption may contribute to the depletion of knowledge creation and utilization in their nations and regions. In Europe, national policymakers and the European Commission are now beginning to look seriously at the increasing offshoring of knowledge-based activities. In the United States, the response from policymakers has often been to focus on the potential downsides in terms of the direct displacement of knowledge-based employment to overseas locations, with little attention given to the potential synergies and complementarities these investments will create between the US and the global market and knowledge economy. This attention on apparent negatives appears to have resulted in rather knee-jerk policymaking in the US, based on proposals for protectionist action such as banning or restricting the use of foreign workers in relation to government contracts.

However, such a protectionist approach makes the assumption that the current shifts in the location pattern of knowledge activities are a zero sum game. As we have shown, in reality knowledge is a resource that produces greater value when different sources and types of knowledge are integrated to create innovation. It is through knowledge networks that these processes occur. For instance, the global knowledge networks being developed by high-technology multinationals such as Intel and Motorola suggest that the knowledge bases these companies are establishing around the globe will be used in a complementary manner, enhancing the innovativeness and competitiveness of all locations involved in the network.[11] These impacts will be multiplied further both at the home and the host of multinationals if there are significant knowledge spillovers between these firms and other geographically proximate companies. Responses to the redrawing of the global map of knowledge creation capacities should be rooted in ensuring that mutual long-term benefits are facilitated through developing and sustaining global networks of knowledge, which capture the obvious upsides of open trade and free enterprise economics.

Appendices

Appendix 1 113 regions in factor analysis

North America

Atlanta–Sandy Springs–Marietta, US
Austin–Round Rock, US
Baltimore–Towson, US
Boston–Cambridge–Quincy, US
Buffalo–Niagara Falls, US
Charlotte–Gastonia–Concord, US
Chicago–Naperville–Joliet, US
Cincinnati–Middletown, US
Cleveland–Elyria–Mentor, US
Columbus, US
Dallas–Fort Worth–Arlington, US
Denver–Aurora, US
Detroit–Warren–Livonia, US
Grand Rapids–Wyoming, US
Greensboro–High Point, US
Hartford–West Hartford–East Hartford, US
Houston–Sugar Land–Baytown, US
Indianapolis, US
Jacksonville, US
Kansas City, US
Las Vegas–Paradise, US
Los Angeles–Long Beach–Santa Ana, US
Louisville, US
Memphis, US
Miami–Fort Lauderdale–Miami Beach, US
Milwaukee–Waukesha–West Allis, US
New York–Northern New Jersey–Long Island, US
Orland–Kissimmee, US
Philadelphia–Camden–Wilmington, US
Phoenix–Mesa–Scottsdale, US
Pittsburgh, US
Portland–Vancouver–Beaverton, US
Raleigh–Cary, US
Richmond, US
Riverside–San Bernardino–Ontario, US
Rochester, US
Sacramento–Arden–Arcade–Roseville, US
Salt Lake City, US
San Antonio, US
San Diego–Carlsbad–San Marcos, US
San Francisco–Oakland–Fremont, US
San Jose–Sunnyvale–Santa Clara, US
Seattle–Tacoma–Bellevue, US
St. Louis, US
Tampa–St. Petersburg–Clearwater, US
Virginia Beach–Norfolk–Newport News, US
Washington–Arlington–Alexandria, US
Alberta, Canada
British Columbia, Canada
Manitoba, Canada
Ontario, Canada
Quebec, Canada
Saskatchewan, Canada

Minneapolis–St. Paul–Bloomington, US
Nashville–Davidson–Murfreesboro, US

Europe

Brussels, Belgium
Vlaams Gewest, Belgium
Denmark
Baden-Württemberg, Germany
Bayern, Germany
Berlin, Germany
Bremen, Germany
Hamburg, Germany
Hessen, Germany
Niedersachsen, Germany
Nordrhein-Westfalen, Germany
Saarland, Germany
Schleswig-Holstein, Germany
Noreste, Spain
Comunidad de Madrid, Spain

Île de France, France
Centre-Est, France
Ireland
Nord Ovest, Italy
Lombardia, Italy
Nord Est, Italy
Emilia-Romagna, Italy
Centro, Italy
Lazio, Italy
Noord-Nederland, Netherlands
West-Nederland, Netherlands
Zuid-Nederland, Netherlands
Ostösterreich, Austria
Westösterreich, Austria
Etelä-Suomi, Finland

Stockholm, Sweden
Sydsverige, Sweden
Småland med öarna, Sweden
Västsverige, Sweden
Eastern, UK
London, UK
South East, UK
Scotland, UK
Norway
Switzerland
Bratislavsky, Slovak Republic
Közép-Magyarország, Hungary
Praha, Czech Republic
Israel

Asia and Oceania

New South Wales, Australia
Victoria, Australia
Western, Australia
New Zealand
Tochigi, Japan

Tokyo, Japan
Kanagawa, Japan
Toyama, Japan
Shizuoka, Japan
Aichi, Japan

Shiga, Japan
Kyoto, Japan
Osaka, Japan
Singapore
Taiwan

Appendix 2 Year of 16 variables in factor analysis

Variable	Year
Employment in IT and computer manufacturing	2002[1]
Employment in high-tech services	2002[1]
Employment in biotech and chemicals	2002[1]
Employment in instrumentation and electrical machinery	2002[1]
Employment in automotive and mechanical engineering	2002[1]
R&D expenditures performed by business sector	2002[2]
R&D expenditures performed by government sector	2002[2]
Patents granted	2002
Private equity investment capital	2002[3]
Number of managers	2002[4]
Employment rate	2002[5]
Economic activity rate	2003[6]
Public expenditures on primary and secondary education	2000[7]
Public expenditures on higher education	2000[8]
Labor productivity	2001[9]
Mean gross monthly earnings	2000[10]

Notes

1 Introduction

1 Thurow, 1996.

2 An indicator of this reliance is the ratio of R&D expenditures to value-added. For instance, R&D expenditures made by firms in the US pharmaceutical and IT hardware industries amount to, on average, 20.2 percent and 30.7 percent of their value-added respectively. This is in stark contrast to less technology-intensive consumer goods industries such as food and textiles. R&D to value-added ratios for the US food and textiles industries are only 1.1 percent and 0.5 percent respectively (figures are for 2000) (Department of Trade and Industry, 2005, Table 3).

Value-added refers to the additional value created at a particular stage of production of a good or a service. If a firm uses $50 worth of intermediate goods (i.e. raw materials, parts and components, and services) to produce a good or service sold at $150, it creates $100 worth of value added. The $100 value added consists of profits, depreciation charges for fixed capital (i.e. equipment, machinery, buildings), and wages of the workers.

3 An example is the change in market leaders in the video game industry. The industry, which exerts significant influences upon lifestyles with a unique combination of advanced technology, art, and entertainment, has its origin in research at the Massachusetts Institute of Technology. Atari created a market for video games – both arcade games and home video games – in the US with its million sellers *Pong* and *Breakout* in the 1970s. In spite of the success, the US market crashed in the early 1980s mainly due to a growing number of clones and their poor quality. Nintendo restored consumer interest in home video games in the US in the late 1980s, subsequently dominating both the US and European markets. Although Nintendo appeared invincible at the time with its expertise as well as the scale economies it was enjoying, Sony entered the market and eventually dethroned Nintendo from the position of market leader with its PlayStation in the mid 1990s. In 2001, the already oligopolistic industry had yet another new entrant – Microsoft with its Xbox console. Again, the market position of Sony has been significantly weakened in the US and European markets. The history of video game industry shows that compatibility between skills and product development changes over the course of industry evolution. With the faster pace of technical progress, advantages such as scale economies and the learning curves associated with the generation of product no longer guarantee the long-term sustainability of a market position. See Izushi and Aoyama, 2006, 1843–61.

4 Paul Krugman suggests that even households at the 95th percentile in the US – namely, households richer than 19 out of 20 households – have seen their real income rise less than 1 percent a year since the late 1970s (Krugman, 2006).

5 In 2001, Taiwan and South Korea were granted by the US Patent and Trademark Office (USPTO) 5,371 and 3,538 utility patents (i.e. 'patents for inventions')

respectively. The number of utility patents granted to inventors in the UK that year was 3,965. During the period between 1991 and 2001, the numbers of USPTO patents granted to Taiwan and South Korea grew at average annual compound rates of 19.5 percent and 24.2 percent respectively. The growth rates of the two countries are much faster than that of the major technology leaders such as the US (5.5 percent) and Japan (4.7 percent), or Germany (3.9 percent), the United Kingdom (3.5 percent), and France (2.9 percent). See: US Patent and Trademark Office, 1999; US Patent and Trademark Office, various years.

6 Ibid.

7 The current members of the OECD include the following 30 countries: Australia, Austria, Belgium, Canada, Czech Republic, Denmark, Finland, France, Germany, Greece, Hungary, Iceland, Ireland, Italy, Japan, South Korea, Luxembourg, Mexico, Netherlands, New Zealand, Norway, Poland, Portugal, Slovak Republic, Spain, Sweden, Switzerland, Turkey, United Kingdom, and United States.

8 National Science Foundation, 2006, Figure 3–36.

9 In 2000, the US accounted for 26 percent of the global distribution of tertiary education graduates. This was followed by China (11 percent), India (8 percent), and Russia (7 percent) (Barro and Lee, 2000). Cited in National Science Foundation, 2006, Figure 3–37.

10 *Business Week*, 2002, 55–6.

11 Friedman, 2005.

12 Ibid.

13 US Department of Education, 2005, Table 8.

14 National Science Foundation, 2003, Table 8; US Census Bureau, various years; cited in Jones, 1995, 759–84.

15 The most notable analysis of the former approach is the five forces framework designed by Michael Porter. The second approach became popular in the 1990s, particularly with a *Harvard Business Review* article by Prahald and Hamel. See Porter, 1980; Prahalad and Hamel, 1990, 79–91.

16 Nonaka and Takeuchi, 1995, 6–7.

17 Charles and Howells, 1992, 126–7.

18 For example, U. Schimank, 1990, 219–28; Lee, 1996, 843–63.

19 Kortum and Lerner, 1999, 1–22.

20 Bozeman, 2000, 627–55.

21 Hawkins with Blackeslee, 2004, 182.

22 Polanyi, 1967.

23 Dixon, 2000, 27.

24 Hawkins with Blackeslee, 2004, 77–80.

25 Polanyi, 1958, 54.

26 Ibid., 102.

27 Nonaka and Takeuchi, 1995.

28 Hawkins with Blackeslee, 2004, 187.

29 Ibid., 184.

30 Johansson, 2004.

31 Rogers and Kincaid, 1981.

32 Love *et al.*, 2006.

33 For example, see, Nelson, 1995, 48–90; Metcalfe, 1998; Malerba, 2002, 247–64.

34 Christensen, 1997.

35 The activities of Leonardo Da Vinci ranged from those as a scientist (topics that came under his inquiry included anatomy, zoology, botany, geology, optics, aerodynamics, and hydrodynamics) and those as an engineer (including architecture, military engineering, canal building, and weapons design) to those as an artist (such as *Mona Lisa* and *The Last Supper*). While the academic contributions of Albert Einstein took place in physics alone, he nonetheless revolutionized the subject in two distinct areas: his

special and general theories of relativity and his seminal work on quantum mechanics. Einstein published five articles within a single year (1905), which all dealt with foundational issues in separate areas of physics, including particle theory of light, investigation of molecular dimensions, kinetic theory of heat, theory of special relativity, and the article in which his most famous equation, $E=mc^2$ first appeared. See Rigden, 2005.

36 In academic circles, these efforts are often studied under the umbrella concept of 'systems of innovation'. Christopher Freeman defines a 'system of innovation' as 'the network of institutions in the public and private sectors whose activities and interactions initiate, import, modify and diffuse new technologies'. While the US tradition of science and technology policy studies focuses on formal institutional mechanisms (i.e. knowledge creation and diffusion from research institutions), the European approach to national innovation systems places greater emphasis on the importance of tacit knowledge and its learning through routine-based activities, such as customer-supplier relationships. See: Freeman, 1987, 1; Lundvall, 1988, 349–69.

37 See Porter, 1990.

38 OECD, 2001.

2 The origin and reality of the knowledge-based economy

1 Department of Trade and Industry, 1998.

2 Smith, 1970 (original 1776).

3 von Tunzelmann, 1995, Chapter 3. Joel Mokyr offers the view that the sustained relationship between technological knowledge and economic growth became possible only when the improved access to technological knowledge emerged in society at large through social networks comprising universities, publishers, professional scientists, and related institutions in the West in the late eighteenth century (Mokyr, 2003).

A similar emphasis upon the importance of a culture receptive to scientific experiments and ideas is found in the works of Nathan Rosenberg and Luther Birdzell Jr. who argue that the West is characterized by autonomy, experiment, and diversity at a level deep down within the society. Rosenberg and Birdzell Jr. write that this results in 'the wide diffusion of the authority and resources necessary to experiment: an absence of more than rudimentary political and religious restrictions on experiment; and incentives which combined ample rewards for success, defined as the widespread economic use of the results of experiment, with a risk of severe penalties for failing to experiment'. Rosenberg and Birdzell, 1986, 33.

In relation to this, Douglas North suggests that economic growth since the rise of the West with Industrial Revolution is to a great extent attributable to the development of institutions such as property rights that removed problems in the transaction of goods. North, 1989, 1319–32.

4 Schumpeter, 1942. Citation is from the Harper Torchbooks edition published in 1975, 82–3.

5 von Tunzelmann, 1995, Chapter 3.

6 Solow, 1957, 312–20.

7 Denison, 1962; Kendrick, 1976.

8 Outside the field of growth accounting, a number of researchers, the late Harvard professor Zvi Griliches among them, studied the relationship between R&D and productivity at the firm and sector level.

9 Harris, 2001, 21–40.

10 US Department of Labor, Bureau of Labor Statistics, 'Major sector multifactor productivity index', Washington, DC: Bureau of Labor Statistics. Available online at www.bles.gov (accessed 10 May 2004). Also see: Baumol and McLennan, 1985, 3–28.

11 Barry Bluestone and Bennett Harrison estimated that approximately 30 million jobs were lost during the 1970s due to closures of business establishments across all sectors of the US economy (not just in manufacturing) (Bluestone and Harrison, 1982). Also for a collection of analyses of the impact upon regional economies in the US, see, Rodwin and Sazanami, 1989.
12 Baumol, 1967, 415–26. Also see Fuchs, 1968.
13 Wolff, 'The magnitude and causes of the recent productivity slowdown in the United States: a survey of recent studies', in Baumol and McLennan, 1985, 29–57.
14 Harris, 2001, 22.
15 Piore and Sabel, 1984.
16 For example, see: Florida and Kenney, 1990.
17 Johnson, 1982; Johnson *et al.*, 1989.
18 Harris, 2001, 22.
19 Prominent proponents of this view include George Gilder and David Birch. See: Gilder, 1984; Birch, 1987.

   Bennett Harrison provides an excellent critique of the view. Harrison shows that although the average size of firms declined in advanced economies since the 1970s, the small firm share of employment remained largely unchanged. An exception to this is the UK in which the share clearly increased. Harrison suggests that the UK economy was more severely hit by deindustrialization than any other country, and a collapse of big companies and the closure of large factories contributed to the employment shift toward small firms. See: Harrison, 1994.
20 Harris, 2001, 23.
21 The key architect of this concept is Danny Quah. Quah arrives at the argument through cross-national analysis of GDP share of services, IT spending, and per capita GDP for OECD economies, 'dynamic' Asian economies, and a selection of others. He recognizes that some manufactured products – such as semiconductors – are examples of dematerialization but adopts the traditional *agriculture, industry, and services* split for his analysis due to data constraints for a wide range of countries at differing levels of development. See: Quah, 1997, 49–56. For discussions of wider impacts of the dematerialization process in the UK, see: Coyle, 1997.
22 Miles, 1990.
23 A pioneering work by Marc Porat estimated that 46 percent of the US gross national product in 1967 originated with the production, processing, and distribution of information goods and services. See Porat, 1977. Subsequent studies adopting a similar approach include: OECD, 1987.
24 Drennan, 2002. The information sector in the study consists of three groups of services: financial producer services (including banking, securities, insurance, and real estate), other producer services (including communication, business, professional, and legal services), and advanced consumer services (including engineering, architecture, accounting, and management consulting).
25 Basu *et al.*, 2003, 28. The percentage of ICT equipment to productive capital stock has increased in major economies. For instance, it amounted to 7.4 percent in the US in 1996. See: Gust and Marquez, 2001, 61.
26 John Jankowski demonstrates that there has been a substantial increase of the share of service R&D in total R&D over recent decades in the US. He argues, however, that this is in large part due to industry's increasing research and technology outsourcing. See: Jankowski, 2001, 323–36.
27 National Science Board, 1989, 63–5.
28 National Science Foundation, 2005, 322–7, Tables 2 and 3.
29 For 1991 figures, OECD, 2001, 154. For 2001 figures, Ministry of Education, Culture, Sports, Science and Technology, 2005, 137, Figure 2–1–22.
30 Tether, 2005, 165.
31 The average figures for European Union are 2.8 percent and 3.7 percent for service

firms and manufacturing firms respectively. This demonstrates strong investment in innovation by UK services firms compared with their counterparts in continental Europe. See: OECD, 1999; OECD, 2001, 174.

32 The proportion of manufacturing output sold to the information sector increased from 2.1 percent in 1972 to 6.1 percent in 1996. See: US Department of Commerce, Bureau of Economic Analysis, 1979, Table 1; US Department of Commerce, Bureau of Economic Analysis, 2000, Table 2. Cited in Drennan, 2002, 37.

33 From 19.1 percent in the 1971–5 period to 31.2 percent in the 1993–7 period. See: US Department of Commerce, Bureau of Economic Analysis, 1998. Cited in Drennan, 2002, 33.

34 During the period between 1998 and 2005, the share of manufacturing output sold to knowledge-based service sectors (including information, finance, insurance, real estate, and professional and business services) grew by 17 percent, while output from the service sectors as a percentage of GDP increased by only 5 percent. US Department of Commerce, Bureau of Economic Analysis, 'Industry Economic Accounts', Washington, DC: Bureau of Economic Analysis. Available online at www.bea.gov/bea/dn2/home/annual_industry.htm (accessed 15 January 2007).

35 By contrast, the share of the information sector's output sold to manufacturing industries declined in the same period. As opposed to the argument of Jankowski mentioned earlier, this suggests that the strong growth in producer services, financial and other knowledge-based services is not accounted for solely by the vertical disintegration of manufacturing, whereby producer services formerly produced in-house become contracted out to producer service firms. See: Drennan, 2002, 38; Jankowski, 2001.

36 Stephen Cohen and John Zysman offered this argument in the middle of the deindustrialization crisis in the US. See: Cohen and Zysman, 1987.

37 Harris, 2001, 23.

38 Tidd *et al.*, 2005, 180.

39 Harris, 2001, 23.

40 Porter, 1990.

41 Basu *et al.*, 2003, 2. Also see: Greenwood and Yorukoglu, 1997, 87.

42 Reverse engineering refers to discovering the technology underpinning a product through analysis of the product's structure, function and operation.

43 Paul Romer is well known for his contributions to this theory. See: Romer, 1986, 1002–37; Romer, 1990, S71–S102. Other important works in the early 1990s include: Aghion and Howitt, 1992, 323–51; Grossman and Helpman, 1991a, 557–86; Grossman and Helpman, 1991b, 43–61.

44 Thurow, 1996.

45 Ibid., 68.

46 US Department of Commerce, Bureau of Economic Analysis, *National Economic Accounts*, various years.

47 US Department of Labor, Bureau of Labor Statistics, 'Major sector multifactor productivity index'.

48 For instance, Paul Romer was named by *Time* magazine in 1997 as one of the most influential people in the US.

49 OECD, 2003, 146.

50 OECD, 2001, 170.

51 OECD, 2003, 175. The UK's knowledge creation and utilization capacity measured in the above terms is only average among the advanced economies. The sum of R&D expenditures, software purchases, and public and private spending on higher education as percent of GDP stood at 4.3 percent in the UK in 2000. This was slightly above the EU average of 4.0 percent but below the OECD average of 4.8 percent (see OECD, 2003, 16–17). Seventeen percent of the UK population aged 25–64 had a bachelor's degree or higher in 1999. The country ranked eighth among OECD

countries in this regard, above the EU average of 12 percent and the OECD average of 14 percent. Yet, educational attainment of the UK labor force is a far cry from the level shown by the US (see OECD, 2001, 170). Researchers per 10,000 persons in the labor force in the UK again show a significantly lower figure than its counterparts across the Atlantic. The UK figure for 1998 was 55 persons, only two-thirds of the US level. This is the same as the EU average but significantly below the OECD average of 63 persons (see OECD, 2003, 175). Particularly, United Kingdom's under-investment in R&D is puzzling to researchers. The ratio of business R&D expenditures to GDP in the UK is significantly lower than its competitor countries. In 2001, the UK ratio was 1.9 percent, as compared with 2.9 percent for the US and the OECD average of 2.3 percent (see OECD, 2003, 170). There is little evidence that differences in industrial structure between the UK and other countries account for this. For instance, John Van Reenen demonstrates that the UK's low business R&D expenditures are due to factors within industries, rather than industry structure. See: Van Reenen, 1997, 493–507. Commentators claim that UK firms do not have sufficient access to external finance, since financial institutions find rates of return to R&D too low to justify investment. However, Mark Rogers shows that the rates of return to R&D for UK firms are broadly similar to other countries. This points to a possibility that management shies away from R&D for other reasons. See: Rogers, 2006.

52 OECD, 2001, 146; OECD, 2003, 16; US Department of Commerce, Bureau of Economic Analysis, *National Economic Accounts*.

53 US Census Bureau, 1996.

54 National Science Foundation, 2003, Table 8.

As the National Science Foundation has revised its definitions of R&D scientists and engineers a number of times, a direct comparison of the 1999 figure with earlier definitions needs care. However, numbers taken from National Science Board, *Science & Engineering Indicators – 1989* (NSB89–1) and various issues of the *Statistical Abstract of the US Economy* show that the number of R&D scientists and engineers per 10,000 labor force increased from about 25 in 1950 to nearly 80 in 1988, an increase of over threefold. See Jones, 1995a, 759–84. Jones finds that the evidence from France, Germany, and Japan shows a similar increase. Ibid., 763.

55 US Department of Labor, Bureau of Labor Statistics, 'Major sector multifactor productivity index'.

56 Ibid. Total factor productivity (TFP) of US manufacturing grew at an average annual rate of 1.69 percent in the period between 1990 and 2000. This is marginally higher than the rate of 1.66 percent in the period between 1949 and 1965 and significantly higher than the rate of 1.19 percent in the period between 1965 and 1972.

57 There are two groups of models aimed at removing the scale effects of the original Romer model (i.e. the larger the R&D workforce, the faster productivity grows). One group assumes increased difficulty of innovation. The other approach asserts divisions of the R&D workforce into smaller groups through product proliferation. For examples of the first approach, see: Jones, 1995a; Jones, 1995b, 495–525; Kortum, 1997, 1389–419; Segerstrom, 1998, 1290–310. For the second approach, see Young, 1998, 41–63; Howitt, 1999, 715–30.

58 Machlup, 1962, 156.

59 Evenson, 1984, 89–123.

60 Griliches, 1990, 1661–707.

61 Cohen *et al.*, 2000, 2.

62 The protection of intellectual property in the software industry underwent a migration from a comparatively weak regime to another that is much more restrictive. The initial protection in the industry was based on copyright laws. This prohibits the users of software from making copies of it without the permission of the software's developer. However, it allows other programmers to use algorithms or techniques contained in the program in their own work. The reliance upon copyrights led to the

'hacker culture'. In the mid 1990s, this regime was replaced as hundreds, even thousands, of patents were awarded for programming processes that ranged from sequences of machine instructions to features of the user interface. See: David and Foray, 1995, 13–68.

63 Cohen *et al.*, 2000, 1–2.

64 Griliches, 1990, 1678.

65 Ibid., 1666; Evenson, 1984, 91.

66 Merton, 1935, 454–74; Gilfillan, 1935, 216–27. Cited in Griliches, 1990, 1697.

67 Machlup, 1962, 170–4.

68 See: Jones, 1995a; Kortum, 1997.

69 Evenson, 1984.

70 For the period up to 1962, US Patent and Trademark Office, 'U.S. patent activity calendar years 1790–2001', Alexandria, VA: US Patent and Trademark Office. Available online at www.uspto.gov/web/offices/ac/ido/oeip/taf/h_counts.htm (accessed 18 May 2004). For the period since 1963, US Patent and Trademark Office, 'U.S. Patent Statistics, Calendar Years 1963–2001', Alexandria, VA: US Patent and Trademark Office. Available online at www.ustpo.gov/web/ offices/ac/ido/oeip/taf/us_stat.pdf (accessed 18 May 2004).

Regarding the surge in patent applications and registrations in the US in absolute numbers, economists offered a number of factors as its source. One is a change in patent registration regimes. The surge in patenting, and notably in ICT, started after important court decisions increased damage awards to plaintiffs in infringement litigation. See: OECD, 2004, 15. An example is the Kodak–Polaroid case in 1986. Polaroid was awarded almost US$1 billion in damages and Kodak was barred from competing in the instant-film camera business. Hall and Ziedonis, 2001, 109.

The extension of patent domain (i.e. areas of technology that can be patented) to include software in ICT and new life forms in biotechnology resulted in a greater number of patents for software and genetic inventions. OECD, 2004, 15.

Furthermore, many firms now 'harvest' patents from their R&D as a means not only to protect their innovations, but also to block rivals from patenting related inventions, to protect against infringement suits, and to win favorable terms in cross-licensing negotiations with other firms. Hall and Ziedonis, 2001, 107; Cohen *et al.*, 2000, 4.

In sum, when coupled with these changes in patent regimes and firm strategies, the stagnating level of patent productivity (i.e. patent applications/registrations per R&D dollar or R&D worker) in the US suggests that the long-run decline in patenting is continuing, although the pace of decline has slowed down since the 1980s. This is consistent with a finding from a study of 17 OECD countries by Furman, Porter and Stern, which is mentioned below.

71 The number of USPTO patent applications per number of business-funded R&D dollars in 1999 remained similar to the level of 1982.

72 The sources of patent statistics include: US Patent and Trademark Office, 'US patent activity calendar years 1790–2001'; US Patent and Trademark Office, 'US Patent Statistics, Calendar Years 1963–2001'. The sources of R&D scientists and engineers include: US Census Bureau, *The Statistical Abstract of the United States*, Washington, DC: US Census Bureau, various years, cited in Jones, 1995a; National Science Board, *1989*; National Science Foundation, 1999; 2003.

73 Furman *et al.*, 2002, 899–933.

74 Evenson, 1984, 108.

75 Kortum, 1993, 450–7.

76 Griliches, 1990, 1702.

77 Ibid., 1700.

78 Case studies showing increased difficulty in discovering inventions include: Baily and Chakrabarti, 1985, 609–32; Henderson and Cockburn, 1996, 32–59.

There is a body of literature called industry life cycle theory, which explores the cycle from a growth stage to maturity and eventual decline. See: Utterback, 1994.

79 Kenneth Arrow approached this issue in relation to the pricing of knowledge. He saw knowledge, particularly knowledge derived from basic research, as a 'public good' and called for government support for basic research. See: Arrow, 1962, 609–25.
80 Mansfield, 1985, 217–23.
81 Ibid., 221.
82 Mansfield *et al.*, 1981, 913.
83 Harris, 2001, 29.
84 Jaffe *et al.*, 1993, 577–98.
85 Breschi and Malerba, 2001, 819.
86 Maskell, 2001, 937.
87 Audretsch and Feldman, 1996, 634.
88 For example, see: Camagni, 1991, 121–44; Izushi, 1997, 117–29; Bathelt *et al.*, 2004, 31–56.
89 Bresnahan *et al.*, 2001, 835–60.
90 Bathelt *et al.*, 2004, 31–56.
91 Simmie, 2002, 885–902.
92 Bottazzi and Peri, 2003, 687–710.
93 Keller, 2002, 120–42.
94 Harris, 2001, 30.
95 David and Foray, 1995, 27.
96 Rosenberg, 1990, 165–74; Nelson, 1992, 57–71; Langlois, 2001, 77–93.
97 Arora and Gambardella, 1994, 523–32; Cowan and Foray, 1997, 595–622.
98 David and Foray, 1995, 43.
99 Brusoni *et al.*, 2002.
100 Langlois, 2001, 80–1.
101 Zucker *et al.*, 1998, 291.
102 Langlois, 2001, 80–1.
103 Cohen and Levinthal, 1990, 128–52; Loasby, 1998, 139–60.
104 Griliches, 1994, 16. Also see, Antonelli, 2000, 536.
105 Stiglitz, 1987, 125–6.
106 Simon, 1985, 3–20; Leonard-Barton, 1995, 20.
107 Peter Drucker notes that the firm's organization is becoming flatter, and teams are flexibly assembled and disbanded according to the requirements of each project. Under the flat organization, managers do not have a full understanding of the expertise of workers working under them any more. The firm has become a place in which 'knowledge workers' with specialized skills and expertise collaborate under the strategic direction of management. See: Drucker, 1999, 18–21.
108 Dixon, 2000, 149.
109 Nelson and Nelson, 2002, 728.
110 Rogers and Bhowmik, 1971, 523–38.
111 Nelson and Nelson, 2002, 728.
112 Jones, 2005.
113 Henderson and Clark, 1990, 9–30.
114 Granstrand, 1998, 74.
115 Miller, 1994, 30.
116 In the model, productivity growth derives from two factors: innovations within each knowledge community, and value added through fusion of previously separate technologies. As 'new growth theory' suggests, the average number of R&D workers within a knowledge community determines the average rate of innovations within knowledge communities. By contrast, the growth of value-added through fusion has its expression in the rate of accumulation of the entire R&D workforce. See: Izushi,

2007a; 2007b. An empirical test of various 'new growth' models is found in: Izushi, forthcoming.

117 See: Jones, 2002, 220–39.
118 Prahalad and Hamel, 1990, 81.
119 Acemoglu, 2002, 15.
120 Atkinson, 1996, 25.
121 Acemoglu, 2002, 7.
122 Ibid., 15–16.
123 Atkinson, 1996, 25.
124 Gosling *et al.*, 1994, 66.
125 Juhn *et al.*, 1993, 411.
126 Acemoglu, 2002, 7.
127 Schmitt, 1995, 178.
128 Berman *et al.*, 1998, 1256–7.
129 Ibid., 1254–5.
130 Ibid., 1268–9.
131 Bound and Johnson, 1992, 371–92; Katz and Murphy, 1992, 35–78.
132 Autor *et al.*, 1998, 1171.
133 For example, see: Berman *et al.*, 1994, 367–97.
134 Acemoglu, 2002, 9.
135 For example, see: Autor *et al.*, 1998.
136 Autor *et al.*, 1998, 1203. However, a plant-level study of factory automation investment shows little correlation between skill upgrading and the adoption of new technologies. According to the study made by Mark Doms, Timothy Dunne, and Kenneth Troske, the adoption of new factory automation technologies is uncorrelated with plant-level changes in workforce skills, although plants that use a large number of new technologies employ more educated workers, employ relatively more managers, professional workers, and precision-craft workers, and pay higher wages. They also find that plants that invest relatively more in computing equipment have larger increases in the share of non-production workers, which is consistent with results of other cross-industry studies. They suggest that the effect of new technologies on workforce structure depends critically on the type of technology being adopted. See: Doms *et al.*, 1997, 253–90.
137 Berman *et al.*, 1994, 390.
138 Frank Levy and Richard Murnane suggest that computerization does not necessarily change skills requirements for a given job. In some cases, skilled workers increase the amount of output through the use of computers by freeing themselves from less skill-intensive elements of their jobs and concentrating on the more skill-intensive elements. See: Levy and Murnane, 1996, 258–62.
139 Krueger, 1993, 54–5.
140 Francesco Caselli and John Coleman show that the computer-skill complementarity is a worldwide phenomenon. See: Caselli and Coleman II, 2001, 328–35.
141 Acemoglu, 2002, 8. The invention of weaving, spinning, and threshing machines led to the Luddite and Captain Swing riots in nineteenth-century Britain, in which skilled artisans destroyed the new machines in the belief that the machines would make their skills redundant.
142 Acemoglu, 2002, 37–9.
143 For example, see: Schmookler, 1966.
144 Acemoglu, 2002, 48–52.
145 Gambardella and Ulph, 2003.
146 *International Herald Tribune*, 2005.
147 Greenwood and Yorukoglu, 1997, 59.
148 Autor *et al.*, 2002, 432–47; Autor *et al.*, 2003, 1279–334.
149 Feenstra and Hanson, 1999, 907–40.

150 Navaretti and Venables, 2004.
151 Global Insight, 2005. A recent study by the McKinsey Global Institute shows that offshoring jobs to India has created wealth for the US as well as for India. According to McKinsey, for every dollar of corporate spending outsourced to India, the US economy captures more than three-quarters of the benefit and gains as much as US$1.14 in return. McKinsey Global Institute, 2003.

3 Knowledge-based capacity of best-performing regions

1 Saxenian, 1981, 1.
2 For example, from 1995 to 1999, housing prices in the region rose by 65 percent, three times faster than the US national average (*Business Week*, 2000, 112).
3 Employment in the region declined by 17.4 percent from December 2001 to April 2003 (*Business Week*, 2004, 110).
4 *Business Week*, 2003, 43.
5 *Business Week*, 2004, 115; Saxenian, 1985, 81.
6 Reinert, 1995, 25.
7 Porter, 1979, 137–45. Also see: Porter, 1980.
8 Porter, 1990.
9 Fagerberg, 1996, 48; Reinert, 1995, 26.
10 Krugman, 1994, 41.
11 Lall, 2001, 10–11.
12 Prahalad and Hamel, 1990, 81.
13 Kay, 1993, 13–14.
14 Mowery *et al.*, 1998, 508. The resource-based view of the firm has its root in Edith Penrose's classic work, *The Theory of the Growth of the Firm*, published in 1959. More recent classics of the resource-based view include Alfred Chandler's study of the growth of managerial capabilities in the US railroad industry in the late nineteenth century, and Richard Nelson and Sidney Winter's study of a firm's innovation process, which they see as selective and evolutionary due to constraints on its internal capabilities. Penrose, 1959; Chandler, 1977; Nelson and Winter, 1982.
15 Jan Fagerberg shows that flows of R&D inputs and outputs, measured by civil R&D as percentage of GDP and external patent applications per capita, are important for medium and long-run differences across 15 OECD countries in the growth of market share between 1961 and 1983. Fagerberg, 1988, 356.
16 For example, Michael Porter argues that labor productivity is the only meaningful concept of competitiveness at the national level. Porter, 1990, 6.
17 Van Biesebroeck, 2003, 2.
18 Needless to say, this difficulty does not arise in the measurement of labor productivity, as it focuses upon a single input (i.e. labor).
19 The first approach, called stochastic frontier production function models, estimates a production function by taking into account randomness in observations. As this approach assumes a certain distribution of randomness, it is less vulnerable to measurement errors in extreme observations. Aigner *et al.*, 1977, 21–37.

By contrast, the second approach, called data envelopment analysis (DEA), does not assume any distribution underlying randomness and instead employs linear programming in identifying a 'frontier', that is, a series of maximum outputs gained from different combinations of inputs. In the case of two inputs and one output, suppose a two-dimensional space, whose horizontal and vertical axes represent output per a first input and output per a second input. All observations (e.g. firms) are plotted on the space. If we view the observations in a narrow scope from the origin, we can then identify one of them situated at the greatest distance. Of the firms falling inside the scope, this firm at the greatest distance from the origin produces the greatest amount of output. When we shift the direction of our scope either clockwise or counterclockwise, we can identify another observation situated at the greatest distance. For such observations situated at the greatest distance from the origin, we can draw a tangential line that touches the point and stays above the rest of the observations. By repeating this, we can define a piece-wise linear production function consisting of a series of short lines. Against this piece-wise frontier, all the observations are situated either below or on it, and those firms on the frontier are labeled 100 percent efficient as best practice firms.

In the operation of DEA in practice, it seeks for each observation a set of weights assigned to output/input ratios that maximizes the weighted sum, with the constraint that no observations have a weighted sum larger than one (or 100 percent). Cooper *et al.*, 2000, 6–8.

20 Using a panel data of manufacturing plants in Columbia, Johannes Van Biesebroeck demonstrates that correlations between alternative productivity estimates based on the three approaches are invariably high (Van Biesebroeck, 2003, 4–5).

21 Harris and Trainor, 1997, 485–6.

22 Tinbergen, 1942, 511–49; English translation, Tinbergen, 1959, 182–221.

23 Solow, 1957, 312–20. In his constructs of TFP, Solow made two assumptions. First, constant returns to scale are assumed. This means that equal rate increases in both labor and physical capital produces a growth in output at the same rate. This assumption is convenient, since an economy can be simply envisaged as the sum of individual firms: the relationship between inputs and an output at the economy level is exactly the same as the relationship observed at the firm level. The second assumption is the profit-maximizing behavior of firms, with them paying competitive market prices for labor and physical capital. With this assumption, when we add up the share of each input to output (e.g. for labor, the ratio of wages to the total value added), the sum equals one. This suggests that there is no profit in production. Although this does not conform with profit-seeking businesses, it comes as a useful assumption when we consider productivity growth. With some rewriting of the production function, Solow reached the formula that the growth rate of output per a bundle of inputs (i.e. the growth rate of TFP) is the growth rate of output minus the sum of the growth rates of inputs (i.e. labor and physical capital).

24 Such studies include: Griliches, 1963, 331–46; Denison, 1967; Kendrick, 1976.

25 Barro and Sala-i-Martin, 1995, 352.

Another limitation of TFP is its inability to distinguish the separate effect of changes in efficiency from technical progress. In the real world, firms (or economies) do not always combine inputs in the most efficient way, often wasting some inputs through the misallocation of resources. This is a different matter from gains by technical progress, which will produce a growth in output for the same combination of inputs. In TFP, these two distinct effects are measured together, whereas DEA and stochastic frontier production function models deal with this issue.

26 Barro and Sala-i-Martin, 1995, 348.

27 Solow, 1957, 316.

28 US Department of Labor, Bureau of Labor Statistics, 'Private business and private nonfarm business MFP tables', Available online at ftp.bls.gov/pub/suppl/prod3.mfptable.zip (accessed 21 February 2006).

29 Quite often human capital is counted as a third production factor following labor and physical capital and removed from TFP. In such cases, TFP refers to the second group, technology and other factors only.

30 Early work includes: Schultz, 1960, 571–83; Schultz, 1961, 1–17; Becker, 1964.

31 Mankiw, 1995, 275–326.

32 Quah, 1999, 13.

33 Ibid., 12.

34 Izushi, forthcoming.

35 Cohen and Levinthal, 1990, 128–52.

36 For instance, see: Jaffe *et al.*, 1993, 577–98; Audretsch and Feldman, 1996, 630–40; Anselin *et al.*, 2000a, 501–15; Anselin *et al.*, 2000b, 435–43; Acs *et al.*, 2002, 1069–85.
37 Quah, 2001, 21.
38 Aghion and Howitt, 1998, 327.
39 Becker, 1964; Lucas, 1988, 3–42. Early empirical work based on this view includes a study in 1970 by Zvi Griliches who estimated that one-third of the Solow residual could be attributed to the growth in the labor force's educational attainments (Griliches, 1970, 71–124). In a similar vein, Edward Denison reported an effect of human capital accumulation upon per capita income growth in the US (Denison, 1979). More recently, a number of cross-national studies have confirmed these positive relationships. They include: Baumol *et al.*, 1989; Barro, 1991, 407–43; Mankiw *et al.*, 1992, 407–37.
40 Nelson and Phelps, 1966, 69–75.
41 Bartel and Lichtenberg, 1987, 1–11; Wolff, 1996, 96–123; Wolff, 2001, 735–59.
42 Benhabib and Spiegel, 1994, 143–73.
43 Aghion and Howitt, 1998, 327–8.
44 Griliches, 1964, 961–74; Evenson, 1968. Jora Minasian also examined chemical firms in the United States using the same framework (Minasian, 1969, 80–5). Griliches himself later shifted his research to an analysis of productivity at a firm level. His works in this line include: Griliches, 1979, 92–116; 1986, 141–54.
45 The 'research capital' model suggests that an increase in productivity during a period arises from the amount of new knowledge created by R&D workers during the same period. Accordingly, *the increment of productivity* is proportional to the number of R&D workers employed during the period. By contrast, the rate of productivity growth becomes proportional to the number of R&D workers when it is assumed that production of new knowledge is also enhanced by the level of existing knowledge or technology.
46 Romer, 1986, 1002–37; 1990, S71–S102.
47 Izushi, 2007a; 2007b.
48 To obtain the average number of R&D workers in a knowledge community, we need to estimate the number of knowledge communities within an economy. We use patent application counts by International Patent Classification categories in this estimation.
49 Stephen Kline and Nathan Rosenberg provide a model of such interactions among a firm's various functions and its external environments, including the market and science base. See Kline and Rosenberg, 1986, 275–305.
50 Whereas the US tradition of science and technology policy studies focus on formal institutional mechanisms (i.e. knowledge creation and diffusion from research institutions), the European approach to national innovation systems places a greater emphasis on the importance of tacit knowledge and its learning through routine-based activities. See Freeman, 1987; Lundvall, 1988, 349–69; Lundvall, 1992.
51 For instance, Nuala Beck uses the proportion of professional, engineering, technical, scientific, and senior management staff to identify knowledge-intensive sectors. Frank Lee and Handan Has combine several knowledge indicators based on R&D activity and human capital content to classify 55 industries into three groups, 'high-knowledge', 'medium-knowledge', and 'low-knowledge'. See: Beck, 1992; Lee and Has, 1996, 39–78.
52 Hatzichronoglou, 1997.
53 Laafia, 1999, 2.
54 According to the NACE classification (which is the statistical classification of economic activities in the European Community), the sectors constituting our five groups are as follows:

  i IT and computer manufacturing: NACE 30 (office machinery and computers); NACE 32 (radio, television, and communication equipment and apparatus)

- ii High-tech services: NACE 64 (post and telecommunications); NACE 72 (computer and related activities); NACE 73 (research and development)
- iii Biotechnology and chemicals: NACE 24 (chemicals and chemical products)
- iv Instrumentation and electrical machinery: NACE 31 (electrical machinery and apparatus); NACE 33 (medical, precision, and optical instruments, watches, and clocks)
- v Automotive and mechanical engineering: NACE 29 (machinery and equipment); NACE 34 (motor vehicles, trailers, and semi-trailers); NACE 35 (other transport equipment).

For regions in other countries, the sectors corresponding with the above are adopted.

55 James Adams suggests that the output of academic research is a major contributor to economic growth, though there is a lag in effect of roughly 20 years. Adam Jaffe finds that university R&D can have spillovers, with an increase of university R&D by 10 percent augmenting corporate patents by roughly 1 percent. See: Adams, 1990, 673–702; Jaffe, 1989, 957–70.

56 When using patent data, a common approach is to calculate patent indicators based on information (filings, grants, etc.) from a particular patent office. While the richness and strength of those indicators are broadly recognized, they are affected by 'home advantage' bias – where domestic applicants tend to file more patents, proportionate to their inventive activity, in their home country compared to foreign applicants. Further, the 'home advantage' bias can exist at three economic block levels – North America, Europe, and Asia – in each of which a major patent office exists, namely, the US Patent and Trademark Office (USPTO), the European Patent Office (EPO), and the Japanese Patent Office (JPO). A method to remove such bias is 'triadic patent families' which combine statistics from the three patent offices by selecting either the optimal geographical filter to determine country coverage (i.e. which and how many patents offices) or the appropriate consolidation filter to relate all patents that refer to the 'same invention'. However, the methods of building triadic patent families are complex. In view of the complexity and further difficulty of extending the methods to a regional level, we use an estimated sum of patents granted by USPTO and patents granted by EPO. For details about 'triadic patent families', see: Dernis and Khan, 2004.

57 Pavitt, 1982, 33–51.

58 Griliches, 1990, 1661–707.

59 For evidence at the national level, see: Fagerberg, 1996, 43. As for evidence at the regional level, Zoltan Acs, Luc Anselin, and Attila Varga demonstrate that patent data developed by the USPTO is in fact a reliable proxy measure of innovative activity at the regional level, as compared to the literature-based innovation output indicator developed by the US Small Business Administration at the sub-state level (Acs *et al.*, 2002).

60 Estimates of private equity investment capital are made on the basis of data from the following sources: European Private Equity and Venture Capital Association (EVCA), 2004; PricewaterhouseCoopers, Thomson Venture Economics, and the National Venture Capital Association, various issues; Martin *et al.*, 2003.

61 For a scheme of occupational classification, Eurostat employs the International Labor Organization's International Standard Classification of Occupations ISCO-88. Estimates of numbers of managers for European regions are based on the category 'Legislators, Senior Officials and Managers'. This includes legislators, senior government officials, traditional chiefs and heads of villages, senior officials of special interest organizations, corporate managers, and general managers. The US Bureau of Labor Statistics adopts its own classification system, the 2000 Standard Occupational Classification (SOC). The category 'Management Occupations' stands as a proxy for ISCO-88's 'Legislators, Senior Officials and Managers', although they are not

complete matches. As for regions in other countries, similar categories in their statistical classification schemes are adopted.

62 Ideally, the average number of years of education completed by the labor force, for example, is a preferred choice. However, the lack of data means that many studies adopt other indicators of human capital. For instance, the OECD uses the proportion of production workers as an indicator of skill intensity in manufacturing industries, assuming that production workers are either less-skilled or unskilled. See: OECD, 1994.

63 Crouch *et al.*, 1999, 227–30.

64 Estimates are made on the basis of numbers of students in primary and secondary education and higher education at the regional level, and total public direct expenditure on primary and secondary education and higher education as a percentage of GDP at the national level. The data on education expenditure at the national level are found in US Department of Education, 2003.

65 Bradley and Taylor, 1996, 1–14.

66 Lall, 2001, 20.

67 Factor analysis maps observations in a space whose dimensions are smaller in number than the number of original variables. A factor is defined as a dimension in which a good part of variations in the original set of variables is displayed. The dimension is shown as a statement of the relationship of the variables to it (called factor loadings). Furthermore, the position of a case (a region in our analysis) in each dimension (i.e. factor) is given as a score called a 'factor score'. The factors identified are orthogonal with one another, and accordingly factor scores are uncorrelated between factors. For each factor, factor scores have a mean of zero and a standard deviation of one. This is achieved by use of the Anderson-Rubin method of estimation for factor scores. As for the extraction of factors and rotation of a factor matrix, we use the maximum likelihood method and the Varimax method respectively. The result of factor analysis can be envisaged as observations mapped in a space of a reduced number of dimensions.

68 As we discussed earlier, a significant component of TFP is a residual consisting of technology and other factors, as well as the human capital component. In addition to our human capital indicators not being perfect, it is most likely that our list of variables does not cover the whole of the residual, particularly the 'other factors'.

69 The 114 regions are a subset of the 125 regions analyzed in our *World Knowledge Competitiveness Index 2005*. The remaining 11 regions are dropped from the current analysis due to the lack of reliable estimates for some of the variables analyzed. Huggins *et al.*, 2005.

70 US regions are metropolitan statistical areas (MSA) defined by the US Census Bureau. The MSA consists of an area with a substantial population center and adjacent counties with a high degree of economic homogeneity. Compared with counties, cities and states, the MSAs analyzed in this study are more robust regional units for economic analysis as they reflect the boundaries of clusters of firms in related industries. The Canadian regions are based on their defined provincial units. The majority of European regions are based on the European Union's definition of regional units (NUTS-1). As a result of this definition, some nations are included as regions (i.e. Denmark, Ireland). Furthermore, regions in Finland and Sweden are based on NUTS-2, a lower level of regional unit. In addition, three non-EU member countries, Switzerland, Norway, and Israel, are included in the analysis. As with Denmark and Ireland, these relatively small nations are treated as regions. The Asian/Oceanic regions consist of prefectures in Japan and are defined by city boundaries for most other nations, along with the inclusion of New Zealand, Taiwan and Singapore as region-states.

71 Factor analysis provides information about how much variance in the original set of indicators is accounted for by each factor identified. The percentage of the variance

accounted for by each factor is as follows: factor 1: 12.0 percent, factor 2: 10.7 percent, factor 3: 7.9 percent, factor 4: 18.8 percent, and factor 5: 7.2 percent. As discussed earlier, the order in this percentage has no bearing on the relative importance of a factor to others in accounting for TFP.

72 Due to the inseparability of employment in biotechnology from other chemical products in our data, none of the factors identify a close association between biotechnology and either patents granted or private equity investment capital.

73 Kondratieff, 1926, 573–609; Kondratieff, 1935, 105–15; Schumpeter, 1939.

74 Hall and Preston, 1988, 21.

75 The share of ICT activity in EPO applications climbed from 28 percent in 1994 to 35 percent in 2001. Another area that witnessed a growth in patent applications is biotechnology: up from 4.3 percent to 5.5 percent. Nearly half of the growth of patenting in the EPO over this period is due to these two technology areas. Patterns in the USTPO are similar. OECD, 2004, 13.

76 The other two regions in top 20 that have a score of higher than zero in all five factors are Boston–Cambridge–Quincy, US and Île de France, France.

77 Saxenian, 1994.

4 Networks and clusters

1 Tapscott 1999; Skyrme, 1999; Dawson, 2003; Cross *et al.*, 2003; Castells, 2004.

2 Kelly, 1999, 5.

3 Coleman, 1988, S95–S120; Putnam, 2000.

4 Tapscott *et al.*, 2000.

5 Lewis, 1999.

6 Lipnack and Stamps, 1995; Nahapiet and Ghoshal, 1998, 242–66; Inkpen and Tsang, 2005, 146–65.

7 Porter, 1990; 1998.

8 Solomon and Flores, 2001; Ciancutti and Steding, 2000; Covey and Merrill, 2006.

9 Hung, 2002, 591–613; Parise and Casher, 2003, 25–39; Hagedoorn, 2006, 670–80.

10 Drucker, 1989.

11 Ibid.

12 Nonaka and Takeuchi, 1995.

13 Oliver, 1997, 697–713.

14 Brown and Duguid, 2001, 198–213.

15 Ibid.

16 Arrow, 1971; Maskell, 2000, 111–23.

17 This means that the competitive advantage a firm is potentially able to gain is dependent upon the resource profiles of its partners (Stuart, 2000, 791–811; Ireland *et al.*, 2002, 413–46; Grant and Baden-Fuller, 2004, 61–84).

18 Burt, 1992.

19 Cowan *et al.*, 2004.

20 Arthur, 1989, 116–31; Adler and Kwon, 2002, 17–40; Labianca and Brass, 2006, 596–614.

21 Darr and Talmud, 2003, 443–61; Reagans and McEvily, 2003, 240–67; Rodan and Galunic, 2004, 541–62.

22 Podolny and Page, 1998, 57–76; Huggins, 2000.

23 Levine, 2005; Podolny and Page, 1998.

24 Huggins, 2000; 2001, 443–58.

25 Axelrod, 1984.

26 Ibid.; Battram, 1998.

27 Yet, players in the knowledge economy have to resist the temptation of cheating the other party, as well as overcoming the fear of being cheated, so that the gains of both parties can be maximized (i.e. both parties remain silent and obtain a relatively short

term in prison as a whole in PDG). For this to happen, PDG's condition of accomplices being held in-communicado has to be lifted. Knowledge workers are likely to use ICT tools to communicate and establish close relationships with their counterparts within a short span of time.

28 Allee, 1997.
29 Kauffman, 1993; 1995.
30 Stacey *et al.*, 2000.
31 Davis and Meyer, 1998.
Although mainly related to computer networks, Metcalfe's Law, named after 3Com founder Robert Metcalfe, further states that the usefulness of networks is proportional to the square of the number of users, while there is a related *network effect* whereby the value of a resource accessible through a network increases in proportion to the square of the number of people that can leverage it. See Welborn and Kasten, 2003.
32 Tapscott *et al.*, 2000.
33 Almeida *et al.*, 2003, 301–15.
34 DiMaggio and Powell, 1983, 147–60; Kim *et al.*, 2006, 704–20.
35 Dalziel, 2005.
36 Tushman and Katz, 1980, 1071–85; Harada, 2003, 1737–51.
37 Inkpen and Tsang, 2005.
38 Coleman, 1988.
39 Putnam, 2000.
40 Portes 1998, 1–24.
41 Coleman, 1988.
42 Ibid.; Sandefur and Laumann, 1998, 481–501.
43 Nahapiet and Ghoshal, 1998.
44 Ibid., 244.
45 Locke, 1999, 8–9.
46 Ibid., 8.
47 Casciaro and Lobo, 2005, 92–9.
48 Cooke and Huggins, 2003, 56.
49 Putnam, 2000; Adler and Kwon, 2002.
50 Putnam, 2000, 176.
51 Ibid., 322.
52 Williamson, 1993, 453–86; Hite and Hesterly, 2001, 275–86.
53 Huggins, 2006.
54 Ibid.
55 Foucault, 1995, 5–34.
56 Storper and Scott, 1995, 505–26.
57 Porter, 1998.
58 Porter, 1990.
59 Some of the key competitive advantages of cluster formation include the following: lower transaction costs, gain access to new and complementary knowledge, capture economies of synergy and interdependent activities, spread risks, promote joint R&D efforts with suppliers and users, obtain reciprocal benefits from the combined use of complementary assets and knowledge, speed up learning processes, and overcome (or create) entry barriers to markets.
See Roelandt and den Hertog, 1998.
60 Brandenburger and Nalebuff, 1996.
61 Scott, 1993.
62 DeVol, 1999, 102–3.
63 Castells, 1987.
64 Ibid.
65 In her work on the 'human side' of the knowledge economy, Carol Kinsey Goman

illustrates the potency of an overlapping business/professional and social environment for corporate performance, precisely because of the resource mobilization based on the two types of capitals. See Goman, 2000.

66 Porter, 1990.

67 Manuel Castells and Peter Hall show that the development of knowledge clusters involves the close integration of the 'usual' factors of production – capital, labor, and raw material – brought together by some form of institutional entrepreneur. In our view, this institutional entrepreneur functions as the glue connecting and mobilizing human capital and other resources. See: Castells and Hall, 1994.

68 Paul Krugman contends that 'given a slightly different sequence of events, Silicon Valley might have been in Los Angeles, Massachusetts, or even Oxfordshire' (Krugman, 1994, 415).

This appears to be quite an exaggeration, ignoring the complex forces at work at both cluster inception and growth stages. The social and cultural differences within these regions are such that even if the same sequence of events were to take place in each, an entirely different form of business evolution, which may involve cluster development, would undoubtedly occur. For instance, although there is evidence to suggest that the creation of knowledge clusters can be associated with the existence of university and research institutions, this is an insufficient explanation since the majority of such institutions around the world have not acted as cluster catalysts. The initial and ensuing conditions are necessarily complex and interrelated, making the deconstruction and isolation of core variables an intricate task.

69 Bresnahan and Gambardella, 2004.

70 Elizabeth Garnsey and Helen Lawton Smith describe the process of knowledge-based development as coevolution and spontaneous order in *ecological succession* that harnesses individual enterprises and relationships. See: Garnsey and Lawton Smith, 1998, 433–50.

71 Audretsch, 1998, 18–29.

72 Romer, 1990, S71–S102.

73 Ridderstråle and Nordström, 2000.

5 Knowledge clusters and their evolution

1 Best, 2000, 459–84.
2 Henton, 2000, 46–58.
3 Hamel, 1999, 70–84.
4 Rosenberg, 2002.
5 Henton, 2000.
6 Collaborative Economics, 2006, 4.
7 Ibid.
8 Kearney, 2004.
9 Kenney, 2000.
10 Kaplan, 1999.
11 Lécuyer, 2005.
12 Berlin, 2005.
13 Castilla *et al.*, 2000, 218–47.
14 Gillmor, 2004.
15 Adams, 2005, 29–51.
16 Gibbons, 2000, 200–17.
17 Saxenian, 1994.
18 Ibid., 2–3.
19 Saxenian, 1994.
20 Koepp, 2002
21 Cohen and Fields, 1999, 108–30.

22 Collaborative Economics, 2002.
23 Rosenberg, 2002, 3.
24 Lewis, 1999.
25 Bronson, 2000.
26 Goman, 2000.
27 Bronson, 2000.
28 Ibid., 88–9.
29 Ibid.
30 Harrison, 1994, 307–28.
31 Ibid., 325.
32 Hobday, 1994, 231–44.
33 Kearney, 2004.
34 Rosenberg, 2002.
35 Kearney, 2004.
36 Ibid.
37 Collaborative Economics, 2006, 50.
38 English-Lueck, 2002.
39 Wolfe, 1999, 707–28.
40 Kotkin and DeVol, 2001.
41 Wolfe, 1999, 711.
42 Kotkin and DeVol, 2001.
43 Ibid.
44 *San Francisco Business Times*, 2001.
45 Indergaard, 2004.
46 *San Francisco Examiner*, 2005.
47 Indergaard, 2004.
48 Huggins *et al.*, 2006.
49 Rosenberg, 2002.
50 Saxenian, 2002, 20–31.
51 Saxenian, 2005, 35–61.
52 Sturgeon, 2003, 199–225.
53 Posadas, 2005.
54 Zhou, 2005, 1113–34.
55 Liefner *et al.*, 2006, 111–30.
56 Zhou and Xin, 2003, 129–52.
57 Wu, 2003, 55–78.
58 Depner and Bathelt, 2005, 53–81.
59 Rosenberg, 2002.
60 Singh, 2003.
61 Patibandla and Petersen, 2002, 1561–77.
62 Parthasarathy, 2004, 664–85.
63 Lee *et al.*, 2002, 14
64 Sako, 2003.
65 Fujita, 2003, 249–81.
66 Ibid.
67 Indergaard, 2004.
68 Doloreux, 2004, 173–89.
69 Ibid.
70 Wolfe, 2002.
71 Shavinina, 2004.
72 Wolfe, 2002.
73 Mallett, 2004, 21–32.
74 Wolfe, 2002.
75 Mallett, 2004.

76 Wolfe and Gertler, 2004, 1071–93.
77 Jackson and Khan, 2003.
78 Doloreux, 2004, 479–92.
79 de la Mothe, 2003.
80 Ibid., 14.
81 Cited in Mallett, 2004.
82 Garnsey and Lawton Smith, 1998, 433–50.
83 Garnsey and Longhi, 2004, 336–55.
84 Library House, 2004.
85 Ibid.
86 Athreye, 2004, 121–59.
87 Library House, 2004.
88 Ibid.
89 Keeble *et al.*, 1999, 319–32; Cooke and Huggins, 2004, 112–32.
90 Ibid.
91 Ibid.
92 Garnsey and Heffernan, 2005, 1127–44; Casper and Karamanos, 2003, 805–22.
93 Garnsey and Heffernan, 2005.
94 Library House, 2004.
95 Garnsey and Heffernan, 2005; Athreye, 2004.
96 Garnsey and Heffernan, 2005.
97 Rosenberg, 2002, 61.
98 SQW Limited, 2001.
99 Lopez-Claros *et al.*, 2005.
100 van der Meer *et al.*, 2003.
101 Steinbock, 2006.
102 Ibid.
103 Huggins and Davies, 2006; Huggins *et al.*, 2005.
104 Roper and Grimes, 2005, 297–313.
105 Castells and Himanen, 2002.
106 Steinbock, 2006.
107 Ibid.
108 Rosenberg, 2002.
109 Steinbock, 2006.
110 Rosenberg, 2002.
111 Ibid.; Steinbock, 2006.
112 Ibid.
113 Hirshfeld and Schmid, 2005.
114 Holstila, 2004.
115 Steinbock, 2006.
116 Ibid.
117 Christensen, 1997.
118 Bison *et al.*, 2004.
119 Hydrios Biotechnology Ltd, 2004.
120 Bison *et al.*, 2004.
121 Ibid.
122 Steinbock, 2006, 133.
123 Storper, 1995, 204.
124 O'Mara, 2004.
125 Storper, 1995.
126 David Audretsch suggests that 'the role of tacit knowledge in generating innovative activity is presumably the greatest during the early stages of the industry life cycle, before product standards have been established and a dominant design has emerged'. Audretsch, 1998, 23.

127 Harrison *et al.*, 2004, 1045–70.
128 Perroux, 1955, 307–20; Hirschman, 1958.
129 Britton, 2004, 369–90.
130 Sturgeon, 2003.
131 Simmie, 2004, 1095–112.
132 Johnson *et al.* 2006, 19–33.
133 Wolfe and Gertler, 2004.
134 Carlsson, 2006, 65.
135 Castells and Hall, 1994.
136 Massey *et al.* 1992, 241.
137 Gittell and Sohl, 2005, 293–312.
138 Moodysson *et al.*, 2005.
139 Alsleben, 2005, 217–48.
140 Pinch *et al.*, 2003, 373–88.
141 Cortright, 2006.
142 Martin and Sunley, 2003, 5–35.
143 Rosenfeld, 2005.

6 Nurturing and attracting talent

1 Finegold, 1999, 60–81.
2 Brown *et al.*, 2001.
3 Doeringer *et al.*, 2002.
4 Cortright, 2005.
5 Finegold *et al.*, 2004, 921–41.
6 Ashton and Green, 1996, 4.
7 Huggins, 2001, 19–34; Huggins and Harries, 2004, 47–68.
8 In this instance the sectors defined as knowledge-based are IT and computer manufacturing, biotechnology and chemicals, automotive and mechanical engineering; instrumentation and electrical machinery, and high-technology services. For details of this classification, see: Hatzichronoglou, 1997; Laafia, 1999.
9 Lisa Lynch finds that the provision of training by private-sector employers plays a significant role in determining the wages and wage growth of 70 percent of young workers in the US who do not graduate from college. However, Lynch warns that such training provision does not widely take place. Lynch, 1992, 299–312.
10 OECD, 2001.
11 Gordon, 2000, xviii.
12 Brown *et al.*, 2001.
13 Campbell, 2002.
14 Ibid.
15 Bassi *et al.*, 2001.
16 Campbell, 2002; Also, for a detailed discussion on the economic returns to investments in education and training, see: Descy and Tessaring, 2004.
17 Campbell, 2002, 78.
18 Kitching and Blackburn, 2002.
19 Campbell, 2002.
20 Finegold, 1996, 235–53.
21 Huggins, 2001, 833–48.
22 Keep and Mayhew, 1996, 305–34.
23 Huggins, 2001.
24 Gray and Mabey, 2005, 467–85.
25 Minniti *et al.*, 2006.
26 As a method for producing a composite rank of global national competitiveness, we have taken a mean of the ranks produced by the IMD's *World Competitiveness*

Scoreboard (Institute for Management Development, 2004) and the World Economic Forum's *Global Competitiveness Report* (Porter *et al.*, 2004). Both produce an annual competitiveness ranking for most nations based on a differing set of secondary and empirically derived indicators. For further details, see: Huggins and Day, 2005.

27 Huggins and Day, 2005.
28 Mueller and Thomas, 2001, 51–75; Hayton *et al.*, 2002, 33–52; Hofstede, 2001.
29 Huggins and Fido, 2002.
30 OECD, 1998.
31 Kitching and Blackburn, 2002.
32 Ibid.
33 Huggins *et al.*, 2006; UNCTAD, 2005.
34 Doeringer *et al.*, 2002.
35 Finegold, 2004.
36 Branstetter, 2000; UNCTAD, 2005.
37 Doeringer *et al.*, 2002.
38 Kotkin, 2000.
39 Drucker, 1989.
40 Florida, 2002, 6.
41 Cairncross, 1997.
42 Kotkin, 2000.
43 Ibid.
44 Florida, 2002.
45 For example, see: Florida, 2002. Florida presents 'Tolerance' (Gay), 'Diversity', 'Bohemian' and 'Melting Pot' index rankings for US regions and highlights their association with economic and technology indicators.
46 Huggins, 2001; Chen *et al.*, 2004, 320–33; Lorenzen and Mahnke, 2002.
47 In the UK, one of the centers of such initiatives was the Welsh Development Agency. A number of studies were undertaken to evaluate its supply-chain development programs. For example, see: Izushi and Morgan, 1998, 75–91; Izushi, 1999, 739–50.
48 Florida, 2002. The term 'quality-of-place' was originally coined by Richard Florida.
49 Kotkin, 2000.
50 Huggins *et al.*, 2003.
51 The term 'smart growth' generally refers to environmentally, fiscally, and economically sustainable and intelligent development. It often takes the form of restoring community and vitality to center cities and older suburbs through the use of innovative land-use planning techniques.
52 Hamilton-Pennell, 2004, 13–15.

7 Managing network capital and innovation

1 Chesbrough, 2003, xxii–xxviii.
2 Ibid.
3 For instance, Jan Faber and Barbara Hesen find that firms that consult with various external sources of information tend to make a higher percentage of the total sales from new and substantially improved products. Robin Teigland and Molly McLure Wasko demonstrate that individuals who rely on other individuals colocated in the same office as a knowledge source report lower levels of creativity. See: Faber and Hesen, 2004, 193–207; Teigland and Wasko, 2003, 261–86.
4 For example, see: Haour, 1992, 177–82.
5 Porter, 1990.
6 This is partly due to the process of technological specialization, which Franco Malerba and Luigi Orsenigo describe as 'creative accumulation'. In this process, those firms continuously active in a certain technological domain accumulate

knowledge and are able to perform successfully in that technology. See: Malerba and Orsenigo, 1995, 59.
7 Quah, 1997, 49–56.
8 Scott, 1982, 111–42.
9 Hitchens *et al.*, 1996, 1299–313; MacPherson, 1997, 52–71.
10 Hitchens *et al.*, 1996.
11 Mackun and MacPherson, 1997, 659–68.
12 Oakey and White, 1993, 147–59.
13 MacPherson, 1988, 953–71; MacPherson, 1997; Mackun and MacPherson, 1997. For evidence in the UK, see: Bennett *et al.*, 2000, 813–28.
14 Keeble *et al.*, 1999, 331.
15 Keeble, 1997, 281–93.
16 Ibid.; Vaessen and Keeble, 1995, 489–505.
17 For example, see: Commission of the European Communities, 1994.
18 Cohen and Levinthal, 1990, 128–52. While the definition given by Cohen and Levinthal is the most widely cited, two other definitions of absorptive capacity exist. David Mowery and Joanne Oxley offer a second definition of absorptive capacity as a broad set of skills needed to deal with the tacit component of transferred knowledge and the need to modify this imported knowledge. Linsu Kim sees the absorptive capacity more broadly than the others, defining it as the capacity to learn and solve problems (Mowery and Oxley, 1995, 67–93; Kim, 1997, 86–100). For this classification of the three definitions of the absorptive capacity, see: Zahra and George, 2002, 186.
19 Cohen and Levinthal, 1990, 128.
20 Howells, 1996, 91–106.
21 Jovanovic, 1995, 16.
22 For instance, see: Arora and Gambardella, 1990, 361–79.
23 Curran and Blackburn, 1994, 170–2.
24 Ibid. Also see: Curran *et al.*, 2000, 128–43.
25 See: Nelson and Winter, 1982; Dosi, 1984; Dosi, 1988, 1126–71.
26 von Tunzelmann, 1995.
27 Utterback and Abernathy, 1975, 639–56; Abernathy and Utterback, 1978, 41–7; Utterback, 1994; Tushman and Rosenkopf, 1992, 311–47. We adopt the names of the four phases used by Edward Roberts and Wenyun Liu. See: Roberts and Liu, 2001, 26–34.
28 Utterback, 1994; Klepper, 1996, 562–83.
29 Tushman and Rosenkopf, 1992, 318.
30 Roberts and Liu, 2001, 31.
31 Pavitt, 1984, 358–9.
32 Christensen, 1997, 118.
33 Izushi and Wang, 2006.
34 Tidd *et al.*, 2005, 24.
35 Tushman and Anderson, 1986, 439–65; Henderson and Clark, 1990, 9–30.
36 Stuart and Podolny, 1996, 22.
37 Ibid., 36; Dixon, 2000, 149. Also see: Wenger, 1998.
38 Rogers and Bhowmik, 1971, 523–38; Rogers and Kincaid, 1981.
39 Conway, 1997, 226–33.
40 Tidd *et al.*, 2005, 430.
41 Allen, 1977.
42 Mowery *et al.*, 1998, 520.
43 Ibid., 510.
44 Stuart and Podolny, 1996, 37.
45 Roberts and Liu, 2001, 33.
46 Stuart and Podolny find evidence that contract-based alliances are less effective conduits for the transfer of complex capabilities (Stuart and Podolny, 1996, 21).

47 Zeithaml, 1981, 186–90.
48 For example, see: Holmstrom, 1985, 183–213; Clark, 1995; Gallouji, 1997, 42–64; Bennett and Robson, 1999, 351–69.
49 Holmstrom, 1985, 184.
50 Zeithaml *et al.*, 1990, 15–26.
51 Glasmeier *et al.*, 1998, 107–24.
52 Tidd *et al.*, 2005, 24; Leonard-Barton, 1995, 41. This lack of foresight on the part of existing customers is eloquently expressed by Gary Hamel and C. K. Prahalad: 'Customers are notoriously lacking in foresight. Ten or fifteen years ago, how many of us were asking for cellular telephones, fax machines and copiers at home, 24-hour discount brokerage accounts, multivalve automobile engines, video dial tone, compact disk players, cars with on-board navigation systems, hand-held global satellite positioning receivers, automated teller machines, MTV, or the Home Shopping Network?' Hamel and Prahalad, 1994, 99–100.
53 Leonard-Barton, 1995, 51.
54 Tushman and Katz, 1980, 1071–85.
55 Tidd *et al.*, 2005, 31.
56 Leonard-Barton, 1995, 156.
57 Izushi, 2003, 771–88.
58 Leonard-Barton, 1995, 156.
59 Daft and Weick, 1984, 284–95; Smeltzer *et al.*, 1988, 55–62.
60 Milliken, 1987, 133–43.
61 Oakey and White, 1993, 151; Lang *et al.*, 1997, 11–23.
62 This is an extension of management's ability to consolidate corporate-wide technologies into competencies, which C. K. Prahalad and Gary Hamel draw attention to as the sources of advantage. See: Prahalad and Hamel, 1990, 81.
63 Such preparation is necessary partly because of difficulties in forecasting the beginning of the discontinuities phase. Anita McGahan suggests that managers are often trapped in a self-fulfilling logic of maturity and wrongly shift their innovative focus to process innovation. Conversely, Dorothy Leonard-Barton warns of the dangers of complacency in believing that the particular technological wave their industry is riding will never peak and level off. See: McGahan, 2000, 2; Leonard-Barton, 1995, 148.

8 But what about the money? Financing and commercializing knowledge

1 Huggins and Emlyn-Jones, 2003. The methodology for this study consisted of a survey of 80 seeds funds in Europe, North America, and Asia Pacific, for which there was a response rate of 30 percent, as well as more in-depth follow-up interviews with the managers of a range of these funds.
2 Huggins, 2006. The methodology for this study consisted of a questionnaire survey of the 39 universities in London, of which 25 questionnaires were completed – a response rate of 64 percent (these respondents accounted for 18 of the top 20 universities in London ranked by total income received, as well as accounting for 88 percent of the income received annually by London's university sector). In-depth interviews were also undertaken with a range of university fund managers, venture capitalists, business angels, business intermediaries and network managers, and the innovation departments of major banks.
3 Murray, 1999, 351–84.
4 Reid and Smith, 2001.
5 Ibid.
6 von Burg and Kenney, 2000, 1135–55.
7 Bygrave, 1998, 11–18.
8 Lockett *et al.*, 2002, 1009–30.

9 Etzkowitz, 1998, 823–33; Bok, 2003.
10 Smilor *et al.*, 1993, 1–11; Slaughter and Leslie, 1997; Etzkowitz *et al.*, 2000, 313–30; Meyer, 2003, 107–15; Powers, 2004, 1–23; Shane, 2004.
11 Ibid.
12 Huggins, 2006.
13 Martin *et al.*, 2003.
14 Etzkowitz, 2003, 293–337.
15 Leleux and Surlemont, 2003, 81–104.
16 Oakey, 2003, 161–79.
17 Franklin *et al.*, 2001, 127–41.
18 Huggins, 2006.
19 Siegel *et al.*, 2004, 115–42.
20 Sapienza, 1992, 9–27; Prevezer, 2001, 17–29; Çetindamar and Laage-Hellman, 2003, 287–303.
21 Mason and Harrison, 2001, 663–8; Mason and Harrison, 2004, 159–73.
22 Podolny, 2001, 33–60; Garmaise and Moskowitz, 2003, 1007–40.
23 Lee *et al.*, 2001, 615–40; Elfring and Hulsink, 2003, 409–22.
24 Huggins, 2006.
25 Shane and Cable, 2002, 364–81.
26 Harding, 2002, 59–76.
27 Shane and Stuart, 2002, 154–70.
28 Di Gregorio and Shane, 2003, 209–27.
29 Powell *et al.*, 2002, 291–305.
30 Sorenson and Stuart, 2001, 1546–88.
31 Higher Education Funding Council for England, 'Higher education-business interaction survey 2001–02', 2004/7, London: Department for Employment and Learning, Higher Education Funding Council for England, Higher Education Funding Council for Wales, Scottish Higher Education Funding Council, Office of Science and Technology, 2004.
32 Carayannis *et al.*, 2000, 603–15.
33 Ibid.
34 Goldfarb and Henrekson, 2003, 639–58.
35 Ibid.
36 Lerner, 2002, F73–F84.

9 Conclusion

1 Stiglitz, 2004, 465–84.
2 Ibid., 470.
3 OECD, 2006.
4 For example, the commercial manufacture of mountain bikes, which originally began when some of the early users built bikes for others, has continued to take up innovations made by the user community. Lüthje *et al.*, 2005, 951–65. Drawing on cases such as open-source software movement and Nestle's custom food products, Eric von Hippel argues that if users are given certain toolkits, they can create a preliminary design, simulate or prototype it, and evaluate its functioning in their own environment. This allows producers to *abandon* their attempts to understand user needs in detail in favor of transferring *need-related* aspects of product and service development to users. See von Hippel, 2005.
5 For example, see: Chesbrough, 2006; Chesbrough *et al.*, 2006.
6 For example, see: Glaeser *et al.*, 1992, 1126–52; Feldman and Audretsch, 1999, 409–29; de Lucio *et al.*, 2002, 241–58.
7 In the 1960s, Martin Seligman and his colleagues at the University of Pennsylvania observed that dogs repeatedly experiencing inescapable shock would not try to escape

even when they were later placed in a situation where escape was possible. In other words, the dogs learned that they had no control over their situation. Seligman extended this theory of learned helplessness to human behavior, providing a model of depression: people who experience repeated failures will stay passive in unpleasant or harmful situations. Seligman, 1975.

8 Dunning, 2000; Teixeira *et al.*, 2006.
9 Le Bas and Sierra, 2002, 589–609; Fredriksson and Liang, 2006.
10 Huggins *et al.*, 2005, 32.
11 Recent evidence suggests that contrary to much political hyperbole, the global redistribution of knowledge creation capacities has not undermined the robustness of advanced economies, particularly in relation to research and development expenditure, patent generation, productivity growth, or the number of researchers and scientists (Bardhan and Jaffee, 2005).

Appendices

1 2000 for British Columbia, Manitoba, and Taiwan; 2001 for Japanese regions; 2003 for the rest of the Canadian regions, and Australian regions
2 2001 for Taiwan
3 Average of 1998–2001 for German regions and UK regions; average of 2001–3 for US regions; 2003 for Canadian regions
4 2001 for Australian regions and Japanese regions: 2003 for Israel
5 2003 for Canadian regions, European regions, and New Zealand
6 2002 for US regions, Australian regions, and Taiwan
7 2001 for New Zealand and Japanese regions; 2002 for Singapore and Taiwan
8 2001 for New Zealand and Japanese regions; 2002 for Singapore and Taiwan; 2003 for Canadian regions
9 2002 for Canadian regions, Israel, New Zealand, and Singapore
10 2002 for US regions, Israel, Australian regions, Singapore, and Taiwan; 2001 for Canadian regions

Bibliography

Abernathy, W. J. and J. M. Utterback, 'Patterns of industrial innovation', *Technology Review* 80 (June/July), 1978, 41–7.

Acemoglu, D., 'Technical change, inequality, and the labor market', *Journal of Economic Literature* 40(1), 2002, 7–72.

Acs, Z. J., L. Anselin, and A. Varga, 'Patents and innovation counts as measures of regional production of new knowledge', *Research Policy* 31(7), 2002, 1069–85.

Adams, J. D., 'Fundamental stocks of knowledge and productivity growth', *Journal of Political Economy* 98(4), 1990, 673–702.

Adams, S. B., 'Stanford and Silicon Valley: lessons on becoming a high-tech region', *California Management Review* 48(1), 2005, 29–51.

Adler, P. S. and S. W. Kwon, 'Social capital: prospects for a new concept', *Academy of Management Review* 27(1), 2002, 17–40.

Aghion, P. and P. Howitt, 'A model of growth through creative destruction', *Econometrica* 60, 1992, 323–51.

Aghion, P. and P. Howitt, *Endogenous Growth Theory*, Cambridge, MA: MIT Press, 1998.

Aigner, D., C. A. K. Lovell, and P. Schmidt, 'Formulation and estimation of stochastic frontier production function models', *Journal of Econometrics* 77(6), 1977, 21–37.

Allee, V., *The Knowledge Evolution: Expanding Organizational Intelligence*, Boston, MA: Butterworth-Heinemann, 1997.

Allen, T. J., *Managing the Flow of Technology: Technology Transfer and the Dissemination of Technological Information Within the R&D Organization*, Cambridge, MA: MIT Press, 1977.

Almeida, P., G. Dokko, and L. Rosenkopf, 'Startup size and the mechanisms of external learning: increasing opportunity and decreasing ability?', *Research Policy* 32(2), 2003, 301–15.

Alsleben, C., 'The downside of knowledge spillovers: an explanation for the dispersion of high-tech industries', *Journal of Economics* 84(3), 2005, 217–48.

Anselin, L., A. Varga, and Z. Acs, 'Geographical spillovers and university research: a spatial econometric perspective', *Growth and Change* 31(4), 2000a, 501–15.

Anselin, L., A. Varga, and Z. J. Acs, 'Geographic and sectoral characteristics of academic knowledge externalities', *Papers in Regional Science* 79(4), 2000b, 435–43.

Antonelli, C., 'Collective knowledge communication and innovation: the evidence of technological districts', *Regional Studies* 34(6), 2000, 535–47.

Arora, A. and A. Gambardella, 'Complementarity and external linkages: the strategies of the large firms in biotechnology', *Journal of Industrial Economics* 38(4), 1990, 361–79.

Arora, A. and A. Gambardella, 'The changing technology of technological change: general and abstract knowledge and the division of innovative labour', *Research Policy* 23(5), 1994, 523–32.

Arrow, K. J., 'Economic welfare and the allocation of resources for invention', in National Bureau of Economic Research (ed.) *The Rate and Direction of Inventive Activity: Economic and Social Factors*, Princeton, NJ: Princeton University Press, 1962, 609–25.

Arrow, K. J., *Essays in the Theory of Risk-Bearing*, Amsterdam: North-Holland, 1971.

Arthur, W. B., 'Competing technologies, increasing returns, and lock-in by historical events', *Economic Journal* 99(394), 1989, 116–31.

Ashton, D. and F. Green, *Education, Training and the Global Economy*, Cheltenham: Edward Elgar, 1996.

Athreye, S., 'Agglomeration and growth: a study of the Cambridge hi-tech cluster', in T. Bresnahan and A. Gambardella (eds) *Building High-Tech Clusters: Silicon Valley and Beyond*, Cambridge: Cambridge University Press, 2004, 121–59.

Atkinson, T., 'Income distribution in Europe and the United States', *Oxford Review of Economic Policy* 12(1), 1996, 15–28.

Audretsch, D. B., 'Agglomeration and the location of innovative activity', *Oxford Review of Economic Policy* 14(2), 1998, 18–29.

Audretsch, D. B. and M. P. Feldman, 'R&D spillovers and the geography of innovation and production', *American Economic Review* 86(3), 1996, 630–40.

Autor, D. H., L. F. Katz, and A. B. Krueger, 'Computing inequality: have computers changed the labor market?', *Quarterly Journal of Economics* 113(4), 1998, 1169–213.

Autor, D. H., F. Levy, and R. Murnane, 'Upstairs, downstairs: computer-skill complementarity and computer-labor substitution on two floors of a large bank', *International Labor Relations Review* 55(3), 2002, 432–47.

Autor, D. H., F. Levy, and R. Murnane, 'The skill content of recent technological change: an empirical exploration', *Quarterly Journal of Economics* 118(4), 2003, 1279–334.

Axelrod, R., *The Evolution of Cooperation*, New York: Basic Books, 1984.

Baily, M. N. and A. K. Chakrabarti, 'Innovation and productivity in US industry', *Brookings Papers on Economic Activity* (2), 1985, 609–32.

Bardhan, A. D. and D. M. Jaffee, 'Innovation, R&D and offshoring', Fisher Center Research Reports No. 1005, Berkeley: Fisher Center for Real Estate & Urban Economics, University of California, Berkeley, 2005.

Barro, R. J., 'Economic growth in a cross section of countries', *Quarterly Journal of Economics* 106(2), 1991, 407–43.

Barro, R. J. and J. W. Lee, 'International data on educational attainment: updates and implications', CID Working Paper No. 42, Cambridge, MA: Center for International Development, Harvard University, 2000.

Barro, R. J. and X. Sala-i-Martin, *Economic Growth*, New York: McGraw-Hill, 1995.

Bartel, A. P. and F. R. Lichtenberg, 'The comparative advantage of educated workers in implementing new technology', *Review of Economics and Statistics* 69(1), 1987, 1–11.

Bassi, L., P. Harrison, J. Ludwig, and D. P. McMurrer, 'Human capital investments and firm performance', Bethesda, MD: Human Capital Dynamics, 2001.

Basu, S., J. G. Fernald, N. Oulton, and S. Srinivasan, 'The case of the missing productivity growth: or, does information technology explain why productivity accelerated in the United States but not the United Kingdom?', NBER Working Paper 10010, Cambridge, MA: National Bureau of Economic Research, 2003.

Bathelt, H., A. Malmberg, and P. Maskell, 'Clusters and knowledge: local buzz, global pipelines and the process of knowledge creation', *Progress in Human Geography* 28(1), 2004, 31–56.

Battram, A., *Navigating Complexity*, London: The Industrial Society, 1998.

Baumol, W. J., 'Macroeconomics of unbalanced growth: the anatomy of urban crisis', *American Economic Review* 57(3), 1967, 415–26.

Baumol, W. J., S. A. B. Blackman, and E. N. Wolff, *Productivity and American Leadership: the Long View*, Cambridge, MA: MIT Press, 1989.

Baumol, W. J. and K. McLennan, 'U.S. productivity performance and its implications', in W. J. Baumol and K. McLennan (eds) *Productivity Growth and US Competitiveness*, New York: Oxford University Press, 1985, 3–28.

Beck, N., *Shifting Gears: Thriving in the New Economy*, Toronto: Harper Collins, 1992.

Becker, G., *Human Capital: A Theoretical and Empirical Analysis, with Special Reference to Education*, New York: National Bureau of Economic Research, 1964.

Benhabib, J. and M. M. Spiegel, 'The role of human capital in economic development: evidence from aggregate cross-country data', *Journal of Monetary Economics* 34(2), 1994, 143–73.

Bennett, R. J., W. A. Bratton, and P. J. Robson, 'Business advice: the influence of distance', *Regional Studies* 34(9), 2000, 813–28.

Bennett, R. J. and P. J. A. Robson, 'Intensity of interaction in supply of business advice and client impact: a comparison of consultancy, business associations and government support initiatives for SMEs', *British Journal of Management* 10(4), 1999, 351–69.

Berlin, L., *The Man Behind the Microchip: Robert Noyce and the Invention of Silicon Valley*, New York: Oxford University Press, 2005.

Berman, E., J. Bound, and Z. Griliches, 'Changes in the demand for skilled labor within US manufacturing: evidence from the Annual Survey of Manufactures', *Quarterly Journal of Economics* 109(2), 1994, 367–97.

Berman, E., J. Bound, and S. Machin, 'Implications of skill-biased technological change: international evidence', *Quarterly Journal of Economics* 113(4), 1998, 1245–79.

Best, M. H., 'Silicon Valley and the resurgence of Route 128: systems integration and regional innovation', in J. H. Dunning (ed.) *Regions, Globalization, and the Knowledge-Based Economy*, Oxford: Oxford University Press, 2000, 459–84.

Birch, D. L., *Job Generation in America*, New York: Free Press, 1987.

Bison, M., A. Dubois, C. Dymèn, S. M. Ezaz, and C. Murray, 'A Helsinki–Tallinn Twin-City study of knowledge transfer: Talliknki for knowledge', Stockholm: KTH Royal Institute of Technology, 2004.

Bluestone, B. and B. Harrison, *The Deindustrialization of America: Plant Closings, Community Abandonment, and the Dismantling of Basic Industry*, New York: Basic Books, 1982.

Bok, D., *Universities in the Marketplace: The Commercialization of Higher Education*, Princeton, NJ: Princeton University Press, 2003.

Bottazzi, L. and G. Peri, 'Innovation and spillovers in regions: evidence from European patent data', *European Economic Review* 47(4), 2003, 687–710.

Bound, J. and G. Johnson, 'Changes in the structure of wages in the 1980s: an evaluation of alternative explanations', *American Economic Review* 82(3), 1992, 371–92.

Bozeman, B., 'Technology transfer and public policy: a review of research and theory', *Research Policy* 20(4–5), 2000, 627–55.

Bradley, S. and J. Taylor, 'Human capital formation and local economic performance', *Regional Studies* 30(1), 1996, 1–14.

Brandenburger, A. and B. J. Nalebuff, *Co-opetition*, New York: Doubleday, 1996.

Branstetter, L., 'Is foreign direct investment a channel of knowledge spillovers? Evidence from Japan's FDI in the USA', NBER Working Paper 8015, Cambridge, MA: National Bureau of Economic Research, 2000.

Breschi, S. and F. Malerba, 'The geography of innovation and economic clustering: some introductory notes', *Industrial and Corporate Change* 10(4), 2001, 817–34.

Bresnahan, T. and A. Gambardella (eds) *Building High-Tech Clusters: Silicon Valley and Beyond*, Cambridge: Cambridge University Press, 2004.

Bresnahan, T., A. Gambardella, and A. Saxenian, '"Old economy" inputs for "new economy" outcomes: cluster formation in the New Silicon Valleys', *Industrial and Corporate Change* 10(4), 2001, 835–60.

Britton, J. N. H., 'High technology localization and extra-regional networks', *Entrepreneurship and Regional Development* 16(5), 2004, 369–90.

Bronson, P., *The Nudist on the Late Shift*, London: Vintage, 2000.

Brown, J. S. and P. Duguid, 'Knowledge and organization: a social-practice perspective', *Organization Science* 12(2), 2001, 198–213.

Brown, P., A. Green, and L. Hugh, *High Skills: Globalization, Competitiveness, and Skill Formation*, Oxford: Oxford University Press, 2001.

Brusoni, S., O. Marsili, and A. Salter, 'The role of codified sources of knowledge in innovation: empirical evidence from Dutch manufacturing', SPRU electronic working paper series No. 80, Sussex: Science and Technology Policy Research, University of Sussex, 2002.

Burt, R. S., *Structural Holes: The Social Structure of Competition*, Cambridge, MA: Harvard University Press, 1992.

Business Week, 'Down and out in Silicon Valley', European edn, 27 March, 2000, 112–14.

Business Week, 'Software: will outsourcing hurt American supremacy?' European edn, 1 March, 2002, 55–6.

Business Week, 'Still the center of this world', European edn, 25 August, 2003, 42–3.

Business Week, 'An old hotbed with new crops', European edn, 11 October, 2004, 110–15.

Bygrave, B., 'Building an entrepreneurial economy: lessons from the United States', *Business Strategy Review* 9(2), 1998, 11–18.

Cairncross, F., *The Death of Distance: How the Communications Revolution Will Change Our Lives*, Boston, MA: Harvard Business School Press, 1997.

Camagni, R., 'Local "milieu", uncertainty and innovation networks: towards a new dynamic theory of economic space', in R. Camagni (ed.) *Innovation Networks: Spatial Perspectives*, London: Belhaven Press, 1991, 121–44.

Campbell, M., *Learn to Succeed: The Case for a Skills Revolution*, Bristol: Policy Press, 2002.

Carayannis, E. G., S. K. Kassicieh, and R. Radosevich, 'Strategic alliances as a source of early-stage seed capital in new technology-based firms', *Technovation* 20(11), 2000, 603–15.

Carlsson, B., 'Internationalization of innovation systems: a survey of the literature', *Research Policy* 35(1), 2006, 56–67.

Casciaro, T. and M. S. Lobo, 'Competent jerks, lovable fools, and the formation of social networks', *Harvard Business Review* 83(6), 2005, 92–9.

Caselli, F. and W. J. Coleman II, 'Cross-country technology diffusion: the case of computers', *American Economic Review Papers and Proceedings* 91(2), 2001, 328–35.

Casper, S. and A. Karamanos, 'Commercializing science in Europe: the Cambridge biotechnology cluster', *European Planning Studies* 11(7), 2003, 805–22.

Castells, M. (ed.) *High Technology, Space and Society, Second edition, Beverly Hills*, 2nd edn, Beverly Hills, CA: Sage Publications, 1987.

Castells, M. (ed.) *The Network Society: A Cross-Cultural Perspective*, Cheltenham: Edward Elgar, 2004.

Castells, M. and P. Hall, *Technopoles of the World: The Making of the Twenty-First-Century Industrial Complexes*, London: Routledge, 1994.

Castells, M. and P. Himanen, *The Information Society and the Welfare State: The Finnish Model*, Oxford: Oxford University Press, 2002.

Castilla, E. J., H. Hwang, E. Granovetter, and M. Granovetter, 'Social networks in Silicon Valley', in C. M. Lee, W. F. Miller, M. G. Hancock, and H. S. Rowen (eds) *The Silicon Valley Edge: A Habitat for Innovation and Entrepreneurship*, Stanford, CA: Stanford University Press, 2000, 218–47.

Çetindamar, D. and J. Laage-Hellman, 'Growth dynamics in the biomedical/biotechnology system', *Small Business Economics* 20(4), 2003, 287–303.

Chandler, A. D. Jr., *The Visible Hand: The Managerial Revolution in American Business*, Cambridge, MA: Belknap Press, 1977.

Charles, D. and J. Howells, *Technology Transfer in Europe: Public and Private Networks*, London: Belhaven Press, 1992.

Chen, T. J., H. Chen, and Y. H. Ku, 'Foreign direct investment and local linkages', *Journal of International Business Studies* 35(4), 2004, 320–33.

Chesbrough, H., *Open Innovation: The New Imperative for Creating and Profiting from Technology*, Boston, MA: Harvard Business School Press, 2003.

Chesbrough, H., *Open Business Models: How to Thrive in the New Innovation Landscape*, Boston, MA: Harvard Business School Press, 2006.

Chesbrough, H., W. Vanhaverbeke, and J. West (eds) *Open Innovation: Researching a New Paradigm*, Oxford: Oxford University Press, 2006.

Christensen, C. M., *The Innovator's Dilemma: When New Technologies Cause Great Firms to Fail*, Boston, MA: Harvard Business School Press, 1997.

Ciancutti, A. R. and T. L. Steding, *Built on Trust: Gaining Competitive Advantage in Any Organization*, New York: McGraw-Hill, 2000.

Clark, T., *Managing Consultants: Consultancy as the Management of Impressions*, Buckingham: Open University Press, 1995.

Cohen, S. S. and G. Fields, 'Social capital and capital gains in Silicon Valley', *California Management Review* 41(2), 1999, 108–30.

Cohen, S. S. and J. Zysman, *Manufacturing Matters: The Myth of the Post-Industrial Economy*, New York: Basic Books, 1987.

Cohen, W. M. and D. A. Levinthal, 'Absorptive capacity: a new perspective on learning and innovation', *Administrative Science Quarterly* 35(1), 1990, 128–52.

Cohen, W. M., R. R. Nelson, and J. P. Walsh, 'Protecting their intellectual assets: appropriability conditions and why US manufacturing firms patent (or not)', NBER Working Paper 7552, Cambridge, MA: National Bureau of Economic Research, 2000.

Coleman, J. S., 'Social capital in the creation of human capital', *American Journal of Sociology* 94, 1988, S95–S120.

Collaborative Economics, 'Joint Venture's 2002 index of Silicon Valley: measuring progress toward the goals of Silicon Valley 2010', San Jose, CA: Joint Venture: Silicon Valley Network, 2002.

Collaborative Economics, 'Index of Silicon Valley 2006', San Jose, CA: Joint Venture: Silicon Valley Network, 2006.

Commission of the European Communities, *Research and Technology Management in*

Enterprises: Issues for Community Policy, Brussels: Office for Official Publications of the European Communities, 1994.

Conway, S., 'Strategic personal links in successful innovation: link-pins, bridges, and liaisons', *Creativity and Innovation Management* 6(4), 1997, 226–33.

Cooke, P. and R. Huggins, 'High-technology clustering in Cambridge', in F. Sforzi (ed.) *The Institutions of Local Development*, Aldershot: Ashgate, 2003, 51–74.

Cooke, P. and R. Huggins, 'A tale of two clusters: high technology industries in Cambridge', *International Journal of Networking and Virtual Organisations* 2(2), 2004, 112–32.

Cooper, W. W., L. M. Seiford, and K. Tone, *Data Envelopment Analysis: A Comprehensive Text with Models, Applications, References and DEA-Solver Software*, Boston: Kluwer Academic, 2000.

Cortright, J., 'The young and the restless in a knowledge economy', Chicago, IL: CEOs for Cities, 2005.

Cortright, J., 'Making sense of clusters: regional competitiveness and economic development', a discussion paper prepared for the Brookings Institution Metropolitan Policy Program, Washington, DC: The Brookings Institution, 2006.

Covey, S. M. R. and R. R. Merrill, *The Speed of Trust: The One Thing that Changes Everything*, New York: Free Press, 2006.

Cowan, R. and D. Foray, 'The economics of codification and the diffusion of knowledge', *Industrial and Corporate Change* 6(3), 1997, 595–622.

Cowan, R., N. Jonard, and J. B. Zimmermann, 'Networks as emergent structures from bilateral collaboration', Infonomics Research Memorandum series 2004–17, Maastricht: Maastricht Economic Research Institute on Innovation and Technology, Maastricht University, 2004.

Coyle, D., *The Weightless World: Strategies for Managing the Digital Economy*, Oxford: Capstone Publishing, 1997.

Cross, R., A. Parker, and L. Sasson (eds) *Networks in the Knowledge Economy*, New York: Oxford University Press, 2003.

Crouch, C., D. Finegold, and M. Sako, *Are Skills the Answer? The Political Economy of Skill Creation in Advanced Industrial Countries*, Oxford: Oxford University Press, 1999.

Curran, J. and R. Blackburn, *Small Firms and Local Economic Networks: The Death of the Local Economy?*, London: Paul Chapman, 1994.

Curran, J., R. Rutherfoord, and S. L. Smith, 'Is there a local business community? Explaining the non-participation of small business in local economic development', *Local Economy* 15(2), 2000, 128–43.

Daft, R. L. and K. E. Weick, 'Toward a model of organizations as interpretation systems', *Academy of Management Review* 9(2), 1984, 284–95.

Dalziel, M., 'Asymmetric interfirm relations', paper presented at the DRUID 10th Anniversary Summer Conference 2005 on the 'Dynamics of Industry and Innovation: Organizations, Networks and Systems', Copenhagen, 27–29 June, 2005.

Darr, A. and I. Talmud, 'The structure of knowledge and seller-buyer networks in markets for emergent technologies', *Organization Studies* 24(3), 2003, 443–61.

David, P. A. and D. Foray, 'Accessing and expanding the science and technology knowledge base', *STI Review* (16), 1995, 13–68.

Davis, S. and C. Meyer, *Blur: The Speed of Change in Connected Economy*, Oxford: Capstone, 1998.

Dawson, R., *Living Networks: Leading Your Company, Customers, and Partners in the*

Hyper-Connected Economy, Upper Saddle River, NJ: Prentice Hall/Financial Times, 2003.

de la Mothe, J., 'The innovation solution: some lessons from Scotland, theory and Canadian cities', Program of Research on Innovation Management and Economy (PRIME) Working Paper 03–18, Ottawa: School of Management, University of Ottawa, 2003.

de Lucio, J. J., J. A. Herce, and A. Goicolea, 'The effects of externalities on productivity growth in Spanish industry', *Regional Science and Urban Economics* 32(2), 2002, 241–58.

Denison, E. F., *The Sources of Economic Growth in the United States and the Alternatives Before Us*, New York: Committee for Economic Development, 1962.

Denison, E. F., *Why Growth Rates Differ: Post-War Experience in Nine Western Countries*, Washington, DC: Brookings Institution, 1967.

Denison, E. F., *Accounting for Slower Economic Growth: the United States in the 1970s*, Washington, DC: Brookings Institution, 1979.

Department of Trade and Industry, UK Government, *Our Competitive Future: Building the Knowledge Driven Economy*, London: Department of Trade and Industry, 1998.

Department of Trade and Industry, UK Government, 'R&D intensive businesses in the UK', DTI Economics Paper No. 11, London: Department of Trade and Industry, 2005.

Depner, H. and H. Bathelt, 'Exporting the German model: the establishment of a new automobile industry cluster in Shanghai', *Economic Geography* 81(1), 2005, 53–81.

Dernis, H. and M. Khan, 'Triadic patent families methodology', STI Working Paper 2004/2, Paris: OECD, 2004.

Descy, P. and M. Tessaring (eds) *Impact of Education and Training, Third Report on Vocational Training Research in Europe: Background Report*, Luxembourg: Office for Official Publications of the European Communities, 2004.

DeVol, R. C., 'America's high-tech economy: growth, development, and risks for metropolitan areas', Santa Monica, CA: Milken Institute, 1999.

Di Gregorio, D. and S. Shane, 'Why do some universities generate more start-ups than others?', *Research Policy* 32(2), 2003, 209–27.

DiMaggio, P. J. and W. W. Powell, 'The iron cage revisited: institutional isomorphism and collective rationality in organizational fields', *American Sociological Review* 48(2), 1983, 147–60.

Dixon, N. M., *Common Knowledge: How Companies Thrive by Sharing What They Know*, Boston, MA: Harvard Business School Press, 2000.

Doeringer, P. B., C. Evans-Klock, and D. G. D. G. Terkla, *Start-Up Factories: High-Performance Management, Job Quality, and Regional Advantage*, Oxford: Oxford University Press, 2002.

Doloreux, D., 'Regional networks of small and medium sized enterprises: evidence from the metropolitan area of Ottawa in Canada', *European Planning Studies* 12(2), 2004, 173–89.

Doloreux, D., 'Regional innovation systems in Canada: a comparative study', *Regional Studies* 38(5), 2004, 479–92.

Doms, M., T. Dunne, and K. R. Troske, 'Workers, wages, and technology', *Quarterly Journal of Economics* 112(1), 1997, 253–90.

Dosi, G., *Technical Change and Industrial Transformation: The Theory and an Application to the Semiconductor Industry*, London: Macmillan, 1984.

Dosi, G., 'Sources, procedures and microeconomic effects of innovation', *Journal of Economic Literature* 26(3), 1988, 1126–71.

Drennan, M. P., *The Information Economy and American Cities*, Baltimore, MD: Johns Hopkins University Press, 2002.

Drucker, P. F., *The New Realities: In Government and Politics, In Economics and Business, In Society and World View*, New York: Harper & Row, 1989.

Drucker, P. F., *Management Challenges for the 21st Century*, Oxford: Butterworth-Heinemann, 1999.

Dunning, J. H., 'Regions, globalization, and the knowledge economy: the issues stated', in J. H. Dunning (ed.) *Regions, Globalization, and the Knowledge-Based Economy*, Oxford: Oxford University Press, 2000.

Elfring, T. and W. Hulsink, 'Networks in entrepreneurship: the case of high-technology firms', *Small Business Economics* 21(4), 2003, 409–22.

English-Lueck, J. A., *Cultures@Silicon Valley*, Stanford, CA: Stanford University Press, 2002.

Etzkowitz, H., 'The norms of entrepreneurial science: cognitive effects of the new university-industry linkages', *Research Policy* 27(8), 1998, 823–33.

Etzkowitz, H., 'Innovation in innovation: the Triple Helix of university-industry-government relations', *Social Science Information* 42(3), 2003, 293–337.

Etzkowitz, H., A. Webster, C. Gebhardt, and B. R. C. Terra, 'The future of the university and the university of the future: evolution of ivory tower to entrepreneurial paradigm', *Research Policy* 29(2), 2000, 313–30.

European Private Equity and Venture Capital Association (EVCA), *EVCA 2004 Yearbook*, Zaventem: EVCA, 2004.

Evenson, R. E., 'The contribution of agricultural research and extension to agricultural production', unpublished PhD dissertation, University of Chicago, 1968.

Evenson, R. E., 'International invention: implications for technology market analysis', in Z. Griliches (ed.) *R&D, Patents, and Productivity*, Chicago: University of Chicago Press, 1984, 89–123.

Faber, J. and B. Hesen, 'Innovation capabilities of European nations: cross-national analyses of patents and sales of product innovations', *Research Policy* 33(2), 2004, 193–207.

Fagerberg, J., 'International competitiveness', *Economic Journal* 98(391), 1988, 355–74.

Fagerberg, J., 'Technology and competitiveness', *Oxford Review of Economic Policy* 12(3), 1996, 39–51.

Feenstra, R. C. and G. H. Hanson, 'The impact of outsourcing and high-technology capital on wages estimates for the United States', *Quarterly Journal of Economics* 114(3), 1999, 907–40.

Feldman, M. P. and D. B. Audretsch, 'Innovation in cities: science-based diversity, specialization and localized competition', *European Economic Review* 43(2), 1999, 409–29.

Finegold, D., 'Market failure and government failure in skills investment', in A. Booth and D. J. Snower (eds) *Acquiring Skills: Market Failures, their Symptoms and Policy Responses*, Cambridge: Cambridge University Press, 1996, 235–53.

Finegold, D., 'Creating self-sustaining, high-skill ecosystems', *Oxford Review of Economic Policy* 15(1), 1999, 60–81.

Finegold, D., P. K. Wong, and T. C. Cheah, 'Adapting a foreign direct investment strategy to the knowledge economy: the case of Singapore's emerging biotechnology sector', *European Planning Studies* 12(7), 2004, 921–41.

Florida, R., *The Rise of the Creative Class: And How It's Transforming Work, Leisure, Community and Everyday Life*, New York: Basic Books, 2002.

Florida, R. and M. Kenney, *The Breakthrough Illusion: Corporate America's Failure to Move from Innovation to Mass Production*, New York: Basic Books, 1990.

Foucault, M., *Power/Knowledge: Selected Interviews and Other Writings, 1972–1977*, New York: Pantheon Books, 1980.

Franklin, S. J., M. Wright, and A. Lockett, 'Academic and surrogate entrepreneurs in university spin-out companies', *Journal of Technology Transfer* 26(1–2), 2001, 127–41.

Fredriksson, T. and G. Liang, 'Features of national innovation systems and determinants of international R&D locations: conceptual framework and empirical exploration', paper presented at the Academy of International Business 2006 Annual Meeting, Beijing, 23–26 June, 2006.

Freeman, C., *Technology, Policy, and Economic Performance: Lessons from Japan*, London: Pinter Publishers, 1987.

Friedman, B. M., *The Moral Consequences of Economic Growth*, New York: Alfred A. Knopf, 2005.

Fuchs, V. R., *The Service Economy*, New York: National Bureau of Economic Research, 1968.

Fujita, K., 'Neo-industrial Tokyo: urban development and globalisation in Japan's state-centred developmental capitalism', *Urban Studies* 40(2), 2003, 249–81.

Fulong, W., 'Globalization, place promotion and urban development in Shanghai', *Journal of Urban Affairs* 25(1), 2003, 55–78.

Furman, J. F., M. E. Porter, and S. Stern, 'The determinants of national innovative capacity', *Research Policy* 31(6), 2002, 899–933.

Gallouji, C., 'Asymmetry of information and the service relationships: selection and evaluation of the service provider', *International Journal of Service Industry Management* 8(1), 1997, 42–64.

Gambardella, A. and D. Ulph, 'Technology, entrepreneurship, and inequality', LEM Working Paper, Sant'Anna School of Advanced Studies, Pisa, 2003.

Garmaise, M. J. and T. J. Moskowitz, 'Informal financial networks: theory and evidence', *Review of Financial Studies* 16(4), 2003, 1007–40.

Garnsey, E. and P. Heffernan, 'High-technology clustering through spin-out and attraction: the Cambridge case', *Regional Studies* 39(8), 2005, 1127–44.

Garnsey, E. and H. Lawton Smith, 'Proximity and complexity in the emergence of high technology industry: the Oxbridge comparison', *Geoforum* 29(4), 1998, 433–50.

Garnsey, E. and C. Longhi, 'High technology locations and globalisation: converse paths, common processes', *International Journal of Technology Management* 28(3/4/5/6), 2004, 336–55.

Gibbons, J. F., 'The role of Stanford University: a Dean's reflections', in C.-M. Lee, W. F. Miller, M. G. Hancock, and H. S. Rowen (eds) *The Silicon Valley Edge: A Habitat for Innovation and Entrepreneurship*, Stanford, CA: Stanford University Press, 2000, 200–17.

Gilder, G., *The Spirit of Enterprise*, New York: Basic Books, 1984.

Gilfillan, S. C., 'The decline of the patenting rate, and recommendations', *Journal of Patent Office* 17, 1935, 216–27.

Gillmor, C. S., *Fred Terman at Stanford: Building a Discipline, a University, and Silicon Valley*, Stanford, CA: Stanford University Press, 2004.

Gittell, R. and J. Sohl, 'Technology centres during the economic downturn: what have we learned?', *Entrepreneurship and Regional Development* 17(4), 2005, 293–312.

Glaeser, E. L., H. D. Kallal, J. A. Scheinkman, and A. Shleifer, 'Growth in cities', *Journal of Political Economy* 100(6), 1992, 1126–52.

Glasmeier, A. K., K. Fuellhart, I. Feller, and M. M. Mark, 'The relevance of firm-learning theories to the design and evaluation of manufacturing modernization programs', *Economic Development Quarterly* 12(2), 1998, 107–24.

Global Insight, 'The comprehensive impact of offshore software and IT services outsourcing on the US economy and the IT Industry', Lexington, MA: Global Insight, 2005.

Goldfarb, B. and M. Henrekson, 'Bottom-up versus top-down policies towards the commercialization of university intellectual property', *Research Policy* 32(4), 2003, 639–58.

Goman, C. K., *The Human Side of High-Tech: Lessons from the Technology Frontier*, New York: John Wiley & Sons, 2000.

Gordon, E. E., *Skill Wars: Winning the Battle for Productivity and Profit*, Boston, MA: Butterworth Heinemann, 2000.

Gosling, A., S. Machin, and C. Meghir, 'What has happened to men's wages since the mid-1960s?' *Fiscal Studies* 15(4), 1994, 63–87.

Granstrand, O., 'Towards a theory of the technology-based firm', *Research Policy* 27(5), 1998, 465–89.

Grant, R. M. and C. Baden-Fuller, 'A knowledge accessing theory of strategic alliances', *Journal of Management Studies* 41(1), 2004, 61–84.

Gray, C. and C. Mabey, 'Management development: key differences between small and large businesses in Europe', *International Small Business* 23(5), 2005, 467–85.

Greenwood, J. and M. Yorukoglu, '1974', *Carnegie-Rochester Conference Series on Public Policy* 46, 1997, 49–95.

Griliches, Z., 'The sources of measured productivity growth: United States agriculture, 1940–60', *Journal of Political Economy* 71(4), 1963, 331–46.

Griliches, Z., 'Research expenditures, education, and the aggregate agricultural production function', *American Economic Review* 54(6), 1964, 961–74.

Griliches, Z., 'Notes on the role of education in production functions and growth accounting', in W. L. Hansen (ed.) *Education, Income, and Human Capital*, New York: National Bureau of Economic Research, 1970, 71–124.

Griliches, Z., 'Issues in assessing the contribution of research and development to productivity growth', *Bell Journal of Economics* 10(1), 1979, 92–116.

Griliches, Z., 'Productivity, R&D, and basic research at the firm level in the 1970's', *American Economic Review* 76(1), 1986, 141–54.

Griliches, Z., 'Patent statistics as economic indicators: a survey', *Journal of Economic Literature* 28(4), 1990, 1661–707.

Griliches, Z., 'Productivity, R&D, and the data constraint', *American Economic Review* 84(1), 1994, 1–23.

Grossman, G. M. and E. Helpman, 'Quality ladders and product cycles', *Quarterly Journal of Economics* 106(2), 1991a, 557–86.

Grossman, G. M. and E. Helpman, 'Quality ladders in the theory of growth', *Review of Economic Studies* 58(1), 1991b, 43–61.

Gust, C. and J. Marquez, 'International comparisons of productivity growth: recent developments', *Business Economics* 36(3), 2001, 55–62.

Hagedoorn, J., 'Understanding the cross-level embeddedness of interfirm partnership formation', *Academy of Management Review* 31(3), 2006, 670–80.

Hall, B. H. and R. H. Ziedonis, 'The patent paradox revisited: an empirical study of patenting in the US semiconductor industry, 1979–1995', *RAND Journal of Economics* 32(1), 2001, 101–28.

Hall, P. and P. Preston, *The Carrier Wave: New Information Technology and the Geography of Innovation 1846–2003*, London: Unwin Hyman, 1988.

Hamel, G., 'Bringing Silicon Valley inside', *Harvard Business Review* 77(5), 1999, 70–84.

Hamel, G. and C. K. Prahalad, *Competing for the Future*, Boston, MA: Harvard Business School Press, 1994.

Hamilton-Pennell, C., 'CI for small businesses: the city of Littleton's economic gardening program', *Competitive Intelligence Magazine* 7(6), 2004, 13–15.

Haour, G., 'Stretching the knowledge-base of the enterprise through contract research', *R&D Management* 22(2), 1992, 177–82.

Harada, T., 'Three steps in knowledge communication: the emergence of knowledge transformers', *Research Policy* 32(10), 2003, 1737–51.

Harding, R., 'Plugging the knowledge gap: an international comparison of the role for policy in the venture capital market', *Venture Capital* 4(1), 2002, 59–76.

Harris, R. G., 'The knowledge-based economy: intellectual origins and new economic perspectives', *International Journal of Management Reviews* 3(1), 2001, 21–40.

Harris, R. I. D. and M. Trainor, 'Productivity growth in the UK regions, 1968–91', *Oxford Bulletin of Economics and Statistics* 59(4), 1997, 485–509.

Harrison, B., 'Concentrated economic power and Silicon Valley', *Environment and Planning A* 26(2), 1994, 307–28.

Harrison, B., *Lean and Mean: The Changing Landscape of Corporate Power in the Age of Flexibility*, New York: Basic Books, 1994.

Harrison, R. T., S. Y. Cooper, and C. M. Mason, 'Entrepreneurial activity and the dynamics of technology-based cluster development: the case of Ottawa', *Urban Studies* 41(5/6), 2004, 1045–70.

Hatzichronoglou, T., 'Revision of the high-technology sector and product classification', STI Working Papers 1997/2, Paris: OECD, 1997.

Hawkins, J. with S. Blakslee, *On Intelligence*, New York: Times Books, 2004.

Hayton, J. C., G. George, and S. A. S. A. Zahra, 'National culture and entrepreneurship: a review of behavioral research', *Entrepreneurship Theory and Practice* 26(4), 2002, 33–52.

Henderson, R. and I. Cockburn, 'Scale, scope, and spillovers: the determinants of research productivity in drug discovery', *RAND Journal of Economics* 27(1), 1996, 32–59.

Henderson, R. M. and K. B. Clark, 'Architectural innovation: the reconfiguration of existing product technologies and the failure of established firms', *Administrative Science Quarterly* 35(1), 1990, 9–30.

Henton, D., 'A profile of the Valley's evolving structure', in C.-M. Lee, W. F. Miller, M. G. Hancock, and H. S. Rowen (eds) *The Silicon Valley Edge: A Habitat for Innovation and Entrepreneurship*, Stanford, CA: Stanford University Press, 2000, 46–58.

Higher Education Funding Council for England, 'Higher education–business interaction survey 2001–02', 2004/7, London: Department for Employment and Learning, Higher Education Funding Council for England, Higher Education Funding Council for Wales, Scottish Higher Education Funding Council, Office of Science and Technology, 2004.

Hirschman, A. O., *The Strategy of Economic Development*, New Haven, CT: Yale University Press, 1958.

Hirshfeld, S. and G. Schmid, 'Globalisation of R&D', Technology Review 184/2005, Helsinki: Tekes, the National Technology Agency of Finland, 2005.

Hitchens, D. M. W. N., P. N. O'Farrell, and C. D. Conway, 'The competitiveness of business services in the Republic of Ireland, Northern Ireland, Wales, and the South East of England', *Environment and Planning A* 28(7), 1996, 1299–313.

Hite, J. M. and W. S. Hesterly, 'The evolution of firm networks: from emergence to early growth of the firm', *Strategic Management Journal* 22(3), 2001, 275–86.

Hobday, M., 'The limits of Silicon Valley: a critique of network theory', *Technology Analysis & Strategic Management* 6(2), 1994, 231–44.

Hofstede, G., *Culture's Consequences: Comparing Values, Behaviors, Institutions, and Organizations Across Nations*, 2nd edn, Thousand Oaks, CA: Sage Publications, 2001.

Holmstrom, B., 'The provision of services in a market economy', in R. P. Inman (ed.) *Managing the Service Economy: Prospects and Problems*, Cambridge: Cambridge University Press, 1985, 183–213.

Holstila, E., 'Building a creative city: the high tech cluster in the Helsinki Metropolitan Region', Helsinki: Culminatum Ltd, 2004.

Howells, J., 'Tacit knowledge, innovation and technology transfer', *Technology Analysis & Strategic Management* 8(2), 1996, 91–106.

Howitt, P., 'Steady endogenous growth with population and R&D inputs growing', *Journal of Political Economy* 107(4), 1999, 715–30.

Huggins, R., *The Business of Networks: Inter-firm Interaction, Institutional Policy and the TEC Experiment*, Aldershot: Ashgate, 2000.

Huggins, R., 'Embedding inward investment through workforce development: experiences in Wales', *Environment and Planning C: Government and Policy* 19(6), 2001, 833–48.

Huggins, R., 'Inter-firm network policies and firm performance: evaluating the impact of initiatives in the United Kingdom', *Research Policy* 30(3), 2001, 443–58.

Huggins, R., 'The skills economy and its development: examples and lessons from a rural region', *Policy Studies* 22(1), 2001, 19–34.

Huggins, R., 'Network capital, social capital, and knowledge networks', paper presented at the 29th National Conference of the Institute for Small Business and Entrepreneurship, Cardiff, 31 October–2 November, 2006.

Huggins, R., 'Universities and knowledge-based venturing: finance, management and networks in London', unpublished manuscript, The Management School, University of Sheffield, 2006.

Huggins, R. and J. Day, *UK Competitiveness Index 2005: The Changing State of the Nation 1997–2005*, Pontypridd: Robert Huggins Associates, 2005.

Huggins, R. and W. Davies, *European Competitiveness Index 2006–07*, Pontypridd: Robert Huggins Associates, 2006.

Huggins, R. and J. Day, *UK Competitiveness Index 2006*, London: The Work Foundation, 2006.

Huggins, R., M. Demirbag, and V. Ratcheva, 'Global knowledge and R&D foreign direct investment flows: recent patterns in Asia Pacific, Europe, and North America', paper presented at European Network on Industrial Policy (EUNIP) 9th International Conference, Limerick, Ireland, 20–22 June, 2006.

Huggins, R. and N. Emlyn-Jones, 'Financing high-technology venture creation: a global study of seed financing mechanisms', paper presented at the 26th Conference of the Institute for Small Business Affairs, Surry, November, 2003.

Huggins, R. and M. Fido, 'Baseline tracking of new entrepreneurs', report prepared for the Welsh Development Agency, Cardiff: Newidiem Consultants, 2002.

Huggins, R. and S. Harries, 'The skills economy and workforce development: a regional approach to policy intervention', *European Journal of Education* 39(1), 2004, 47–68.

Huggins, R., H. Izushi, and W. Davies, *World Knowledge Competitiveness Index 2005*, Pontypridd: Robert Huggins Associates, 2005.

Huggins, R., H. Izushi, J. Day, N. Emlyn-Jones, J. Liu, and K. Sootarsing, *World Knowledge Competitiveness Index 2003–2004: Benchmarking the Globe's Leading Knowledge Economy Regions*, Cardiff: Robert Huggins Associates, 2003.

Hung, S.-C., 'Mobilising networks to achieve strategic difference', *Long Range Planning* 35(6), 2002, 591–613.

Hydrios Biotechnology Ltd, 'Helsinki-Tallinn Twin City of Science: life science and biotechnology report', Helsinki: Culminatum Ltd, 2004.

Indergaard, M., *Silicon Alley: The Rise and Fall of a New Media District*, New York: Routledge, 2004.

Inkpen, A. C. and E. W. K. Tsang, 'Social capital, networks, and knowledge transfer', *Academy of Management Review* 30(1), 2005, 146–65.

Institute for Management Development, *The World Competitiveness Yearbook*, Lausanne: International Institute for Management Development, 2004.

International Herald Tribune, 'College diploma loses some economic luster', 14 January, 2005.

Ireland, R. D., M. A. Hitt, and D. Vaidyanath, 'Alliance management as a source of competitive advantage', *Journal of Management* 28(3), 2002, 413–46.

Izushi, H., 'Conflict between two industrial networks: technological adaptation and inter-firm relationships in the ceramics industry in Seto, Japan', *Regional Studies* 31(2), 1997, 117–29.

Izushi, H., 'Can a development agency foster co-operation among local firms? The case of the Welsh Development Agency's Supplier Association Programme', *Regional Studies* 33(8), 1999, 739–50.

Izushi, H., 'Impact of the length of relationships upon the use of research institutes by SMEs', *Research Policy* 32(5), 2003, 771–88.

Izushi, H., 'Boundary spanning and the "knowledge community"', in P. Cooke and D. Schwartz (eds) *Creative Regions: Technology, Culture and Knowledge Entrepreneurship*, London: Routledge, 2007.

Izushi, H., '"Knowledge communities": knowledge spillovers, specialisation, and their contributions to productivity growth', paper presented at the Kiel Institute for the World Economy workshop on Agglomeration and Growth in Knowledge-Based Societies, Kiel, 20–21 April, 2007.

Izushi, H., 'What does endogenous growth theory tell about regional economies? Empirics of R&D worker-based productivity growth', *Regional Studies*, forthcoming.

Izushi, H. and Y. Aoyama, 'Industry evolution and cross-sectoral skill transfers: a comparative analysis of the video game industry in Japan, the United States, and the United Kingdom', *Environment and Planning A* 38(10), 2006, 1843–61.

Izushi, H. and K. Morgan, 'Management of supplier associations: observations from Wales', *International Journal of Logistics: Research and Applications* 1(1), 1998, 75–91.

Izushi, H. and S. Wang, 'How does external knowledge sourcing change over industry life cycle? A comparative study of UK electronics and automotive firms', unpublished manuscript, Aston Business School, 2006.

Jackson, E. T. and R. Khan, 'Seeking sustainable livelihoods: constructing a role for community economic development in technology–cluster growth', Ottawa: The Caledon Institute of Social Policy, 2003.

Jaffe, A. B., 'Real effect of academic research', *American Economic Review* 79(5), 1989, 957–70.

Jaffe, A. B., M. Trajtenberg, and R. Henderson, 'Geographic localization of knowledge spillovers as evidenced by patent citations', *Quarterly Journal of Economics* 108(3), 1993, 577–98.

Johansson, F., *The Medici Effect: Breakthrough Insights at the Intersection of Ideas, Concepts, and Cultures*, Boston, MA: Harvard Business School Press, 2004.

Johnson, C., *MITI and the Japanese Miracle: The Growth of Industrial Policy, 1925–1975*, Stanford, California: Stanford University Press, 1982.

Johnson, C., L. D. A. Tyson, and J. Zysman (eds) *Politics and Productivity: How Japan's Development Strategy Works*, New York: Harper Business, 1989.

Johnson, D. K. N., N. Siripong, and A. S. Brown, 'The demise of distance? The declining role of physical proximity for knowledge transmission', *Growth and Change* 37(1), 2006, 19–33.

Jones, B. F., 'Age and great invention', NBER Working Paper 11359, Cambridge, MA: National Bureau of Economic Research, 2005.

Jones, C. I., 'R&D-based models of economic growth', *Journal of Political Economy* 103(4), 1995, 759–84.

Jones, C. I., 'Time series tests of endogenous growth models', *Quarterly Journal of Economics* 110(2), 1995, 495–525.

Jones, C. I., 'Sources of US economic growth in a world of ideas', *American Economic Review* 92(1), 2002, 220–39.

Jovanovic, B., 'Learning and growth', NBER Working Paper 5383, Cambridge, MA: National Bureau of Economic Research, 1995.

Juhn, C., K. M. Murphy, and B. Pierce, 'Wage inequality and the rise in returns to skill', *Journal of Political Economy* 101(3), 1993, 410–42.

Kaplan, D. A., *The Silicon Boys and Their Valley of Dreams*, New York: William Morrow, 1999.

Katz, L. F. and K. M. Murphy, 'Changes in relative wages, 1963–1987: supply and demand factors', *Quarterly Journal of Economics* 107(1), 1992, 35–78.

Kauffman, S. A., *Origins of Order: Self-Organization and Selection in Evolution*, New York: Oxford University Press, 1993.

Kauffman, S. A., *At Home in the Universe: The Search for Laws of Self-Organization and Complexity*, New York: Oxford University Press, 1995.

Kay, J., *Foundations of Corporate Success: How Business Strategies Add Value*, Oxford: Oxford University Press, 1993.

Kearney, A. T., 'The future of Bay Area jobs: the impact of offshoring and other key trends', San Francisco, CA: Bay Area Economic Forum, Joint Venture: Silicon Valley Network, and Stanford Project on Regions of Innovation and Entrepreneurship, 2004.

Keeble, D., 'Small firms, innovation and regional development in Britain in the 1990s', *Regional Studies* 31(3), 1997, 281–93.

Keeble, D., C. Lawson, B. Moore, and F. Wilkinson, 'Collective learning process, networking and "institutional thickness" in the Cambridge region', *Regional Studies* 33(4), 1999, 319–32.

Keep, E. and K. Mayhew, 'Evaluating the assumptions that underlie training policy', in A. Booth and D. J. Snower (eds) *Acquiring Skills: Market Failures, their Symptoms and Policy Responses*, Cambridge: Cambridge University Press, 1996, 305–34.

Keller, W., 'Geographic localization of international technology diffusion', *American Economic Review* 92(1), 2002, 120–42.

Kelly, K., *New Rules for the New Economy: 10 Ways the Network Economy is Changing Everything*, New edn, London: Fourth Estate, 1999.

Kendrick, J. W., *The Formation and Stocks of Total Capital*, New York: National Bureau of Economic Research, 1976.

Kenney, M. (ed.) *Understanding Silicon Valley: The Anatomy of an Entrepreneurial Region*, Stanford, CA: Stanford University Press, 2000.

Kim, L., 'The dynamics of Samsung's technological learning in semiconductors', *California Management Review* 39(3), 1997, 86–100.

Kim, T.-Y., H. Oh, and A. Swaminathan, 'Framing interorganizational network change: a network inertia perspective', *Academy of Management Review* 31(3), 2006, 704–20.

Kitching, J. and R. Blackburn, 'The nature of training and motivation to train in small firms', DfES Research Report 330, London: Department for Education and Skills, 2002.

Klepper, S., 'Entry, exit, growth, and innovation over the product cycle', *American Economic Review* 86(3), 1996, 562–83.

Kline, S. J. and N. Rosenberg, 'An overview of innovation', in R. Landau and N. Rosenberg (eds) *The Positive Sum Strategy: Harnessing Technology for Economic Growth*, Washington, DC: National Academy Press, 1986, 275–305.

Koepp, R., *Clusters of Creativity: Enduring Lessons on Innovation and Entrepreneurship from Silicon Valley and Europe's Silicon Fen*, Hoboken, NJ: John Wiley & Sons, 2002.

Kondratieff, N. D., 'Die langen Wellen der konjunktur', *Archiv für Sozialwissenschaft* 56, 1926, 573–609.

Kondratieff, N. D., 'The long waves in economic life', *Review of Economic Statistics* 17(6), 1935, 105–15.

Kortum, S. and J. Lerner, 'What is behind the recent surge in patenting', *Research Policy* 28(1), 1999, 1–22.

Kortum, S. S., 'Equilibrium R&D and the patent-R&D ratio: US evidence', *American Economic Review Papers and Proceedings* 83, 1993, 450–7.

Kortum, S. S., 'Research, patenting, and technological change', *Econometrica* 65(6), 1997, 1389–419.

Kotkin, J., *The New Geography: How the Digital Revolution is Reshaping the American Landscape*, New York: Random House, 2000.

Kotkin, J. and R. DeVol, 'Knowledge-value cities in the digital age', Santa Monica, CA: Milken Institute, 2001.

Krueger, A. B., 'How computers have changed the wage structure: evidence from microdata, 1984–1989', *Quarterly Journal of Economics* 108(1), 1993, 33–60.

Krugman, P., 'Competitiveness: a dangerous obsession', *Foreign Affairs* 73(2), 1994, 28–44.

Krugman, P., 'Complex landscapes in economic geography', *American Economic Review Papers and Proceedings* 84, 1994, 412–6.

Krugman, P., 'Inequality's apologists', *International Herald Tribune*, 9–10 September, 2006.

Laafia, I., 'Regional employment in high technology', Statistics in Focus, Research and Development Theme 9–1/1999, Luxembourg: Eurostat, 1999.

Labianca, G. and D. J. Brass, 'Exploring the social ledger: negative relationships and negative asymmetry in social networks in organizations', *Academy of Management Review* 31(3), 2006, 596–614.

Lall, S., 'Comparing national competitive performance: an economic analysis of World Economic Forum's Competitiveness Index', Queen Elizabeth House Working Paper 61, Oxford: Development Studies, University of Oxford, 2001.

Lang, J. R., R. J. Calantone, and D. Gudmundson, 'Small firm information seeking as a response to environmental threats and opportunities', *Journal of Small Business Management* 35(1), 1997, 11–23.

Langlois, R. N., 'Knowledge, consumption, and endogenous growth', *Journal of Evolutionary Economics* 11(1), 2001, 77–93.

Le Bas, C. and C. Sierra, '"Location versus home country advantages" in R&D activities: some further results on multinationals' locational strategies', *Research Policy* 31(4), 2002, 589–609.

Lécuyer, C., *Making Silicon Valley: Innovation and the Growth of High Tech, 1930–1970*, Cambridge, MA: MIT Press, 2005.

Lee, C., K. Lee, and J. M. Pennings, 'Internal capabilities, external networks, and performance: a study on technology-based ventures', *Strategic Management Journal* 22(6–7), 2001, 615–40.

Lee, C.-M., W. F. Miller, M. G. Hancock, and H. S. Rowen, 'The Silicon Valley habitat', in C.-M. Lee, W. F. Miller, M. G. Hancock, and H. S. Rowen (eds) *The Silicon Valley Edge: A Habitat for Innovation and Entrepreneurship*, Stanford, CA: Stanford University Press, 2000, 1–15.

Lee, F. C. and H. Has, 'A quantitative assessment of high-knowledge industries versus low-knowledge industries', in P. Howitt (ed.) *The Implications of Knowledge-Based Growth for Micro-Economic Policies*, Calgary: University of Calgary Press, 1996, 39–78.

Lee, Y. S., '"Technology transfer" and the research university: a search for the boundaries of university-industry collaboration', *Research Policy* 25(6), 1996, 843–63.

Leleux, B. and B. Surlemont, 'Public versus private venture capital: seeding or crowding out? A pan-European analysis', *Journal of Business Venturing* 18(1), 2003, 81–104.

Leonard-Barton, D., *Wellsprings of Knowledge: Building and Sustaining the Source of Innovation*, Boston, MA: Harvard Business School Press, 1995.

Lerner, J., 'When bureaucrats meet entrepreneurs: the design of effective "public venture capital" programmes', *Economic Journal* 112(477), 2002, F73–F84.

Levine, S. S., 'The strength of performative ties: three essays on knowledge, social networks, and exchange', unpublished PhD dissertation, University of Pennsylvania, 2005.

Levy, F. and R. J. Murnane, 'With what skills are computers a complement?' *American Economic Review Papers and Proceedings* 86, 1996, 258–62.

Lewis, J. D., *Trusted Partners, How Companies Build Mutual Trust and Win Together*, New York: Free Press, 1999.

Lewis, M., *The New New Thing: A Silicon Valley Story*, New York: W.W. Norton, 1999.

Library House, 'Cambridge cluster report 2004', Cambridge: Library House, 2004.

Liefner, I., S. Hennemann, and L. Xin, 'Cooperation in the innovation process in developing countries: empirical evidence from Zhongguancun, Beijing', *Environment and Planning A* 38(1), 2006, 111–30.

Lipnack, J. and J. Stamps, *The Age of the Network: Organizing Principles for the 21st Century*, New York: John Wiley & Sons, 1995.

Livingstone, D. N., 'The spaces of knowledge: contributions towards a historical geography of science', *Environment and Planning D: Society and Space* 13(1), 1995, 5–34.

Loasby, B. J., 'The organisation of capabilities', *Journal of Economic Behavior & Organization* 35(2), 1998, 139–60.

Locke, E. A., 'Some reservations about social capital', *Academy of Management Review* 24(1), 1999, 8–9.

Lockett, A., G. Murray, and M. Wright, 'Do UK venture capitalists still have a bias against investment in new technology firms', *Research Policy* 31(6), 2002, 1009–30.

Lopez-Claros, A., M. E. Porter, and K. Schwab, *Global Competitiveness Report 2005–2006: Policies Underpinning Rising Prosperity*, New York: Palgrave Macmillan, 2005.

Lorenzen, M. and V. Mahnke, 'Global strategy and the acquisition of local knowledge: how MNCs enter regional knowledge clusters', DRUID Working Paper No. 02–08, Aalborg: Danish Research Unit for Industrial Dynamics, 2002.

Love, J. H., S. Roper, and G. Mangiarotti, 'Organizing innovation: complementarities between cross-functional teams', Aston Business School Working Paper Series, Birmingham: Aston Business School, 2006.

Lucas, R. E. Jr., 'On the mechanics of economic development', *Journal of Monetary Economics* 22(1), 1988, 3–42.

Lundvall, B.-Å., 'Innovation as an interactive process: from user-producer interaction to the national system of innovation', in G. Dosi, C. Freeman, R. Nelson, G. Silverberg, and L. Soete (eds) *Technical Change and Economic Theory*, London: Pinter Publishers, 1988, 349–69.

Lundvall, B.-Å. (ed.) *National Systems of Innovation: Towards a Theory of Innovation and Interactive Learning*, London: Pinter Publishers, 1992.

Lüthje, C., C. Herstatt, and E. von Hippel, 'User-innovators and "local" information: The case of mountain biking', *Research Policy* 34(6), 2005, 951–65.

Lynch, L. M., 'Private-sector training and the earnings of young workers', *American Economic Review* 82(1), 1992, 299–312.

Machlup, F., 'The supply of inventors and inventions', in National Bureau of Economic Research (ed.) *The Rate and Direction of Inventive Activity: Economic and Social Factors*, Princeton, NJ: Princeton University Press, 1962, 143–69.

Machlup, F., *The Economics of Information and Human Capital*, Princeton, NJ: Princeton University Press, 1984.

Mackun, P. and A. D. MacPherson, 'Externally-assisted product innovation in the manufacturing sector: the role of location, in-house R&D and outside technical support', *Regional Studies* 31(7), 1997, 659–68.

MacPherson, A., 'Industrial innovation in the small business sector: empirical evidence from metropolitan Toronto', *Environment and Planning A* 20(7), 1988, 953–71.

MacPherson, A., 'The role of producer service outsourcing in the innovation performance of New York State manufacturing firms', *Annals of the Association of American Geographers* 87(1), 1997, 52–71.

Malerba, F., 'Sectoral systems of innovation and production', *Research Policy* 31(2), 2002, 247–64.

Malerba, F. and L. Orsenigo, 'Schumpeterian patterns of innovation', *Cambridge Journal of Economics* 19(1), 1995, 47–65.

Mallett, J. G., 'Silicon Valley North: the formation of the Ottawa innovation cluster', in L. V. Shavinina (ed.) *Silicon Valley North: A High-Tech Cluster of Innovation and Entrepreneurship*, Amsterdam: Elsevier, 2004, 21–32.

Mankiw, N. G., 'The growth of nations', *Brookings Papers on Economic Activity* (1), 1995, 275–326.

Mankiw, N. G., D. Romer, and D. N. Weil, 'A contribution to the empirics of economic growth', *Quarterly Journal of Economics* 107(2), 1992, 407–37.

Mansfield, E., 'How rapidly does new industrial technology leak out?' *Journal of Industrial Economics* 34(2), 1985, 217–23.

Martin, R., C. Berndt, B. Klagge, P. Sunley, and S. Herten, 'Regional venture capital policy: UK and Germany compared', London: Anglo-German Foundation, 2003.

Martin, R. and P. Sunley, 'Deconstructing clusters: chaotic concept or policy panacea?', *Journal of Economic Geography* 3(1), 2003, 5–35.

Maskell, P., 'Social capital, innovation, and competitiveness', in S. Baron, J. Field, and

T. Schuller (eds) *Social Capital: Critical Perspectives*, Oxford: Oxford University Press, 2000, 111–23.

Maskell, P., 'Towards a knowledge-based theory of the geographical cluster', *Industrial and Corporate Change* 10(4), 2001, 921–43.

Mason, C. M. and R. T. Harrison, '"Investment readiness": a critique of government proposals to increase the demand for venture capital', *Regional Studies* 35(7), 2001, 663–8.

Mason, C. M. and R. T. Harrison, 'Improving access to early stage venture capital in regional economies: a new approach to investment readiness', *Local Economy* 19(2), 2004, 159–73.

Massey, D., P. Quintas, and D. Wield, *High-Tech Fantasies: Science Parks in Society, Science and Space*, London: Routledge, 1992.

McGahan, A. M., 'How industries evolve', *Business Strategy Review* 11(3), 2000, 1–16.

McKinsey Global Institute, 'Offshoring: is it a win-wing game?', San Francisco, CA: McKinsey Global Institute, 2003.

Merton, R. K., 'Fluctuations in the rate of industrial invention', *Quarterly Journal of Economics* 49(3), 1935, 454–74.

Metcalfe, J. S., *Evolutionary Economics and Creative Destruction*, London: Routledge, 1998.

Meyer, B., 'Academic entrepreneurs or entrepreneurial academics? Research-based ventures and public support mechanisms', *R&D Management* 33(2), 2003, 107–15.

Miles, I., *Mapping and Measuring the Information Economy*, London: British Library Research and Development Department, 1990.

Miller, R., 'Global R&D networks and large-scale innovations: the case of the automobile industry', *Research Policy* 23(1), 1994, 27–46.

Milliken, F. J., 'Three types of perceived uncertainty about the environment: state, effect, and response uncertainty', *Academy of Management Review* 12(1), 1987, 133–43.

Minasian, J. R., 'Research and development, production functions, and rates of return', *American Economic Review Papers and Proceedings* 59(2), 1969, 80–5.

Ministry of Education, Culture, Sports, Science and Technology (MEXT), Japanese Government, *White Paper on Science and Technology 2005*, Tokyo: Ministry of Education, Culture, Sports, Science and Technology, 2005.

Minniti, M., W. D. Bygrave, and E. Autio, *Global Entrepreneurship Monitor: 2005 Executive Report*, Wellesley, MA and London: Babson College and London Business School, 2006.

Mokyr, J., *The Gifts of Athena: Historical Origins of the Knowledge Economy*, Princeton, NJ: Princeton University Press, 2003.

Moodysson, J., M. Nilsson, and M. Svensson Henning, 'Contextualizing clusters in time and space: long-term dynamics, systems of regions, and extra-regional interdependencies', paper presented at the DRUID Tenth Anniversary Summer Conference on Dynamics of Industry and Innovation: Organizations, Networks and Systems, Copenhagen, 27–29 June, 2005.

Mowery, D. C. and J. E. Oxley, 'Inward technology transfer and competitiveness: the role of national innovation systems', *Cambridge Journal of Economics* 19(1), 1995, 67–93.

Mowery, D. C., J. E. Oxley, and B. S. Silverman, 'Technological overlap and interfirm cooperation: implications for the resource-based view of the firm', *Research Policy* 27(5), 1998, 507–23.

Mueller, S. L. and A. S. Thomas, 'Culture and entrepreneurial potential: a nine country study of locus of control and innovativeness', *Journal of Business Venturing* 16(1), 2001, 51–75.

Murray, G., 'Early-stage venture capital funds, scale economies and public support', *Venture Capital* 1(4), 1999, 351–84.

Nahapiet, J. and S. Ghoshal, 'Social capital, intellectual capital, and the organizational advantage', *Academy of Management Review* 23(2), 1998, 242–66.

National Science Board, *Science & Engineering Indicators – 1989* (NSB 89–1), Washington, DC: US Government Printing Office, 1989.

National Science Foundation, 'National patterns of R&D resources: 1998', (NSF99–335), Arlington, VA: National Science Foundation, 1999.

National Science Foundation, 'National patterns of R&D resources: 2002 data update', (NSF 03–313), Arlington, VA: National Science Foundation, 2003.

National Science Foundation, *Scientists, Engineers, and Technicians in the United States: 2001* (NSF 05–313), Arlington, VA: National Science Foundation, 2005.

National Science Foundation, *Science and Engineering Indicators 2006* (NSB 06–01), Arlington, VA: National Science Foundation, 2006.

Navaretti, G. B. and A. J. Venables, *Multinational Firms in the World Economy*, Princeton, NJ: Princeton University Press, 2004.

Nelson, K. and R. Nelson, 'On the nature and evolution of human know-how', *Research Policy* 31(5), 2002, 719–33.

Nelson, R. R., 'What is "commercial" and what is "public" about technology, and what should be?', in N. Rosenberg, R. Landau, and D. C. Mowery (eds) *Technology and the Wealth of Nations*, Stanford, CA: Stanford University Press, 1992, 57–71.

Nelson, R. R., 'Recent evolutionary theorizing about economic change', *Journal of Economic Literature* 33(1), 1995, 48–90.

Nelson, R. R. and E. S. Phelps, 'Investment in humans, technological diffusion, and economic growth', *American Economic Review Papers and Proceedings* 56(2), 1966, 69–75.

Nelson, R. R. and S. G. Winter, *An Evolutionary Theory of Economic Change*, Cambridge, MA: Belknap Press, 1982.

Nonaka, I. and H. Takeuchi, *The Knowledge-Creating Company: How Japanese Companies Create the Dynamics of Innovation*, New York: Oxford University Press, 1995.

North, D. C., 'Institutions and economic growth: an historical introduction', *World Development* 17(9), 1989, 1319–32.

O'Mara, M. P., *Cities of Knowledge: Cold War Science and the Search for the Next Silicon Valley*, Princeton, NJ: Princeton University Press, 2004.

Oakey, R. P., 'Funding innovation and growth in UK new technology-based firms: some observations on contributions from the public and private sectors', *Venture Capital* 5(2), 2003, 161–79.

Oakey, R. P. and T. White, 'Business information and regional economic development: some conceptual observations', *Technovation* 13(3), 1993, 147–59.

OECD, *Trends in the Information Economy*, Paris: OECD, 1987.

OECD, *Jobs Study: Evidence and Explanations. Labour Market Trends and Underlying Forces of Change*, Paris: OECD, 1994.

OECD, *Fostering Entrepreneurship*, Paris: OECD, 1998.

OECD, *The Knowledge-Based Economy: A Set of Facts and Figures*, Paris: OECD, 1999.

OECD, *OECD Education Policy Analysis*, Paris: OECD, 2001.

OECD, *OECD Science, Technology and Industry Scoreboard: Towards a Knowledge-Based Economy*, Paris: OECD, 2001.

OECD, *OECD Science, Technology and Industry Scoreboard*, 2003 edn, Paris: OECD, 2003.

OECD, *Patents and Innovation: Trends and Policy Challenges*, Paris: OECD, 2004.

OECD, *OECD Science, Technology and Industry Outlook 2006*, Paris: OECD, 2006.

Oliver, C., 'Sustainable competitive advantage: combining institutional and resource-based views', *Strategic Management Journal* 18(9), 1997, 697–713.

Parise, S. and A. Casher, 'Alliance portfolios: designing and managing your network of business-partner relationships', *Academy of Management Executive* 17(4), 2003, 25–39.

Parthasarathy, B., 'India's Silicon Valley or Silicon Valley's India? Socially embedding the computer software industry in Bangalore', *International Journal of Urban and Regional Research* 28(3), 2004, 664–85.

Patibandla, M. and B. Petersen, 'Role of transnational corporations in the evolution of a high-tech industry: the case of India's software industry', *World Development* 30(9), 2002, 1561–77.

Pavitt, K., 'R&D, patenting and innovative activities: a statistical exploration', *Research Policy* 11(1), 1982, 33–51.

Pavitt, K., 'Sectoral patterns of technical change: towards a taxonomy and a theory', *Research Policy* 13(6), 1984, 343–73.

Penrose, E. T., *The Theory of the Growth of the Firm*, Oxford: Blackwell, 1959.

Perroux, F., 'Note sur la notion de pôle de croissance', *Economic Appliquée* 8, 1955, 307–20.

Pinch, S., N. Henry, M. Jenkins, and S. Tallman, 'From "industrial districts" to "knowledge clusters": a model of knowledge dissemination and competitive advantage in industrial agglomerations', *Journal of Economic Geography* 3(4), 2003, 373–88.

Piore, M. J. and C. F. Sabel, *The Second Industrial Divide: Possibilities for Prosperity*, New York: Basic Books, 1984.

Podolny, J. M., 'Networks as the pipes and prisms of the market', *American Journal of Sociology* 107(1), 2001, 33–60.

Podolny, J. M. and K. L. Page, 'Network forms of organization', *Annual Review of Sociology* 24(1), 1998, 57–76.

Polanyi, M., *Personal Knowledge: Towards a Post-Critical Philosophy*, London: Routledge & Kegan Paul, 1958.

Polanyi, M., *The Tacit Dimension*, London: Routledge & Kegan Paul, 1967.

Porat, M. U., *The Information Economy: Definition and Measurement*, Washington DC: Office of Telecommunications, US Department of Commerce, 1977.

Porter, M. E., 'How competitive forces shape strategy', *Harvard Business Review* 57(2), 1979, 137–45.

Porter, M. E., *Competitive Strategy: Techniques for Analyzing Industries and Competitors*, New York: Free Press, 1980.

Porter, M. E., *The Competitive Advantage of Nations*, New York: Free Press, 1990.

Porter, M. E., *On Competition*, Boston, MA: Harvard Business School Press, 1998.

Porter, M. E., K. Schwab, X. Sala-i-Martin, and A. Lopez-Claros, *Global Competitiveness Report 2004–2005*, New York: Palgrave Macmillan, 2004.

Portes, A., 'Social capital: its origins and applications in modern sociology', *Annual Review of Sociology* 24(1), 1998, 1–24.

Posadas, D., *Rice Bowl & Chips: How Asian Countries Are Using the Silicon Valley Model to Develop Technology Startups*, New York: iUniverse, 2005.

Powell, W. W., K. W. Koput, J. I. Bowie, and L. Smith-Doerr, 'The spatial clustering of science and capital: accounting for biotech firm-venture capital relationships', *Regional Studies* 36(3), 2002, 291–305.

Powers, J. B., 'R&D funding sources and university technology transfer: what is stimulating universities to be more entrepreneurial?', *Research in Higher Education* 45(1), 2004, 1–23.

Prahalad, C. K. and G. Hamel, 'The core competence of the corporation', *Harvard Business Review* 68(3), 1990, 79–91.

Prevezer, M., 'Ingredients in the early development of the US biotechnology industry', *Small Business Economics* 17(1/2), 2001, 17–29.

PricewaterhouseCoopers, Thomson Venture Economics and the National Venture Capital Association, 'MoneyTree Survey', New York: PricewaterhouseCoopers, various issues.

Putnam, R. D., *Bowling Alone: The Collapse and Revival of American Community*, New York: Simon & Schuster, 2000.

Quah, D., 'Cross-country growth comparison: theory to empirics', Discussion Paper No. 2294, London: Centre for Economic Policy Research, 1999.

Quah, D., 'Technology dissemination and economic growth: some lessons for the New Economy', Discussion Paper No. 522, London: Centre for Economic Performance, London School of Economics, 2001.

Quah, D. T., 'Increasingly weightless economies', *Bank of England Quarterly Bulletin* 37(1), 1997, 49–56.

Reagans, R. and B. McEvily, 'Network structure and knowledge transfer: the effects of cohesion and range', *Administrative Science Quarterly* 48(2), 2003, 240–67.

Reid, G. C. and J. A. Smith, 'How do venture capitalists handle risk in high-technology ventures? – some preliminary results', CRIEFF Discussion Paper No. 0107, St. Andrews: Centre for Research into Industry, Enterprise, Finance and the Firm, University of St. Andrews, 2001.

Reinert, E. S., 'Competitiveness and its predecessors – a 500-year cross-national perspective', *Structural Change and Economic Dynamics* 6(1), 1995, 23–42.

Ridderstråle, J. and K. Nordström, *Funky Business: Talent Makes Capital Dance*, Harlow: Pearson Education, 2000.

Rigden, J. S., *Einstein 1905: The Standard of Greatness*, Cambridge, MA: Harvard University Press, 2005.

Roberts, E. B. and W. K. Liu, 'Ally or acquire? How technology leaders decide', *Sloan Management Review* 43(1), 2001, 26–34.

Rodan, S. and C. Galunic, 'More than network structure: how knowledge heterogeneity influences managerial performance and innovativeness', *Strategic Management Journal* 25(6), 2004, 541–62.

Rodwin, L. and H. Sazanami (eds) *Deindustrialization and Regional Economic Transformation: The Experience of the United States*, Boston: Unwin Hyman, 1989.

Roelandt, T. and P. den Hertog, 'Cluster analysis and cluster-based policy in OECD-countries', paper presented at OECD Workshop on Cluster Analysis and Cluster-based Policy, Vienna, May, 1998.

Rogers, E. M. and D. K. Bhowmik, 'Homophily-heterophily: relational concepts for communication research', *Public Opinion Quarterly* 34(4), 1971, 523–38.

Rogers, E. M. and D. L. Kincaid, *Communication Networks: Toward a New Paradigm for Research*, New York: Free Press, 1981.

Rogers, M., 'R&D and productivity in the UK: evidence from firm-level data in the 1990s', Working Paper Series 255, Oxford: Department of Economics, Oxford University, 2006.

Romer, P. M., 'Increasing returns and long-run growth', *Journal of Political Economy* 94(5), 1986, 1002–37.

Romer, P. M., 'Endogenous technological change', *Journal of Political Economy* 98(5), 1990, S71–S102.

Roper, S. and S. Grimes, 'Wireless valley, silicon wadi and digital island – Helsinki, Tel Aviv and Dublin and the ICT global production network', *Geoforum* 36(3), 2005, 297–313.

Rosenberg, D., *Cloning Silicon Valley: The Next Generation High Tech Hotspots*, London: Pearson Education, 2002.

Rosenberg, N., 'Why do firms do basic research (with their own money)?' *Research Policy* 19(2), 1990, 165–74.

Rosenberg, N. and L. E. Birdzell, Jr., *How the West Grew Rich: The Economic Transformation of the Industrial World*, New York: Basic Books, 1986.

Rosenfeld, S., 'Industry clusters: business choice, policy outcome, or branding strategy', Carrboro, NC: Regional Technology Strategies, 2005.

Sako, M., 'Between Bit Valley and Silicon Valley: hybrid forms of business governance in the Japanese Internet economy', in B. Kogut (ed.) *The Global Internet Economy*, Cambridge, MA: MIT Press, 2003.

San Francisco Business Times, 'Multimedia Gulch turns into Multimedia Mulch', 30 March, 2001.

San Francisco Examiner, 'Act 2 for Multimedia Gulch', 18 September, 2005.

Sandefur, R. L. and E. O. Laumann, 'A paradigm for social capital', *Rationality and Society* 10(4), 1998, 481–501.

Sapienza, H. J., 'When do venture capitalists add value?', *Journal of Business Venturing* 7(1), 1992, 9–27.

Saxenian, A., 'Silicon chips and spatial structure: the industrial basis of urbanization in Santa Clara County, California', IURD Working Paper No. 345, Berkeley, CA: Institute of Urban and Regional Development, University of California at Berkeley, 1981.

Saxenian, A., 'Silicon Valley and Route 128: regional prototypes or historic exceptions?', in M. Castells (ed.) *High Technology, Space, and Society*, Beverly Hills, CA: Sage, 1985, 81–105.

Saxenian, A., *Regional Advantage: Culture and Competition in Silicon Valley and Route 128*, Cambridge, MA: Harvard University Press, 1994.

Saxenian, A., 'Silicon Valley's new immigrant high-growth entrepreneurs', *Economic Development Quarterly* 16(1), 2002, 20–31.

Saxenian, A., 'From brain drain to brain circulation: transnational communities and regional upgrading in India and China', *Studies in Comparative International Development* 40(2), 2005, 35–61.

Schimank, U., 'Technology policy and technology transfer from state-financed research institutions to the economy: some German experiences', *Science and Public Policy* 17(4), 1990, 219–28.

Schmitt, J., 'The changing structure of male earnings in Britain, 1974–1988', in R. B. Freeman and L. F. Katz (eds) *Differences and Changes in Wage Structures*, Chicago: University of Chicago Press, 1995, 177–204.

Schmookler, J., *Invention and Economic Growth*, Cambridge, MA: Harvard University Press, 1966.

Schultz, T. W., 'Capital formation by education', *Journal of Political Economy* 68(6), 1960, 571–83.

Schultz, T. W., 'Investment in human capital', *American Economic Review* 51(1), 1961, 1–17.

Schumpeter, J. A., *Business Cycles*, New York: McGraw-Hill, 1939.

Schumpeter, J. A., *Capitalism, Socialism and Democracy*, New York: Harper & Brothers, 1942.

Scott, A. J., 'Locational patterns and dynamics of industrial activity in the modern metropolis', *Urban Studies* 19(2), 1982, 111–42.

Scott, A. J., *Technopolis: High-Technology Industry and Regional Development in Southern California*, Berkeley: University of California Press, 1993.

Segerstrom, P. S., 'Endogenous growth without scale effects', *American Economic Review* 88(5), 1998, 1290–310.

Seligman, M. E. P., *Helplessness: On Depression, Development, and Death*, San Francisco: W. H. Freeman, 1975.

Shane, S., *Academic Entrepreneurship: University Spinoffs and Wealth Creation*, Cheltenham: Cheltenham, 2004.

Shane, S. and D. Cable, 'Network ties, reputation, and the financing of new ventures', *Management Science* 48(3), 2002, 364–81.

Shane, S. and T. Stuart, 'Organizational endowments and the performance of university start-ups', *Management Science* 48(1), 2002, 154–70.

Shavinina, L. V. (ed.) *Silicon Valley North: A High-Tech Cluster of Innovation and Entrepreneurship*, Amsterdam: Elsevier, 2004.

Siegel, D. S., D. A. Waldman, L. E. Atwater, and A. N. Link, 'Toward a model of the effective transfer of scientific knowledge from academicians to practitioners: qualitative evidence from the commercialization of university technologies', *Journal of Engineering and Technology Management* 21(1–2), 2004, 115–42.

Simmie, J., 'Knowledge spillovers and reasons for the concentration of innovative SMEs', *Urban Studies* 39(5–6), 2002, 885–902.

Simmie, J., 'Innovation and clustering in the globalised international economy', *Urban Studies* 41(5/6), 2004, 1095–112.

Simon, H. A., 'What we know about the creative process', in R. L. Kuhn (ed.) *Frontiers in Creative and Innovative Management*, Cambridge, MA: Ballinger, 1985, 3–20.

Singh, I., 'Can government catalyze clusters? Examples of government actions', paper presented at the 6th Annual International Conference of the Competitiveness Institute, Gothenburg, Sweden, September, 2003.

Skyrme, D. J., *Knowledge Networking: Creating the Collaborative Enterprise*, Oxford: Butterworth-Heinemann, 1999.

Slaughter, S. and L. L. Leslie, *Academic Capitalism: Politics, Policies, and the Entrepreneurial University*, Baltimore, MD: Johns Hopkins University Press, 1997.

Smeltzer, L. R., G. L. Fann, and V. N. Nikolaisen, 'Environmental scanning practices in small business', *Journal of Small Business Management* 26(3), 1988, 55–62.

Smilor, R. W., G. B. Dietrich, and D. V. Gibson, 'The entrepreneurial university: the role of higher education in the United States in technology commercialization and economic development', *International Social Science Journal* 45(135), 1993, 1–11.

Smith, A., *An Inquiry into the Nature and Causes of the Wealth of Nations*, Harmondsworth: Penguin, 1970 (original 1776).

Solomon, R. C. and F. Flores, *Building Trust in Business, Politics, Relationships, and Life*, New York: Oxford University Press, 2001.

Solow, R. M., 'Technical change and the aggregate production function', *Review of Economics and Statistics* 39, 1957, 312–20.

Sorenson, O. and T. E. Stuart, 'Syndication networks and the spatial distribution of venture capital investments', *American Journal of Sociology* 106(6), 2001, 1546–88.

SQW Limited, 'The Oxford-Cambridge Arc: final report to a group of partners from across the Arc', Cambridge: SQW Limited, 2001.

Stacey, R. D., D. Griffin, and P. Shaw, *Complexity and Management: Fad or Radical Challenge to Systems Thinking?*, London: Routledge, 2000.

Steinbock, D., 'Finland's innovative capacity', Regional Development 13/2006, Helsinki: Ministry of the Interior, Government of Finland, 2006.

Stiglitz, J. E., 'Learning to learn, localized learning and technological progress', in P. Dasgupta and P. Stoneman (eds) *Economic Policy and Technological Performance*, Cambridge: Cambridge University Press, 1987, 125–53.

Stiglitz, J. E., 'Globalization and growth in emerging markets', *Journal of Policy Modeling* 26(4), 2004, 465–84.

Storper, M., 'The resurgence of regional economics, ten years later: the region as a nexus of untraded interdependencies', *European Urban and Regional Studies* 2(3), 1995, 191–221.

Storper, M. and A. J. Scott, 'The wealth of regions: market forces and policy imperatives in local and global context', *Futures* 27(5), 1995, 505–26.

Stuart, T. E., 'Interorganizational alliances and the performance of firms: a study of growth and innovation rates in a high-technology industry', *Strategic Management Journal* 21(8), 2000, 791–811.

Stuart, T. E. and J. M. Podolny, 'Local search and the evolution of technological capabilities', *Strategic Management Journal* 17(Summer Special Issue), 1996, 21–38.

Sturgeon, T. J., 'What really goes on in Silicon Valley? Spatial clustering and dispersal in modular production networks', *Journal of Economic Geography* 3(2), 2003, 199–225.

Tapscott, D. (ed.) *Creating Value in the Network Economy*, Boston, MA: Harvard Business School Press, 1999.

Tapscott, D., D. Ticoll, and A. Lowy, *Digital Capital: Harnessing the Power of Business Webs*, London: Nicholas Brealey, 2000.

Teigland, R. and M. M. Wasko, 'Integrating knowledge through information trading: examining the relationship between boundary spanning communication and individual performance', *Decision Science* 34(2), 2003, 261–86.

Teixeira, A., P. Santos, and A. Oliveira Brochado, 'Does proximity really matter in international R&D cooperative projects?', paper presented at European Network on Industrial Policy (EUNIP), 9th International Conference, Limerick, 20–22 June, 2006.

Tether, B. S., 'Do services innovate (differently)? Insights from the European Innobarometer Survey', *Industry and Innovation* 12(2), 2005, 153–84.

Thurow, L. C., *The Future of Capitalism: How Today's Economic Forces Shape Tomorrow's World*, New York: William Morrow and Company, 1996.

Tidd, J., J. Bessant, and K. Pavitt, *Managing Innovation: Integrating Technological, Market and Organizational Change*, 3rd edn, Chichester: Wiley & Sons, 2005.

Tinbergen, J., 'Zur theorie der langfristigen wirtschaftsentwicklung', *Weltwirtschaftliches Archiv* 55(1), 1942, 511–49.

Tinbergen, J., 'On the theory of trend movements', in L. H. Klaassen, L. M. Koyck and H. J. Witteveen (eds) *Jan Tinbergen, Selected Papers*, Amsterdam: North-Holland, 1959, 182–221.

Tödtling, F., 'Regional networks of high-technology firms: the case of the Greater Boston region', *Technovation* 14(5), 1994, 323–43.

Tushman, M. L. and P. Anderson, 'Technological discontinuities and organizational environments', *Administrative Science Quarterly* 31(3), 1986, 439–65.

Tushman, M. L. and R. Katz, 'External communication and project performance: an investigation into the role of gatekeepers', *Management Science* 26(11), 1980, 1071–85.

Tushman, M. L. and L. Rosenkopf, 'Organizational determinants of technological change: toward a sociology of technological evolution', *Research in Organizational Behavior* 14, 1992, 311–47.

US Census Bureau, 'Educational attainment in the United States: March 1995' (P20–489), Washington, DC: US Census Bureau, 1996.

US Census Bureau, *Statistical Abstract of the United States*, Washington, DC: US Census Bureau, various years.

US Census Bureau, *Statistical Abstract of the United States*, Washington, DC: US Census Bureau, various years.

US Department of Commerce, Bureau of Economic Analysis, 'Industry Economic Accounts', Washington, DC: Bureau of Economic Analysis.. Available online at http://www.bea.gov/bea/dn2/home/annual_industry.htm (accessed 15 January 2007).

US Department of Commerce, Bureau of Economic Analysis, 'Input-output accounts for the US economy, 1972', *Survey of Current Business* 59(4), 1979.

US Department of Commerce, Bureau of Economic Analysis, *National Income and Product Accounts*, Washington, DC: Bureau of Economic Analysis, 1998.

US Department of Commerce, Bureau of Economic Analysis, 'Input-output accounts for the US economy, 1996', *Survey of Current Business* 80(1), 2000.

US Department of Commerce, Bureau of Economic Analysis, *National Economic Accounts*, Washington, DC: Bureau of Economic Analysis, various years.

US Department of Education, *Digest of Education Statistics 2003*, Washington, DC: US Department of Education, 2003.

US Department of Education, *Digest of Education Statistics 2005*, Washington, DC: US Department of Education, 2005.

US Department of Labor, Bureau of Labor Statistics, 'Major sector multifactor productivity index', Washington, DC: Bureau of Labor Statistics. Available online at http://www.bles.gov/ (accessed 10 May, 2004).

US Department of Labor, Bureau of Labor Statistics, 'Private business and private nonfarm business MFP tables', Washington, DC: Bureau of Labor Statistics. Available online at ftp://ftp.bls.gov/pub/suppl/prod3.mfptable.zip (accessed 21 February, 2006).

US Patent and Trademark Office, 'U.S. patent activity calendar years 1790–2001', Alexandria, VA: US Patent and Trademark Office. Available online at http://www.uspto.gov/web/offices/ac/ido/oeip/taf/h_counts.htm (accessed 18 May, 2004).

US Patent and Trademark Office, 'U.S. Patent Statistics, calendar years 1963–2001', Alexandria, VA: US Patent and Trademark Office. Available online at http://www.ustpo.gov/web/offices/ac/ido/oeip/taf/us_stat.pdf (accessed 18 May, 2004).

US Patent and Trademark Office, 'All technologies report, January 1963 – December 1998', Alexandria, VA: US Patent and Trademark Office, 1999.

US Patent and Trademark Office, 'Patent counts: states and countries of origin', Alexandria, VA: US Patent and Trademark Office, various years.

UNCTAD, *World Investment Report 2005: Transnational Corporations and the Internalization of R&D*, New York and Geneva: United Nations Conference on Trade and Development, 2005.

Utterback, J. M., *Mastering the Dynamics of Innovation: How Companies Can Seize Opportunities in the Face of Technological Change*, Boston, MA: Harvard Business School Press, 1994.

Utterback, J. M. and W. J. Abernathy, 'A dynamic model of process and product innovation', *Omega* 3(6), 1975, 639–56.

Vaessen, P. and D. Keeble, 'Growth-oriented SMEs in unfavourable regional environment', *Regional Studies* 29(6), 1995, 489–505.

Van Biesebroeck, J., 'Revising some productivity debates', NBER Working Paper 10065, Cambridge, MA: National Bureau of Economic Research, 2003.

van der Meer, A., W. van Winden, and P. Woets, 'ICT clusters in European cities during the 1990s: development patterns and policy lessons – The cases of Amsterdam, Cork, Dublin, Groningen, Helsinki, Jönköping, Oulu, and Stockholm', Euricur Report (R2003–2), Rotterdam: European Institute for Comparative Urban Research (Euricur), Erasmus University, 2003.

Van Reenen, J., 'Why has Britain had slower R&D growth?', *Research Policy* 26(4–5), 1997, 493–507.

von Burg, U. and M. Kenney, 'Venture capital and the birth of the local area networking industry', *Research Policy* 29(9), 2000, 1135–55.

von Hippel, E., *Democratizing Innovation*, Cambridge, MA: MIT Press, 2005.

von Tunzelmann, N., Technology and Industrial Progress: The Foundations of Economic Growth, Aldershot: Edward Elgar, 1995.

Welborn, R. and V. Kasten, *The Jericho Principle: How Companies Use Strategic Collaboration to Find New Sources of Value*, Hoboken, NJ: John Wiley & Sons, 2003.

Wenger, E., *Communities of Practice: Learning, Meaning, and Identity*, Cambridge: Cambridge University Press, 1998.

Williamson, O. E., 'Calculativeness, trust, and economic organization', *Journal of Law and Economics* 36(1), 1993, 453–86.

Wolfe, D. A., 'Knowledge, learning and social capital in Ontario's ICT clusters', paper presented at the Annual Meeting of the Canadian Political Science Association, University of Toronto, Toronto, 29–31 May, 2002.

Wolfe, D. A. and M. S. Gertler, 'Clusters from the inside and out: local dynamics and global linkages', *Urban Studies* 41(5/6), 2004, 1071–93.

Wolfe, M. R., 'The wired loft: lifestyle innovation diffusion and industrial networking in the rise of San Francisco's Multimedia Gulch', *Urban Affairs Review* 34(5), 1999, 707–28.

Wolff, E. N., 'The magnitude and causes of the recent productivity slowdown in the United States: a survey of recent studies', in W. J. Baumol and K. McLennan (eds) *Productivity Growth and US Competitiveness*, New York: Oxford University Press, 1985, 29–57.

Wolff, E. N., 'Technology and the demand for skills', *OECD Science, Technology and Industry Review* 18, 1996, 96–123.

Wolff, E. N., 'The role of education in the postwar productivity convergence among OECD countries', *Industrial and Corporate Change* 10(3), 2001, 735–59.

Young, A., 'Growth without scale effects', *Journal of Political Economy* 106(1), 1998, 41–63.

Zahra, S. A. and G. George, 'Absorptive capacity: a review, reconceptualization, and extension', *Academy of Management Review* 27(2), 2002, 185–203.

Zeithaml, V. A., 'How consumer evaluation processes differ between goods and services', in J. H. Donnelley and W. R. George (eds) *Marketing of Services*, Chicago: American Marketing Association, 1981, 186–90.

Zeithaml, V. A., A. Parasuraman, and L. L. Berry, *Delivering Quality Service*, New York: Free Press, 1990.

Zhou, Y., 'The making of an innovative region from a centrally planned economy: institutional evolution in Zhongguancun Science Park in Beijing', *Environment and Planning A* 37(6), 2005, 1113–34.

Zhou, Y. and T. Xin, 'An innovative region in China: interaction between multinational corporations and local firms in a high-tech cluster in Beijing', *Economic Geography* 79(2), 2003, 129–52.

Zucker, L. G., M. R. Darby, and M. B. Brewer, 'Intellectual human capital and the birth of US biotechnology enterprises', *American Economic Review* 88(1), 1998, 290–306.

Index